W9-AGJ-975

Don't Stop Laughing Now!

BOOKS BY ANN SPANGLER

A Miracle a Day

An Angel a Day

Daily Secrets of the Christian Life, Hannah Whitall Smith (compiled by Ann Spangler)

Don't Stop Laughing Now! compiled by Ann Spangler and Shari MacDonald

He's Been Faithful, Carol Cymbala with Ann Spangler

She Who Laughs, Lasts! compiled by Ann Spangler

Women of the Bible, coauthored with Jean Syswerda

Men of the Bible, coauthored with Robert Wolgemuth

Look Who's Laughing! compiled by Ann Spangler and Shari MacDonald

BOOKS BY SHARI MACDONALD

A Match Made in Heaven

Don't Stop Laughing Now! compiled by Ann Spangler and Shari MacDonald

Humor for a Woman's Heart, compiled by Shari MacDonald

Humor for the Heart, compiled by Shari MacDonald

Love on the Run

The Perfect Wife

Look Who's Laughing! compiled by Ann Spangler and Shari MacDonald

Stories to Tickle Your Funny Bone and Strengthen Your Faith

WOMEN OF FAITH℠

Don't Stop Laughing Now!

STORIES BY

BARBARA JOHNSON, PATSY CLAIRMONT, THELMA WELLS,

LUCI SWINDOLL, SHEILA WALSH, MARILYN MEBERG,

BECKY FREEMAN, KAREN LINAMEN, CHONDA PIERCE,

AND MORE!

COMPILED BY ANN SPANGLER AND SHARI MACDONALD

ZONDERVAN™

GRAND RAPIDS, MICHIGAN 49530

WWW.ZONDERVAN.COM

ZONDERVAN™

Don't Stop Laughing Now!
Copyright © 2002 by Ann Spangler

Requests for information should be addressed to:
Zondervan, *Grand Rapids, Michigan 49530*

ISBN 0-7394-3807-7

All Scripture quotations, unless otherwise indicated, are taken from the *Holy Bible, New International Version®*. NIV®. Copyright © 1973, 1978, 1984 by International Bible Society. Used by permission of Zondervan. All rights reserved.

Scripture references marked LB are from the *Living Bible,* copyright © 1971. Used by permission of Tyndale House Publishers, Inc., Wheaton, Illinois 60189. All rights reserved.

All rights reserved. No part of this publication may be reproduced, stored in a retrieval system, or transmitted in any form or by any means — electronic, mechanical, photocopy, recording, or any other — except for brief quotations in printed reviews, without the prior permission of the publisher.

Interior design by Susan Ambs
Printed in the United States of America

Contents

Chapter Fourteen:
Life Is Unpredictable, but God Is Good

ACKNOWLEDGMENTS

We want to thank Sandy VanderZicht, executive editor at Zondervan, for her support for this book as well as for its predecessor, *She Who Laughs, Lasts!* In both cases her insightful commentary has resulted in a stronger and, we hope, funnier book. Thanks to Dirk Buursma and Rachel Boers for their care in editing the manuscript. Thanks also to Steve Arterburn and Mary Graham of Women of Faith and to Thelma Wells, Sheila Walsh, Luci Swindoll, Marilyn Meberg, Barbara Johnson, and Patsy Clairmont for dispensing so much real wisdom and joy at Women of Faith Conferences throughout the country. Special thanks to Sara Wachtel for relating the story retold by Shari MacDonald in "When in Rome." We also wish to acknowledge with gratitude the publishers and individuals who gave permission to reprint the material that follows.

PREFACE

Frenzied, fearful, frazzled, frustrated—if these words all too frequently describe your state of mind, you are not alone. The world has suddenly become a much different place than the one we have taken for granted all our lives. We long for our sense of peace to be restored, for our safety to be assured. We pray with greater fervor than ever that God will bless our country and draw us near to him in humility and trust.

Ultimately, we know that our future rests in the hands of the God who is in complete control of the universe no matter how shaky our world may seem. This book won't tell you everything you need to know in order to restore a sense of peace and trust to your life. It won't teach you anything about prayer, which, of course, is essential to both trust and peace. But it will offer you something you may need right now, this very minute—an enjoyable break from everything difficult, stressful, and challenging in your life.

Don't Stop Laughing Now! is the sequel to *She Who Laughs, Lasts!* Like its predecessor, it is a collection of some of the funniest stories, quips, and jokes around, written by men and women who are doing their best to respond to life's challenges with faith and hope.

As we were completing work on this book, we received a letter from a reader of *She Who Laughs, Lasts!* that further confirmed our sense that women, even women of faith, need to lighten up and find ways to take themselves a little less seriously. Tammy MacKay is a self-proclaimed overachiever with a nice sense of humor. We'll let her tell you about her life in her own words:

> I've just finished reading *She Who Laughs, Lasts!* and I am still chuckling to myself. Believe me when I tell you it was much needed "soul food." I have been feeling so empty the last few months, completely overwhelmed as a single mom of three beautiful yet very energetic boys, ages four, six, and

nine. I am a nursing student preparing to enter my clinical portion of schooling, am working three jobs, and am "on call" to my patients whenever they need someone to talk to. Recently, three of my patients died; several others are suffering from terminal cancer. My pager goes off constantly as friends and patients know I am "the strong one," always willing to lend an ear or offer a prayer.

Additionally, I am on every committee known to man. I am secretary of the PTO and chairperson of the school fun fair. I help with the church nursery and the church groundskeeping. I also make sure my three sons get to hockey games, Boy Scouts, birthday parties, and so on. At one point when my nine-year-old son asked to have a couple of hockey friends over for a sleepover and couldn't decide which ones, what did good ol' Mom say? "Honey, just invite the whole team! It will be fun!" By 3:00 A.M. the next morning, with all thirteen kids still awake and having already consumed groceries that cost as much as the national debt, I knew I had lost my sanity.

This past Friday, having spent the past couple of weeks crying after my boys were in bed, and then biting my lip and praying hard that I wouldn't scream like a monster at the next child who dared to say "Moooommmm!" I decided it was time for a little retreat just for me! I headed for a Christian bookstore and came out two hours later with thirteen, count 'em, thirteen books and three new CDs and then went straight to the local park. I justified the expense thinking, Heck, it's cheaper than a therapist and I don't have to wait three months for an appointment!

Freedom! Fresh air! No children! I felt like it had been forever since I laughed. So I settled down on my blanket, opened to the first page of *She Who Laughs, Lasts!* and indeed I did laugh! People must have thought I was a crazy woman, but I did not care. I read and prayed and read some more. I related to so many of the stories. For two days I laughed out loud, so much so that I feel like a new woman as I await the arrival of my children today, knowing I can once again be the responsible, strong woman God made me—the one who laughs at spilled milk and messes and delights in hearing the word "Moooommm!"

As Tammy discovered, laughter has a way of renewing our souls and restoring our perspective when all else fails. It's a powerful antidote to the stressed-out, speeded-up, overcommitted style of life we live today.

Someone once told a story about an American explorer who hired a crew to guide him through a portion of the Amazon jungle. The first day the crew worked hard, hacking out a path through the undergrowth. The same thing happened the second day. But the third morning was different. The crew just sat around, making no effort to get started.

When the explorer asked why nothing was being done, one of the guides explained. "It's a very serious problem. The men say they cannot move any farther until their souls have caught up with their bodies."*

What an image! Our bodies running so far ahead that our souls become disconnected. No wonder we feel out of sorts!

We hope that *Don't Stop Laughing Now!* will offer not just a few good laughs but that it will also help you, whatever your circumstances, to put body and soul back together. So relax, settle down, get ready to laugh a little and enjoy yourself. For, as a great philosopher once said: "I laugh, therefore I am!"

*James Truslow Adams, "Time for the Soul," quoted in Mark Link, S.J., *Illustrated Sunday Homilies* (Allen, Tex.: Resources for Christian Living, 1987).

Chapter One

Psst...Has Anyone Seen a Table I Can Crawl Under?

Things are going to get a lot worse before they get worse.
—Lily Tomlin

*I try to take one day at a time, but sometimes
several days attack me at once.*
—Jennifer Unlimited

*If you can't be a good example, then you'll just have
to be a horrible warning.*
—Catherine Aird

Inevitably, the funniest stories are usually the ones we tell on ourselves. Sometimes these stories are downright embarrassing. But once we put away our punctured pride and dust off our damaged dignity, they can become an endless source of amusement. The ability to laugh at ourselves is surely a sign that all is well with our souls.

Humbled by a Pine Tree

Stan Toler

*M*any years ago, I was privileged to serve as the first pastoral staff member of John Maxwell at Faith Memorial Church in Lancaster, Ohio. John, a noted author, lecturer, and former senior pastor of the Skyline Wesleyan Church, has been my mentor for more than twenty years. He has guided me in matters of leadership, preaching, evangelism, and church growth. And from time to time, John, who is an excellent golfer, has felt the need to mentor me in the great game of golf.

On one rainy fall day many years ago in Lancaster, I was working on a project when the intercom buzzer sounded. "Toler," the booming voice of Maxwell said, "let's play 18!"

What a welcome diversion! I thought to myself. In a matter of minutes, we loaded our golf clubs into John's 1972 Ford Pinto and hurried to the nearby Carrollwood golf course. Since it was raining steadily, the course was not crowded and we were able to tee off immediately.

For the first five holes, it appeared that the Maxwell Mentoring Course on golf was working. "What a great game—thanks for asking me to come along," I said to John.

As we approached the sixth tee box, I courageously asked John to loan me his three-wood. He was proud of his new clubs and most willing to share them with his prized pupil. I stepped up to the tee box and took a practice swing. Feeling ready, I swung mightily at the little white ball.

To this day, I don't remember whether I actually hit that ball, but what I do remember is the club slipping out of my hands and sailing twenty feet into the air. Embarrassing? You bet! And if that wasn't humbling enough, the three-wood landed in a pine tree. Maxwell was in a state of utter disbelief.

"You just threw my new club into a tree!" he cried. "How on earth are we going to get it down?"

Mustering all the confidence I had, I said, "Give me your shoe." Obediently, John sat down on the cart and handed me his golf shoe. I carefully aimed his shoe at the club and gave it a mighty heave, expecting it to knock the club out of the pine tree. To my dismay, his shoe got stuck in the same tree.

Undaunted, I said, "Give me your other shoe." Again, without arguing, John handed his other shoe to me. Taking better aim, I tossed his shoe at the club, and missed again! Can you believe it? The second shoe stayed in the tree also.

As the drizzle started to become a downpour, Maxwell stood up and said, "Toler, you big dummy! No, wait a minute—I'm the dummy! Stan, give me your shoe!"

In a spirit of cooperation—and fear—I took off my shoe and handed it to him. And why not? He had a three-wood and two golf shoes in that pine tree. Taking careful aim, he threw my shoe at the club. Up it went, approximately eighteen feet in the air, and missed everything. Feeling more confident, I picked up my shoe and tossed it at the club. It missed the club, but as it fell downward, it knocked one of John's shoes loose. In the process, however, my shoe got stuck in the tree. John immediately grabbed his shoe that had fallen to the ground and clutched it defensively. Now neither of us had a complete pair of shoes, and still the golf club was stuck in the tree.

By this time, several other golfers had passed the sixth tee, observing this Laurel and Hardy comedy routine. Remarkably, most did not speak or offer to help us. (Can you blame them?)

When every effort had failed in retrieving the golf club, my esteemed friend finally climbed the huge pine tree and personally retrieved the club and our shoes. At that point, it began to thunder, and the rain was coming down even harder. The only thing left to do was quit for the day and go to the clubhouse for hot chocolate.

Feeling embarrassed and helpless, we drove rapidly across the course to the clubhouse. As John opened the door, the room became silent. And that's when paranoia instantly gripped us. Sure enough, the other golfers had told on us! As we stood in the doorway, laughter erupted like you've never heard.

We shut the door, turned right around, and went straight home. And believe me, it was a long time before we played golf there again.

THE ALMOND JOY INCIDENT

Cathy Lee Phillips

It all started with a simple glass of water. It was Day Fourteen of my Weight Watchers diet, and I was doing great! I'd lost seven pounds by carefully keeping track of my food exchanges. For two weeks I'd successfully avoided hamburgers and cheesecake. I was following the regime religiously in all areas but one—I simply couldn't drink eight glasses of water a day. Impossible! I could never get further than glass number six. I spent the rest of the day trotting to the nearest bathroom.

Nevertheless, on this particular Saturday, I was determined that nothing would deter me from consuming the prescribed eight glasses. Nothing! So I panicked at 11:36 P.M. when I realized I'd only had seven glasses of water. Only twenty-four meager minutes until midnight. Could I do it?

Despite the late hour and the danger of bladder-related sleep deprivation, I braced myself for one more glass of water. In the kitchen I grabbed a glass and sliced a fresh, juicy lemon. The nightmare began when I opened the freezer for a few cubes of ice. It was lying there, innocently tucked behind a few stray cartons of frozen yogurt and two packs of Weight Watchers frozen lasagna. How it got there is still a mystery. I only know that my eyes grew wide and my heart beat wildly.

An Almond Joy! Two simple bits of coconut, each bathed in milk chocolate and crowned with a large crunchy almond, swaddled in a beautiful blue wrapper. An Almond Joy!

17

Rationalization was easy. I'd been on my diet for two weeks and had lost seven pounds. Surely one simple candy bar wouldn't harm me. I probably needed the sugar in my system after not having had any for, lo, these fourteen days. And it was an awfully hot night so the candy bar would be especially cool and refreshing. Besides, it wasn't as if I'd been looking for an Almond Joy. On the contrary, the Almond Joy had found me!

Best of all, my husband, Jerry, was sleeping soundly. He would never know. No one would ever know. It was all so perfect. Surely it was God's will that I eat this Almond Joy!

Grabbing the candy bar and my number eight glass of water, I raced for the sofa. I crossed my legs underneath me, aimed the TV remote, and found a *MASH* rerun. Perfect! Quite deliberately I unwrapped my newfound treasure from its bright blue cover and held it aloft. Life was suddenly very exciting.

The candy bar was frozen but not too firm against my teeth. It was cool and sweet. And it was all mine. No one would ever know that I'd surrendered my diet for this piece of heaven that had so unexpectedly entered my life.

I ate it all. Every bit of coconut, every dab of chocolate, every crumb of almond. And because I had something to eat, it was so much easier to drink my number eight glass of water.

Turning off the TV, I placed my empty glass in the sink and popped the bright blue wrapper in the trash can. Risking a mouthful of cavities, I didn't even stop to brush my teeth. I fell asleep with the taste of Almond Joy still dancing in my mouth.

My husband, a pastor, awoke early the next morning to put the finishing touches on his sermon. While I slept soundly, he puttered in the kitchen, toasting some bread and pouring himself a tall glass of orange juice. Emptying the carton, he opened the pantry door and reached for the garbage can. The bag was full. As he bent to remove it, Jerry discovered the remains of a bright blue Almond Joy wrapper perched atop the other miscellaneous garbage.

What is this? he thought to himself. He didn't remember eating a candy bar. And knowing I was religiously following the Weight Watchers diet, he was puzzled by the object that had somehow found its way into our garbage can. Clutching the wrapper to his chest, he walked quietly back to the bedroom where I slept, unaware of the trouble at hand.

"Cathy," he nudged me gently. Opening one eye slowly, I looked into his loving face. He smiled at me. I smiled back. Was he feeling romantic at this hour? And on a Sunday morning? Then, almost immediately, I caught sight of a familiar bright blue piece of paper in his hand. Could it be? Jerry dangled the wrapper above me, a clever smirk on his face.

"Do you want to tell me about this?" he asked. The smirk grew larger.

It wasn't that my husband noticed every pound I gained or lost. He loved me regardless of my weight or the number of Almond Joys I might consume. I knew that without question.

It was the smirk.

That arrogant little grin told me that my late-night escapade was no longer my little secret. I'd been found out.

So, why not just admit I'd found an Almond Joy and, in a moment of weakness, had eaten it? I knew I should have told the truth, but in the heat of the moment I panicked. I can only blame my actions on the "sinful" chocolate in my stomach and the smirk on my husband's face.

"The candy bar belonged to Ray Lathem," I blurted.

Ray Lathem, a good friend of ours and member of our church, lived across the street from our parsonage. Recently Ray had been placed on a strict eating program by his doctor, so he and I often shared our dieting successes and failures. I knew, therefore, that Ray would understand my Almond Joy experience. I would tell him about it after church and we would have a good laugh together.

"Last night, Ray Lathem knocked on our door," the lie began. "He'd been craving a candy bar all day but knew his family would never let him have one. Finally, he couldn't stand it! In a moment of weakness, he ate an Almond Joy he'd hidden in his truck. But he didn't know what to do with the wrapper. If his wife found it, she'd know he'd abandoned his diet. So Ray sneaked out of his house and knocked on our door. He had one simple request: Could he place the wrapper in our garbage can? What could I do? Of course I would let my friend and fellow dieter place the wrapper in our garbage can," I concluded with great emotion.

"That's your story?" Jerry's smirk filled the room.

"And I'm sticking to it," I replied, rather proud of the creativity I'd exhibited at such an early hour. I pulled the blanket over my head while Jerry, chuckling loudly, returned to his sermon and orange juice.

I put the story out of my mind until 11:35 A.M. when Jerry, beginning his sermon, reached inside his pocket and held the familiar wrapper before the entire congregation.

"Ray Lathem, does this belong to you?" the voice from the pulpit inquired.

Ray and his wife, Leila, were in their usual pew. Confused, Ray looked innocently at Leila, begging to be believed.

Knowing I had a sense of humor and had agreed to having the details of my life shared with the entire congregation, my husband relayed the story and then thanked me for providing the perfect illustration for his sermon entitled, appropriately enough, "The Devil Made Me Do It." The congregation laughed and laughed. And they kept laughing.

In fact, Ray laughed the loudest, delighted that I'd included him in my elaborate tale.

Afterwards, many people came up to me saying I was a good sport for being able to laugh at myself. And, before the day was done, more than two dozen Almond Joys had been brought to our home by sympathetic friends who themselves had fallen off the diet wagon at least once. With his wife's permission, I shared the goods with Ray Lathem.

During his sermon, Jerry shared the passage in Numbers 32 in which Moses told the Israelites their sins would find them out. Jerry said our sins would always find us out sooner or later too.

Mine sure did. I just pray I can learn to limit my sins to Almond Joys.

Icebreaker SOS

Sheri Rose Shepherd

*W*hen a group of women get together for a retreat without their husbands and children, there's no telling what will happen. At one particular gathering, the planners decided to have an icebreaker game before I began my presentation. They divided us into Group A and Group B and had a contest to see which group could turn in the most items from their collective purses.

First they called for lipsticks, and we all dug around in our purses to fish out our Cantaloupe Blush, Pouty Persimmon, or whatever, and passed it to the front. The next category was receipts, then breath mints, and so on down the line. The sides were pretty evenly matched, and by the final round the score was tied at nine points each. Whoever won the next round would be Purse Scavenger Champs, with bragging rights for the whole weekend.

I was in Group A, and we smelled victory right around the corner. We were pumped. The moderator prepared to announce the last category, pausing for dramatic effect as we sat with hands poised over our pocketbooks. "And now the championship category is . . . tweezers."

One of my teammates in the back of the room pulled a pair of tweezers out of her bag and, instead of passing them, launched them toward the front, since time was an essential element of going for the gold. The tweezers flew through the air to where I sat in the front row and stuck like a blow dart in the back of my head. When I turned to see what happened—was the other side attacking us?—

the tweezers fell out of my scalp, bounced off my shoulder, ricocheted off my lap, and ran my hose from knee to heel.

Of course it was now time for me to speak. Bloodied, battle scarred, and with no time to repair the damage (at least we won!), I took my place at the lectern. To my left was a big speaker box. "Is this in your way?" I asked the audience. "Yes!" they all shouted. Trying to be useful, I began loosening the clamp on the stand so I could lower it. Unfortunately, gravity had other plans. With a hair-raising screech, the speaker cabinet slid down the stand and pinched my hand. My eyes bulged. My heart pounded. My hand throbbed.

Five hundred women gasped at the sight of their guest being attacked by a cabinet full of woofers and tweeters. I didn't think I was seriously hurt—nothing ice packs and a week of bed rest wouldn't fix—and I tried to make light of the whole thing. "Sometimes I break a nail right before I speak," I joked, "and I always think that means my message is going to be anointed. Since I've just punctured my head, run my hose, and broken my hand, this will probably be the best message I've ever given."

Everyone laughed, the tension was broken, and I launched into the presentation. About thirty seconds into it, I said, "I don't think the Devil wants me to deliver this message today." At that instant a potted plant above me tipped over on its side, sending a substantial shower of mulch, dirt, and vermiculite all over me and the lectern. I had expected to teach by word rather than by example that day, but God had other plans.

The title of my program? "How Do You React to Trial and Tribulation?"

A Complete Ensemble

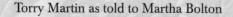

Torry Martin as told to Martha Bolton

Shortly after moving from Washington, D.C., to the Los Angeles area to attend college, I decided I needed to go shopping for some new shorts. I was down to only one pair and everyone knows shorts and a T-shirt is the southern California uniform. So when I happened upon a sidewalk sale and discovered numerous pairs of shorts in my size, I was elated. I grabbed about ten pairs and began trying them on in their dressing room. Five pairs fit, so I took both bundles up to the checkout counter.

"I'd like to buy all these," I told the clerk as I handed him the stack of shorts that I wanted to buy. "And you can have these," I said, handing him the stack of shorts that I didn't want to buy.

"You don't want any of these?" he asked, looking over the rejected stack.

"No. Just those five I've picked out," I said.

"You're sure?" he pressed.

"I'm sure," I said, wondering why he was being so pushy. I was buying five pairs of shorts. Wasn't that enough? Was he working on a quota system or something?

"You're really sure these are all you want?" he continued.

"Yes," I said, emphatically. "These are the only ones I want." I could feel the veins in my neck beginning to bulge.

"All right," he said as he began to ring them up. "I just thought you might like to take these," he said, holding up the pair of shorts

I had worn into the store. I didn't even have to look down. I knew at that instant I was standing there in my underwear and shirt. I grabbed my shorts and rushed back to the dressing room to finish dressing. California's casual, but not that casual!

AWKWARD SITUATIONS

Becky Freeman with Ruthie Arnold

$\mathcal{H}$ave you ever had one of those experiences when you wish you could just disappear? Often I want to do that, especially when I find myself in a situation where it is rude, sacrilegious, or unthinkable to do what I have an uncontrollable urge to do—laugh. My husband, Scott, has been so embarrassed by my outbursts in the past that he is now skittish about sitting next to me in any formal situation. It's an awful affliction, and I honestly don't know what to do about it.

It's pure agony to try to suppress the laughter. I bite into the flesh of my cheeks, cover my mouth and nose, and still . . . I somehow manage to blow. I once got tickled at a prayer meeting—not at a lighthearted women's prayer meeting, but a serious, down-on-your-knees prayer meeting in Glen Eyrie, Colorado. A nice young fellow was leading us in prayer, and I know this is no excuse, but he had the most nasal tone I have ever heard from the mouth of a human being.

On top of "the voice" came a string of requests addressed to the Almighty with an incredible preponderance of "eths." "Dear Father, blesseth Thoueth the meetingeth hereth in our presenceth." The giggle bubbled up from the belly, threatening to pour forth through my mouth and nose. I slapped my mouth and held my nose. The sound I issued resembled a suckling pig. My shoulders began to shake, and I could sense Scott's presence seething next to me. Then there was a blessed pause, and I thought I might be saved. But no. "Andeth ifeth it pleaseth Thine heart, maketh useth . . ." At that point I began to wheeze. There was to be no mercy. It waseth the prayer that hadeth no endeth.

Finally, I grabbed a Kleenex, feigned being overcome with emotion, and ran out the door pretending to sob. Actually, by the time I got out of there, I was laughing so hard I began to weep. After the service, Scott was livid with shame and embarrassment. I apologized profusely, but then I noticed how Scott's nostrils flared when he got mad and how his ears twitched when his voice got loud, and I found myself once again in a situation where fools laugh and angels fear to tread.

Everyone I'm sure has had the experience of going into the wrong rest room a time or two. Granted, there are some of us who have done this a bit more often than others, but my mild-mannered, deeply spiritual father has the prize for the most embarrassing example of this awkward situation. The horrible part is that he was stuck in the women's rest room at no less than the prestigious Dallas Theological Seminary, where he was taking a layman's course. He came to realize that something was awry when he saw a woman's purse drop down in the stall next to him.

All he could think of was how he would explain his presence to Dr. Howard Hendricks if he should come strolling down the hall-way just as Daddy ran in panic out of the ladies' room.

Chapter Two

I'm Okay . . . You, I'm Not So Sure About

The closest distance between two people is a good laugh.
−Victor Borge

Why is it that most of the jokes we hear are credited to that prolific author named "anonymous"? Perhaps it's because we're so hungry for good laughs that we simply gobble them up before we notice who said what to whom. Some of the stories that follow have no doubt passed around the globe faster than the speed of light. Whether or not the pieces are jokes or stories taken from real life, you'll note that each one concerns the funniest two creatures on earth−men and women.

THE PERFECT WOMAN

Anonymous

*O*nce upon a time, a perfect man and a perfect woman met. After a perfect courtship, they had a perfect wedding. Their life was, of course, "perfect."

One snowy, stormy Christmas Eve, this perfect couple was driving their perfect car (an SUV) along a winding road, when they noticed someone at the side of the road in distress. Being the perfect couple, they stopped to help.

There stood Santa Claus with a huge bundle of toys. Not wanting to disappoint any children on the eve of Christmas, the perfect couple loaded Santa and his toys into their vehicle. Soon they were driving along delivering the toys.

Unfortunately, the driving conditions deteriorated and the perfect couple and Santa Claus had an accident. Only one of them survived the accident.

Who was the survivor?

Answer: The perfect woman survived. She's the only one who really existed in the first place. Everyone knows there is no Santa Claus and there is no such thing as a perfect man.

* Women stop reading here, that is the end of the joke. Men keep reading. *

So, if there is no perfect man and no Santa Claus, the perfect woman must have been driving. This explains why there was an accident.

ADAM'S BARGAIN

Anonymous

*A*dam was walking around the Garden of Eden feeling very lonely, so God asked Adam, "What is wrong with you?"

Adam said he didn't have anyone to talk to.

God said, "I was going to give you a companion, and it would be a woman."

God continued: "This person will cook for you and wash your clothes. She will always agree with every decision you make. She will bear your children and never ask you to get up in the middle of the night to take care of them. She will not nag you, and will always be the first to admit she was wrong when you've had a disagreement. She will never have a headache, and will freely give you love and compassion whenever needed."

Adam asked God, "What would a woman like this cost me?"

God said, "An arm and a leg."

Adam asked, "What can I get for just a rib?"

READ MY LIPS

Karen Scalf Linamen

I saw this great bumper sticker yesterday. It said, "Oh, Evolve."

I saw another bumper sticker a couple weeks ago. It wasn't nearly as subtle. It said, "Men Are Idiots and I Married Their King."

What was particularly funny is that the King was driving the car.

We love to make statements, don't we? On our bumpers, our T-shirts . . .

And speaking of clothing statements, the one I've never quite understood is the whole deal with B.U.M. Equipment. Why a man would wear a shirt announcing something like that to the entire world is beyond me.

The truth is, personal statements fascinate me, whether we're talking about someone using their car, clothing, or their computer to say, "This is who I am, and here's what I think about this or that."

And what about statements of faith? I don't know about your household, but there are more WWJD [What Would Jesus Do?] bracelets floating around mine than wrists to wear them. And plenty of T-shirts sporting Bible verses or faith-inspired phrases too.

Although here's the thing with wearing your faith on your sleeve, so to speak. It helps if you put your actions where your mouth is. It's like the time about ten years ago when I was driving down the road and pulled in behind a sedan sporting the bumper sticker that said, "Honk If You Love Jesus!" (Remember those?) So

I honked. Now, it's possible the man driving the sedan thought I was trying to hurry him along. In any case, he indicated his displeasure by twisting around in his seat and flashing me a lone finger (and it wasn't the "One Way" sign either!).

I'm all for catchy slogans. "Honk If You Love Jesus" was catchy. "Smile, Jesus Loves You" was catchy. Even WWJD was catchy.

I've got one that's not so catchy, but I'd love to see it catch on nonetheless. However, as illustrated by our finger-waving friend in the sedan, it's got to be accompanied by the right actions to really carry any punch.

It goes like this:

HCILJLYTM?

Now, *there's* a great statement. I realize it's about as pronounceable as the name of The Artist Formerly Known As Prince, but it's a great statement nonetheless. In fact, I'd love to launch a national campaign with this statement. I'd love to print it on billboards and bumper stickers and T-shirts (okay, so they'd have to be size XL to handle all the letters, but still . . .).

And February would be a great month to begin. It's the month of love, the perfect time for showing folks how much we care about them, and an even better month to show them how much Jesus cares for them.

HCILJLYTM?

It could revolutionize your world.

The meaning? Simple:

How Can I Let Jesus Love You Through Me?

Okay, so I don't have the shirts printed yet, the bumper stickers are still in the art department, and we had to go back to the drawing board with the earrings. (Too heavy. Potential spinal column compression.)

But even if you don't have the paraphernalia, wear the attitude. Be an instrument of God's love in the lives of those around you. Offer an encouraging word, a helping hand, a sacrificial gift. Better yet, take the guesswork out of it—just go up to your husband or your kids or your mom or your best friend or your pastor and ask outright: "How can I let Jesus love you through me today?"

And then do it.

In the meantime, I'll keep working on those T-shirts. Watch for them this spring in the Plus Size department of your local Christian bookstore.

WOMEN TELL WHAT THEY WANT IN A MAN

Anonymous

What I Want in a Man, Original List (age 22)

1. Handsome
2. Charming
3. Financially successful
4. A caring listener
5. Witty
6. In good shape
7. Dresses with style
8. Appreciates finer things
9. Full of thoughtful surprises
10. An imaginative, romantic lover

What I Want in a Man, Revised List (age 32)

1. Nice looking—prefer hair on his head
2. Opens car doors, holds chairs
3. Has enough money for a nice dinner
4. Listens more than talks
5. Laughs at my jokes
6. Carries bags of groceries with ease
7. Owns at least one tie
8. Appreciates a good home-cooked meal
9. Remembers birthdays and anniversaries
10. Seeks romance at least once a week

What I Want in a Man, Revised List (age 42)

1. Not too ugly–bald head okay
2. Doesn't drive off until I'm in the car
3. Works steady–splurges on dinner at Denny's on occasion
4. Nods head when I'm talking
5. Usually remembers punch lines of jokes
6. Is in good enough shape to rearrange the furniture
7. Wears a shirt that covers his stomach
8. Knows not to buy champagne with screw-top lids
9. Remembers to put the toilet seat down
10. Shaves on most weekends

What I Want in a Man, Revised List (age 52)

1. Keeps hair in nose and ears trimmed
2. Doesn't belch or scratch in public
3. Doesn't borrow money too often
4. Doesn't nod off to sleep when I'm venting
5. Doesn't retell same joke too many times
6. Is in good enough shape to get off couch on weekends
7. Usually wears matching socks and fresh underwear
8. Appreciates a good TV dinner
9. Remembers my name on occasion
10. Shaves some weekends

What I Want in a Man, Revised List (age 62)

1. Doesn't scare small children
2. Remembers where the bathroom is
3. Doesn't require much money for upkeep
4. Snores only lightly when awake (*loudly* when asleep)
5. Remembers why he's laughing
6. Is in good enough shape to stand up by himself
7. Usually wears some clothes
8. Likes soft foods
9. Remembers where he left his teeth
10. Remembers that it is a weekend

What I Want in a Man, Revised List (age 72)

1. Breathing

They Need Help!

Thelma Wells

*D*uring the first few years of my marriage, I dedicated myself to changing my husband, George. When I married him, he was perfect. Then, shortly after the honeymoon, he changed! Little things started to annoy me. His grammar wasn't perfect. He was too quiet. He never planned any fun activities for us. In short, he needed help! And as his wife, it was my duty to remake him into a perfect being, according to my own ideals.

Now, when we would discuss *his issues,* he'd reply, "Thelma, this is the way I am and you can't change me. If anyone has changed in this relationship, it's you." Can you believe that? He was accusing *me* of changing! Hmmmph.

As the years ticked by, our idea of the perfect marriage revolved around lifestyle and luxuries. But I wasn't happy. It wasn't enough. Our marriage needed changing. *George* needed changing.

During that same period, I noticed that our oldest daughter, Vikki, needed changing too. She was a lot like her father—a loner. She would hibernate in front of the television set or hide out in her room and read a book. She was too quiet, especially at times when I needed her to be charming. I would introduce her to people and she would look at them, without smiling or even attempting to look friendly, and mumble a cold, disinterested "Hi." Nothing else, just "Hi."

One day when she was twelve, I introduced her to some church members and she barely spoke. I had had it. When we got in the car, I yelled at her and told her I would no longer tolerate her indifference and "rudeness." I explained what an appropriate greeting was, how embarrassed I was, how impolite she was. On and on I told her about herself, for forty-five loud minutes.

When I finished, she said something I will never forget. With her arms folded in a "get out of my life" posture, she quietly, yet firmly, stated, "Mama, I love you. But I'm not you. I don't even want to be like you."

What? You don't want to be like me! Say what? How dare you! My head was swimming. *Why doesn't my own daughter want to be like me? I'm wonderful. Does she not understand that I'm a Proverbs 31 woman?!*

I allowed myself to get so angry with that girl that I didn't even want to feed her, but I had to. She *was* my child. But my feelings were crushed. After all, she came from me. She ought to want to be like me. *(Whine-whine.)*

But after a few weeks, I understood her statement. What she was really saying was, "Mother, God made me different from you and everybody else. I am a unique person with my own personality, preferences, and desires. Please accept me the way I am and respect my individuality."

I started asking myself why I *needed* to change the people around me. Why was I so stubborn about having things and people my way?

After much soul-searching, I had to admit that the issues I perceived as others' problems were really my own. I observed my own behavior and became consciously aware of my own shortcomings. The change needed to happen in *me*. Ouch.

Once I realized I had been blind to my own faults, I saw just how much love and patience others had with me. During those stormy years of our marriage, my husband never gave up. He loved me with a gracious, unfailing love. He was never angry for an extended length of time. He always tried to reason with me. He made a very few demands on me, and he trusted me. My goodness, once I removed the stick out of my own eye, I saw I had me a righteous man!

I'm glad I got over my obsession to change George, Vikki, and others. George and I have been married nearly forty years now, and not only do we love each other, but we like each other too.

And Vikki and I are thick as thieves. We are a prime example of how true love can survive turmoil. We have learned that even in the face of adversity, godly love is patient and kind. It is not fault-finding. It is not selfish. It never fails.

THE LOVING SPOUSE

Anonymous

A woman accompanied her husband to the doctor's office for his checkup. Afterward the doctor took the wife aside and said, "Unless you do the following things, your husband will surely die."

The doctor went on to say, "Here's what you need to do. Every morning make sure you serve him a good healthy breakfast. Meet him at home every day and serve him a well-balanced lunch. Also, feed him a good hot meal each evening.

"Don't overburden him with stressful conversation, nor ask him to perform any household chores. Also, keep the house spotless and clean so he doesn't get exposed to any threatening germs. Be available to serve his every whim."

On the way home the husband asked the wife, "What did the doctor say?"

She replied, "He said you're going to die."

REALLY BAD DAY

Anonymous

$\mathcal{A}$ woman came home to find her husband in the kitchen, shaking frantically with what looked like a wire running from his waist towards the electric kettle. Intending to jolt him away from the deadly current she whacked him with a handy plank of wood left by the back door, breaking his arm in two places. A shame, as he had merely been dancing while listening to his Walkman.

Steaming in the Southwest

Charlene Ann Baumbich

Vacations are wonderful for an old married couple. Two people, sharing an adventure, seeing the sights, being together nearly every minute, becoming acutely aware they don't like the same activities, working on different time clocks, being trapped in the car together for hours on end ... Whoops!

Okay, so after many years some of the vacation glow may be gone, but that doesn't mean you can't fan the embers and look for suitable compromises. Right?

So with bellows pumping, George and I headed off alone together from Albuquerque (where we were visiting family) to Santa Fe (where yet more tourists were) for a two-day romantic respite. Maybe we'd even take a drive up to Taos.

We didn't get out of Albuquerque until late afternoon and I was hungry; we'd eaten a late breakfast and just never got around to lunch. Hunger brings out the extra bad of my worst side(s). Trust me on this. George wanted to check into our motel before eating. Usually he's good about stopping when I need to, but this day found him a man with a mission. Before we got to the Super 8, I was whining.

"George, do you know that no matter where we go in this country, it looks the same because we always stay at a Super 8? I know they have clean, dependable rooms and are in our budget, but what's the point of traveling halfway across the country to see the same thing every place we go? Milwaukee, Minnesota, San Francisco, and now Santa Fe will all feel the same when I go to bed. Why, George, can't we stay in a different place just once in a while? A place that ... *blah blah blah.*"

George finally spoke. "What road is the Super 8 on? Are you looking at the map? Is this where we exit?"

"George, you're not listening to a word I say."

"Yes, I am. You're complaining about why we always stay in a Super 8."

"Right. So?"

"So remember the time the Super 8 was full in Winona? That other place cost us $98. And for what? A bed?"

"No, George. It had a whirlpool bathtub and a swimming pool. It had a sauna and a weight room. It had a game room and cable. It had continental breakfast. It felt like vacation."

"I'd rather spend the money on something else. What do we do in the room anyway? Get in late, go to sleep, and then get up early and go eat because you're hungry, right? We're barely in the room. Why pay big bucks for a bed?"

"George, maybe we'd spend more time in the room if it were a little nicer. More exciting. More exotic. Get my drift?"

"Is this where I turn? I'm turning."

"George, you just don't care what I think, do you?"

"Yes, I care."

"But we're staying at the Super 8 anyway, right?"

"Right."

The ride to the Super 8 was quiet. I'm sure George was happy. We found it without much trouble, took our bags to the room, went to the desk, and asked about the location of a very close place to eat. The desk clerk recommended a "nice family restaurant right down the street." Back into the car we went, down the four-lane divided highway toward the middle of town. Before we'd ventured very far, I spotted it.

"There it is, George. Get in the other lane."

"I see it."

"George! Get in the other lane."

"I'll handle it. I can't pull over right now. There's a car coming up."

"You can't pull over right now because there's a car coming up because you didn't pull over back there when I first told you to. Now you're going to miss the turn," I said as we whizzed by the restaurant.

Two things are at work here: one, I was starving, not hungry, but starving; and two, George is always in the wrong lane. It's a miracle he found the right chute at birth.

After traveling several blocks before we could turn around and finally get back to the restaurant, I had done a lot of internal talking. *Shut up, Charlene. You're on vacation. Just because George drives like a Gomer doesn't mean you have to keep chiding. What's the point of arguing? Does it get you anywhere faster?*

And so we entered the restaurant on a quiet but hungry note. We were the only ones there. If there was an atmosphere more hostile than our little family, it was this little family restaurant. It permeated the place.

Finally we asked if they were open.

"Yes!" snapped a woman. She headed for the seating area without offering so much as a "follow me." We sat across from one another trying to ignore the fact that an older woman was cleaning tables and seat covers and flinging the chairs around. Seriously. They were nearly airborne.

In the meantime, the woman who had seated us was on the phone. Screaming. "You don't appreciate a thing I do for you! You can't even pick up when I ask you to. I can't believe. . . !"

George and I decided our own friction was enough for us. It was emotionally too hot in there. We left.

Now we had no plan for a restaurant. George spotted a nearby McDonalds and suggested we eat there.

"First we have to stay at a Super 8, then you want me to travel halfway across the country to eat at McDonalds?"

"I thought you were starving."

"I am, but for vacation food."

"Where do you want to eat?"

"I don't know. Just head toward the square. How many miles are we from the square anyway? Super 8s are always on the outskirts of town. Wouldn't it be nice if we could occasionally just walk to a restaurant? Maybe even eat in our hotel lobby?"

"Well, you can't. Just tell me where you want to go." As soon as those words left George's mouth, a thought occurred to him. "Hey, didn't we get a sheet of coupons from the rental car place? Didn't they say, 'If you get to Santa Fe, here's some coupons for free hors d'oeuvres'?"

"Yes," I said in my starving, weakened state. I began thrashing through the glove compartment. "Here it is." I read him a list of about eight restaurants. "What do you have a taste for?"

"I don't care. What do you want? You're the one who's hungry."

"Italian. Pasta sounds real good," I chirped.

"I don't have a taste for Italian."

"Then don't tell me to pick a place! Where do you want to go?"

"I'm driving. I can't read the map. Just pick something and tell me what lane to get into."

Finally I decided on Thai food. I looked location number six up on the coupon map and tried to get a read on the next intersection. Of course we were in the wrong lane. Of course we missed our turn—twice. Of course it took us a very long time to finally see the sign. The volume on our voices had escalated to Mach 9.

Finally we pulled up across the street from the place and George began to enter the parking lot. I clutched the door handle for a quick exit.

"Pay parking? I'm not paying to park to go eat!"

"George! You're getting a free appetizer. You're on vacation. Park."

There was no way George was pulling into the pay lot. We cruised around until we found a parking spot with a meter. Gimme a break! Like meters are free?

George went to the meter and plunked in a dime. The red arm in the meter barely made a clinking noise, then registered only twenty minutes. George was furious. Good, we were even.

He put in two more dimes, then asked me how long it would take to eat. Wrong question, George. "If you think I'm cramming down my food now after waiting all this time so you don't have to . . ." He emptied his pockets of change, stuffed each coin in the meter, and we headed for the restaurant—only to find out they didn't open for another hour.

We slammed our car doors and began another quick study of the map. We settled on the Blue Corn Café. It didn't look too far away. One-way, wrong-way, around the block we went.

"There, George. There's a lot."

"What? I'm not paying to park in a lot. I'll find a place. Just be quiet."

The only way I could follow that directive was to leave the car. I announced I was heading for the restaurant to order a beverage and our free appetizer.

"Fine."

"Fine." I leaped out of the car in the middle of the intersection. *Slambang.* George peeled off.

I accidentally set off in the right direction. I almost missed it, however, because the entrance was on the corner, and the sign wasn't visible as you looked down the street. The restaurant was upstairs and quite cute. I was seated immediately and was very happy to see a bowl of chips and salsa as soon as my backside hit the chair. I began cramming them into my mouth and could barely speak when the waiter came to take my order. I explained I was waiting for someone, but that we'd like our free appetizer. Two bowls of chips, half the free guacamole, and twenty minutes later, George still had not arrived.

It occurred to me he wasn't able to: (1) remember the name of the restaurant; (2) couldn't find it because of its hidden location; or (3) had headed for Chicago without me.

I called over the waiter and said, "I'm beginning to envision a very bad evening. I'm not skipping out, but I need to leave for a few minutes to find my husband. I'll be back."

Down the stairs I headed, then up and down the street. No George. I decided to stay put; that's what we always used to tell the kids when they were lost.

Suddenly I heard his yelling voice. "Where am I supposed to park?" George's head hung out the window as he passed through the intersection in our two-door Thunderbird rental car, smoke rolling out of his ears, looking every bit the maniacal man. "No one will give me change for the meter, and I put it all in the last place!"

I couldn't believe it. He was still driving around trying to avoid the lot. I simply pointed, shook my head, and headed back to the guacamole.

Yes, vacations are a wonderful thing for an old married couple. Two people, sharing an adventure, seeing the sights, being together nearly every minute, becoming acutely aware they don't like the same activities, working on different time clocks, being trapped in the car together for hours on end . . .

Chapter Three

You Can't Kid a Kid

A ten-year-old, under the tutelage of her grandmother, was becoming quite knowledgeable about the Bible. Then one day she floored her grandmother by asking, "Which virgin was the mother of Jesus: the Virgin Mary or the King James Virgin?"
—from christianwomentoday.com/

You know children are growing up when they start asking questions that have answers.
—John Plomp

Part of what makes something funny is the element of surprise. And what more surprising creatures than those mischievous beings we call children? Always making trouble with a big grin. Always looking at life from some strange new corner of the universe. Always upsetting the status quo by blurting out the most disarming and truthful statements about anything and everything. No wonder they both keep us young and threaten to send us to an early grave. Our definition of a kid is simply this: A kid is the shortest distance between two laughs.

THE REVISED NONSTANDARD BIBLE

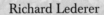

Richard Lederer

A Sunday school teacher was talking about Christmas and the coming of Christ and she asked, "And what was Jesus' mother's name?"

"Mary," all said.

"Now what was his father's name?"

One little fellow raised his hand, "Virg."

"Virg? Where did you get that idea?"

"Well," answered the boy, "they always talk about the Virg 'n' Mary!"

Another religion teacher was telling her class the story of Lot. "Lot was warned to take his wife and flee out of the city, but his wife looked back and she was turned to salt." She looked around the class, and one little girl tentatively raised her hand. "Yes?" said the teacher.

"I was wondering," said the girl, "what happened to the flea?"

When a Hebrew school teacher intoned, "The Lord Our God is one," little Benjamin asked, "When will he be two?"

An art teacher in a Maine elementary school also taught Sunday school, where she had the little ones draw pictures of Bible stories. Little Emma proudly presented her picture of the journey to Bethlehem. The drawing showed an airplane flying over the desert. In the passenger area were seated Joseph and Mary and little Jesus.

"The drawing is fine," said the teacher, "but who's that up front flying the plane?"

Answered Emma, "Why, that's Pontius the Pilot."

Another religion teacher told her first-graders to draw a big picture of the story of Adam and Eve and the Garden of Eden. One little boy drew a big car with God at the wheel driving Adam and Eve out of Paradise.

When yet another teacher asked her student why there was a dog in the nativity drawing, the fledgling artist explained that it was a German shepherd. That dog has been joined in the gallery of Sunday school portraiture by a grinning bear with crossed eyes— Gladly, the Cross-Eyed Bear, of course.

Sunday school boys and girls produce not only graphic misinterpretations of the Bible in their drawings. They also rewrite biblical history with amazing grace. It is truly astonishing what happens to Bible stories when they are retold by young scholars around the world:

The Bible is full of many interesting caricatures. Michael Angelo painted them on the Sixteen Chapels.

The first five books of the Bible are Genesis, Exodus, Laxatives, Deuteronomy, and Numbers. In the first book of the Bible, Guinessis, God got tired of creating the world, so he took the Sabbath off. Adam and Eve were created from an apple tree. One of their children, Cain, asked, "Am I my brother's son? My punishment is greater than I can bare."

Noah's wife was called Joan of Ark. He built an ark, which the animals came on to in pears. Lot's wife was a pillar of salt by day, but a ball of fire by night. Saddam and Gomorrah were twins.

Abraham begat Isaac and Isaac begat Jacob and Jacob begat twelve partridges. God asked Abraham to sacrifice Isaac on Mount Montezuma. Abraham took Isaac up the mountain to be circumcised. Jacob, son of Isaac, stole his brother Esau's birthmark. Esau was a man who wrote fables and sold his copyright for a mess of potash. Jacob was a patriarch who brought up his twelve sons to be patriarchs, but they did not take to it. One of Jacob's sons, Joseph, gave refuse to the Israelites.

The Jews were a proud people and throughout history they had trouble with the unsympathetic Genitals. Samson was a strongman who let himself be led astray by a Jezebel like Delilah. Samson slayed the Philistines with the axe of the apostles. He slayed them by pulling down the pillows of the temple.

Pharaoh forced the Hebrew slaves to make beds without straw. Moses was an Egyptian who lived in a hark made of bullrushes. Moses led the Hebrews to the Red Sea, where they made unleavened bread, which is bread made without any ingredients. The Egyptians were all drowned in the dessert.

Afterwards, Moses went up on Mount Cyanide to get the Ten Amendments. The First Commandment was when Eve told Adam to eat the apple. The Fifth Commandment is humor thy father and mother. The Seventh Commandment is thou shalt not admit adultery. The Ninth Commandment is thou salt not bare faults witness.

Moses ate nothing but whales and manner for forty years. He died before he ever reached Canada. Then, Joshua led the Hebrews in the battle of Geritol. The greatest miracle in the Bible is when Joshua told his son to stand still and he obeyed him.

David was a Hebrew king skilled at playing the liar. He wrote psalms. They are called psalms because he sang them while playing the harmonica. David also fought with the Finkelsteins, a race of people who lived in biblical times. Solomon, one of David's sons, had 300 wives and 700 porcupines.

Later came Job, who had one trouble after another. Eventually, he lost all his cattle and all his children and had to go live alone with his wife in the desert. Then came Shadrach, Meshach, and To Bed We Go, and then Salome, who was a wicked woman who wore very few clothes and took them off when she danced before Harrods.

When Mary heard that she was the Mother of Jesus, she sang the Magna Carta. When the three wise guys from the East Side arrived, they found Jesus in the manger wrapped in waddling clothes. In the Gospel of Luke they named him Enamel. Jesus was born because Mary had an immaculate contraption. St. John, the Blacksmith, dumped water on his head.

Jesus enunciated the Golden Rule, which says to do one to others before they do one to you. He also explained, "Man doth not live by sweat alone." Jesus was crucified on his way to Calgary. It was a miracle when he rose from the dead and managed to get the tombstone off the entrance.

The people who followed the Lord were called the twelve decibels. The epistles were the wives of the apostles. One of the opossums was St. Matthew, who was by profession a taximan.

St. Paul cavorted to Christianity. He preached holy acrimony, which is another name for marriage. A Christian should have only one wife. This is called monotony. The natives of Macedonia did not believe in Paul, so he got stoned.

Other Christians were condemned to death in large groups. They entered the arena to face wild lions singing hymns of praise in the name of the Father, the Son, and In-the-Hole-He-Goes. The Romans went to the coliseum to watch the Christians die for the fun of it. But, as Mel Brooks says, "The meek shall inherit the earth."

Struck by Wimpiness

Anonymous

*O*ne summer evening during a violent thunderstorm, a mother was tucking her small boy into bed. She was about to turn off the light when he asked with a tremor in his voice, "Mommy, will you sleep with me tonight?"

The mother smiled and gave him a reassuring hug. "I can't, dear," she said. "I have to sleep in Daddy's room."

A long silence was broken at last by his shaky, little voice: "The big sissy."

Just Kidding Around

Various Authors

*O*ne evening my husband, Mark, and our preschooler, Krystal, were on the couch chatting. "Daddy, you're the boss of the house, right?" I overheard her ask sweetly.

My husband proudly replied, "Yes, I'm the boss of the house."

But Krystal quickly burst his bubble when she added, "'Cause Mommy put you in charge, huh, Daddy?"

— Rhonda Mony

While visiting a neighbor, five-year-old Andrew pulled out his kindergarten class picture and immediately began describing each classmate. "This is Robert; he hits everyone. This is Stephen. He never listens to the teacher. This is Mark. He chases us and is very noisy." Pointing to his own picture, Andrew commented, "And this is me. I'm just sitting here minding my own business."

— Kathy Plate

Living in Florida all their lives, my children weren't used to wearing certain winter apparel. Before going outside one particularly cold day, I told my four-year-old son, Kyle, to be sure to cover his ears.

"It's okay, Mom," he assured me. "I've got my ear mittens on."

As my eleven-year-old daughter, Kayla, and I giggled behind our hands, she whispered, "He meant to say, 'ear muffins'!"

— Karin C. Wooten

My first-grade daughter, Jenny, loves to sing. One day as I drove her to school, we were "accompanying" Michael W. Smith on his song "Angels Unaware." When we got to the line, "Maybe we are entertaining angels unaware," I heard her version loud and clear: "Maybe we are irritating angels unaware." I couldn't have said it better myself.

— Nancy LaDuke

When my grandson asked me how old I was, I teasingly replied, "I'm not sure."

"Look in your underwear, Grandma," he advised. "Mine says I'm four."

— Elizabeth Sphar

In an attempt to prolong the going-to-bed process, Jackson, my five-year-old nephew, asked for one more glass of juice.

"No, sir," my brother answered. "You may not have another sip. I'm king of the juice in this house."

"That's not right, Daddy," Jackson rebutted. "Our Sunday school teacher said Jesus is king of the juice."

— Rhonda Reese

Once a week I get together with my great-grandsons—Joshua, Danny, and Andrew. As we were playing games, I happened to mention I had three boys before I had a girl. On hearing that, Danny (almost five) got up, came over to me, and with a loving punch to my shoulder said, "Grammy, why didn't you tell me you had kids?"

— Mary Alderfer

My aunt and uncle had a missionary family visiting. When the missionary children were called in for dinner, their mother said, "Be sure to wash your hands." The little boy scowled and said, "Germs and Jesus. Germs and Jesus. That's all I hear, and I've never seen either one of them."

— Vesper Bauer

When my husband, Greg, left his nine-to-five job and started a home business, we explained to our three- and five-year-old girls, Anna and Laura, that Daddy didn't have to go to an office anymore. He had a new office in the basement, and people would pay him to do projects.

It sounded somewhat suspicious though when we overheard Anna tell her friend, "Daddy doesn't have to go to work anymore. He just makes money in the basement."

– Judi Gaudio

My six-year-old son, David, and his grandmother were taking a walk and detoured through the local graveyard. Stopping to read the tombstones, Grandma explained that the first date was the day the person was born and the second date was the day the person died.

"Why do some tombstones only have one date?" David asked.

"Because those people haven't died yet," his grandmother explained.

That night, David couldn't stop talking about the excursion. "Mom," he said with wide eyes, "some of the people buried there aren't even dead yet!"

– Kathy Dinnison

Sometimes the distinction between Jews and Gentiles is difficult for young children to grasp. My nephew Art and his children, Claire, five, and Jesse, three, were strolling through the mall one day when Jesse asked out of the blue, "Dad, why didn't God make us Jews?"

Before Art could answer, Claire said in a serious tone, "Because he made us reptiles, Jesse."

– Carol Reasoner

My son was a bit anxious about his first dental exam. The dentist asked Jamie to open wide, but he refused. The dentist then asked softly, "What's the matter? Don't you want your teeth checked?"

With a horrified look, Jamie stammered, "You mean I can't keep them white?"

– Gary Severson

My twelve-year-old daughter's personality had changed drastically. Teachers and friends advised me that much of the problem was puberty and to try to ignore it. Recently, though, my daughter shed some light on the cause: "You know, Mom, I don't understand why I had to have this measles, mumps, and rebellion booster when I started the seventh grade."

– Stephanie Gates

Following our church's Easter musical, our four-year-old daughter went through the house shouting, "Give us the rabbits! Give us the rabbits!" Finally I asked why she was shouting this.

"Daddy, that's what all those people were yelling on the stage," she explained. I thought for a moment and then it dawned on me. The crowd was actually yelling, "Give us Barabbas!"

– Marc C. Whitt

My kids were eagerly shoveling snow off the driveway to make a mound for sledding. When I stepped outside to check their progress, my youngest informed me of our neighbors' incredible offer.

"Guess what?" my eight-year-old said in near amazement. "The neighbors said we could have the snow off their driveway too!"

– Sheri Lynn Essian

After visiting grandparents, we were two hours into a seven-hour return trip. The freezing rain had turned to snow, and we almost slid into a ditch. To make matters worse, our two-year-old son, Philip, was fussy. Finally I asked in my nicest voice, "Philip, did you put on your crabby pants this morning?"

"No!" he retorted.

"Why don't you go to sleep?" I asked, only to hear again, "No!"

Then his father entered the conversation. "Philip, why don't you just stay awake and be crabby?"

"Okay, Daddy," Philip happily replied.

– Tracy Potter

My husband was delighted when our three-year-old daughter climbed up onto his knee and said, "Daddy, you're handsome." But his grin quickly faded when she added, "And I'm Gretel."

– Sheila O'Connor

Ever since my son Luke was born, I'd sing "Rocky Top" to calm him down. As he grew older, he would sometimes ask me to sing "his song" before he went to bed. Always shy about my singing ability, I was proud Luke appreciated it.

One day the song was on the radio, so I called Luke in to hear it. He listened and then said, "Mom, I like that song, but I've never heard it before."

– Martha Andersen

My granddaughter came home from the mall excited about buying her first training bra. Forgoing all modesty, she lifted her shirt up to show off her new apparel to her five-year-old brother. "Oh, that's no big deal," he shrugged. "Before long I'll be wearing one too!"

– Rachel Swan

A friend of mine took her four-year-old daughter to a baptismal service at her church. Later that night, her daughter took all of her dolls into the bathtub with her and held her own "baptism."

As she dunked each doll under the water, she repeated, "Now I baptize you in the name of the Father, the Son, and hold your nose."

– Vonda P.

One night our family was doing a devotional that included the story of the Ten Commandments. My husband asked, "How many commandments did God give to Moses?" Seth, our five-year-old son, quickly replied, "Too many!"

– Sandy Y.

My husband and I are always talking to our son about all the wonderful things God has made. We ask him questions like "Who made the sun?" and "Who made the rain?"

One evening, I looked at the toys scattered on the floor and asked, "Who made this mess?" After thinking for a few minutes, my son said, "God did!"

— Shawne B.

One night my five-year-old hugged me and said, "I love you, Mommy, but I love God more." I was pleased and told her, "That's the way it should be, Katie."

But then she added, "I love God more because he's never boring and sometimes you're a little boring, Mom."

— Mary H.

When my cousin was three, she was asked, "Where did you get those big, brown eyes?" She thought a minute, then answered, "Um, they came with my head!"

— Shannon C.

My father-in-law was showing the new minister some construction work that was taking place in the church. The minister's six-year-old son picked up a nail and said, "Look, Dad, it's one of us!" Surprised, my father-in-law asked, "What do you mean?"

"Well," said the boy, "Dad told me yesterday that Mom and my sisters were females, and he and I were nails."

— Rajendra P.

My sons and I were enjoying a beautiful day at the park when the boys began to race each other. Right before the finish line, my six-year-old, Benjamin, stepped in a small hole and twisted his ankle. As we prayed for his ankle to get better, Benjamin constructed his own request: "Dear God, if you heal my ankle, I'll forgive you for tripping me."

— Michele G.

Our three-year-old son, Michael, received Superman pajamas for Christmas last year and wore them to bed that night. The next morning, I could hear Michael jumping off a chair over and over again. After several minutes, he broke down, "These pajamas don't work. I still can't fly!"

– Wendy S.

One day during my seventh month of pregnancy I was playing with my four-year-old nephew.

He started getting too aggressive and was pressing on my belly to the point of discomfort. I said to him, "Connor, please don't press on my tummy–there's a baby in there."

With a look of shock he said, "You mean . . . *you ate a baby?*"

– Gina Doll

Love Tips as Explained by Kids

Anonymous

All questions answered by kids aged 5–10.

What is the proper age to get married?

"Eighty-four! Because at that age, you don't have to work anymore, and you can spend all your time loving each other in your bedroom." *(Judy, 8)*

"Once I'm done with kindergarten, I'm going to find me a wife!" *(Tom, 5)*

What do most people do on a date?

"On the first date, they just tell each other lies, and that usually gets them interested enough to go for the second date." *(Mike, 10)*

When is it okay to kiss someone?

"You should never kiss a girl unless you have enough bucks to buy her a big ring and her own VCR, 'cause she'll want to have videos of the wedding." *(Jim, 10)*

"Never kiss in front of other people. It's a big embarrassing thing if anybody sees you. But if nobody sees you, I might be willing to try it with a handsome boy, but just for a few hours." *(Kelly, 9)*

The great debate: Is it better to be single or married?

"It's better for girls to be single but not for boys. Boys need somebody to clean up after them!" *(Lynette, 9)*

"It gives me a headache to think about that stuff. I'm just a kid. I don't need that kind of trouble." *(Kenny, 7)*

Why does love happen between two particular people?

"No one is sure why it happens, but I heard it has something to do with how you smell. That's why perfume and deodorant are so popular." *(Jan, 9)*

"I think you're supposed to get shot with an arrow or something, but the rest of it isn't supposed to be so painful." *(Harlen, 8)*

"One of the people has freckles and so he finds somebody else who has freckles too." *(Andrew, 6)*

How do people in love typically behave?

"Mooshy—like puppy dogs—except puppy dogs don't wag their tails nearly as much." *(Arnold, 10)*

"All of a sudden, the people get movie fever so they can sit together in the dark." *(Sherm, 8)*

What is it like to fall in love?

"Love is the most important thing in the world, but baseball is pretty good too." *(Greg, 8)*

"Like an avalanche where you have to run for your life." *(Roger, 9)*

"If falling in love is anything like learning how to spell, I don't want to do it. It takes too long." *(Leo, 7)*

"I'm in favor of love as long as it doesn't happen when *The Simpsons* is on television." *(Anita, 6)*

"Love will find you, even if you are trying to hide from it. I have been trying to hide from it since I was five, but the girls keep finding me." *(Bobby, 8)*

"I'm not rushing into being in love. I'm finding fourth grade hard enough." *(Regina, 10)*

"Love is foolish—but I still might try it sometime." *(Floyd, age 9)*

What do good looks have to do with being in love?

"If you want to be loved by somebody who isn't already in your family, it doesn't hurt to be beautiful." *(Jeanne, 8)*

"It isn't always just how you look. Look at me. I'm handsome like anything and I haven't got anybody to marry me yet." *(Gary, 7)*

"Beauty is skin deep. But how rich you are can last a long time." *(Christine, 9)*

Why do lovers often hold hands?

"They want to make sure their rings don't fall off because they paid good money for them." *(Dave, 8)*

"They are just practicing for when they might have to walk down the aisle someday and do the holy matchimony thing." *(John, 9)*

What personal qualities are necessary to be a good lover?

"One of you should know how to write a check. Because even if you have tons of love, there is still going to be a lot of bills." *(Ava, 8)*

"Sensitivity doesn't hurt." *(Robbie, 8)*

What is a surefire way to make a person fall in love with you?

"Tell them that you own a whole bunch of candy stores." *(Del, 6)*

"Yell out that you love them at the top of your lungs—and don't worry if their parents are right there." *(Manuel, 8)*

"Don't do things like have smelly, green sneakers. You might get attention, but attention ain't the same thing as love." *(Alonzo, 9)*

"One way is to take the girl out to eat. Make sure it's something she likes to eat. French fries usually work for me." *(Bart, 9)*

How can you tell if two adults eating dinner at a restaurant are in love?

"Just see if the man picks up the check. That's how you can tell if he's in love." *(John, 9)*

"Lovers will just be staring at each other and their food will get cold. Other people care more about the food." *(Brad, 8)*

"It's love if they order one of those desserts that are on fire. They like to order those because it's just like how their hearts are . . . on fire." *(Christine, 9)*

"Romantic adults usually are all dressed up, so if they are just wearing jeans it might mean they used to go out or they just broke up." *(Sarah, 9)*

"See if the man has lipstick on his face." *(Sandra, 7)*

What are most people thinking when they say "I love you"?

"The person is thinking: Yeah, I really do love him. But I hope he showers at least once a day." *(Michelle, 9)*

"Some lovers might be real nervous, so they are glad they finally got it out and said it and now they can go eat." *(Dick, 7)*

How was kissing invented?

"I know one reason that kissing was created. It makes you feel warm all over, and they didn't always have electric heat or fireplaces or even stoves in their houses." *(Gina, 8)*

How does a person learn to kiss?

"You can have a big rehearsal with your Barbie and Ken dolls." *(Julia, 7)*

"You learn it right on the spot when the gooshy feelings get the best of you." *(Doug, 7)*

"It might help to watch soap operas all day." *(Carin, 9)*

When is it okay to kiss someone?

"When they're rich." *(Pam, 7)*

"It's never okay to kiss a boy. They always slobber all over you. That's why I stopped doing it." *(Jean, 10)*

"If it's your mother, you can kiss her anytime. But if it's a new person, you have to ask permission." *(Roger, 6)*

How do you make love last?

"Spend most of your time loving instead of going to work." *(Tom, 7)*

"Don't forget your wife's name . . . That will mess up the love." *(Roger, 8)*

"Be a good kisser. It might make your wife forget that you never take out the trash." *(Bobby, 9)*

"Don't say you love somebody and then change your mind. Love isn't like picking what movie you want to watch." *(Natalie, 9)*

What would be a good title for a love ballad you could sing to your beloved?

"How Do I Love Thee When You're Always Picking Your Nose?" *(Arnold, 10)*

"You Are My Darling Even Though You Also Know My Sister" *(Larry, 8)*

"I Love Hamburgers, I Like You!" *(Eddie, 6)*

"I Am in Love with You Most of the Time, but Don't Bother Me When I'm with My Friends" *(Bob, 9)*

"Hey, Baby, I Don't Like Girls but I'm Willing to Forget You Are One!" *(Will, 7)*

I'll Catch a Later Bus

Al Sanders

The sixth-grade Sunday school class was coming to an end. The earnest teacher had planned her lesson well, and she knew it was time to ask that strategic question. When everyone seemed to be listening intently, she said, "How many of you children would like to go to heaven?"

As you would expect, every hand shot up—except for one boy's. He simply stared at her, remaining passive and indifferent.

The teacher thought she had either failed with the lesson or he hadn't understood the question. With a kind follow-up, she smiled and pressed the inquiry. "Son, don't you want to go to heaven?" she asked.

The boy quickly responded, "Well, sure, I mean, eventually. But the way you put the question, I thought you were makin' up a load right now!"

Chapter Four

"Weird" Is a Two-Way Street

Marriage is the alliance of two people, one of whom never remembers birthdays and the other who never forgets.
—Ogden Nash

As to marriage or celibacy, let a man take the course he will.
He will be sure to repent.
—Socrates

Marrying a man is like buying something you've been admiring for a long time in a shop window. You may love it when you get it home, but it doesn't always go with everything in the house.
—Jean Kerr

One of the greatest tools for building a healthy marriage is the ability to maintain a sense of humor about that "weird" creature you've promised to love and to cherish for "as long as you both shall live." Humor, as you can see from the following stories, can change even the most frustrating experience into an occasion of laughter. And remember, when it comes to marriage, "weird" is always a two-way street.

If You Could Read My Mind

G. Ron Darbee

I've heard it said that after many years of marriage, spouses begin to acquire certain traits from their partners. They assume the same body language, share many of the same colloquialisms in their speech, and even begin to resemble each other in attitude and appearance. Sue always gets very emotional when we discuss this subject. So deep is her love for me that the conversation often reduces her to tears, and she spends the following weeks buying new outfits and experimenting with hairstyles. Try as she might, I don't think they make her look at all like me.

What I have noticed, though, is that while she may not be able to match my receding hairline or the soft, subtle curves of my expanding waist, she has developed a knack for following my train of thought. It is a short and slow-moving train, to be sure; a coal-burning engine in this day of electric rails, but follow it she does. Sometimes I wonder if she is not the engineer, and I'm just a passenger relaxing in the safety of my own private caboose.

Why, just the other day, while I was sitting in my favorite chair watching the Knicks battle the Lakers in double overtime, my sweet Amazing Karnack of a wife stared right through my eyes and read the very thoughts from my brain before I even realized they were there.

"I bet you were just getting ready to go outside and weed those flower beds you've been promising to take care of for the last six weeks," she said.

"Is that what I was thinking?" I asked, one eye on the television and the other straining to make contact with hers. "I felt a thought developing deep down in there somewhere, but the word *pretzel* was loosely tied to it. Oh well, I guess it's gone now."

"Just as well," Sue said, "you finished the pretzels late in the third quarter."

"Really," I said. "Tell me something, sweetheart. Was I thinking about weeding the flower beds right this minute during the most exciting game of the year, or did I plan to wait until after the postgame interviews and the highlight clips?"

"Let me see," Sue said, and she looked deep and thoughtfully into my eyes. "As best I can tell, you were hoping to pull weeds right after the buzzer sounded and to skip all that senseless banter about a game you watched in its entirety."

"You know something, Sue? I think you're right. It's becoming very clear to me now. Boy, it sure is a good thing I have you, or I might have sat in this chair and wasted an entire afternoon."

"I'm here to help," Sue said.

Frankly, I don't know how I ever got along without her. I can't begin to list the number of times Sue has been able to read my mind and dredge up a thought that has saved me from wasting a potentially productive day engaged in some needless and idle pursuit like a sporting event or a nap on the couch. It amazes me that I accomplished anything during the years prior to our marriage.

This woman is a blessing to me; there are no two ways about it. Yet, somehow I have failed to reciprocate in like fashion. Certainly, I have assumed some of her mannerisms. The way I answer the telephone or fold a shirt can be easily traced to her. But when it comes to reading her mind, I don't know where to start.

Sue's mind is like a Tolstoy novel—beautiful and well constructed. She has an incredible depth of character, a thoroughly imaginative plot, combined with a strong and consistent theme. And as with Tolstoy's *War and Peace,* I can't seem to muddle my way through the first chapter. Not for lack of trying, no sir; I have read and reread the opening lines, pondered over the cover for hours on end. Too many twists and turns—try as I might, something always gets lost in the translation.

"Surprise, sweetheart!" I said one evening. "I picked up four tickets to the monster truck rally at the arena."

"Why?" she asked.

"Because I thought you liked monster trucks."

"Not even a little bit," she said. "What gave you that idea?"

"You said something about it the other night when I was reading the paper."

"What I said was, 'The kids were acting like monsters on the way home from the grocery store, and we almost got sideswiped by a truck.'"

"Are you sure?" I asked. She provided a convincing argument, following which we were both absolutely sure.

I don't know why I find it so difficult to follow my wife's thought patterns, but at least I'm in pretty good company. Other men I know suffer from the same shortcoming. We even discussed it one evening during our weekly discipleship meeting.

"I know exactly what you mean," Jerry said. "It's eerie. Like some sort of *Twilight Zone* thing. Kathy always knows what I'm thinking before I do. Hours before, sometimes even days."

"Have you ever tried to read her mind?" I asked.

"I think it's one of those things you shouldn't even mess around with," Steve said. "There's a lot of potential for trouble when you start poking into things we're not meant to understand."

"Like what?" I asked.

"Like, suppose you got lucky and actually figured out what she was thinking," Steve said. "Then what happens? You've shown you have the ability to read her mind, and the next time you do something dumb and insensitive, your best defense is reduced to nothing more than another lame excuse."

"I don't follow you," I said.

"You've heard the statement 'Ignorance is bliss,'" Steve said.

"Yeah."

"Well, stay happy."

Being the sensitive, caring man of the nineties that I was at the time, I was not the least bit discouraged by the cynical comments of my peers. I left the group with my determination intact, even more intent than before on uncovering the key to Sue's mind. When I got home, we started with the experiments.

"Okay, sweetheart," I said, "just sit right there."

"What do I have to do?" she asked.

"Nothing. Just sit there and look pretty while I attempt to read your mind." Her bout of uncontrolled hysterics nearly destroyed my concentration.

"I mean it," I said. "You sit there, while I try to tell you what you're thinking."

"Maybe you should start smaller," Sue suggested, "and work your way up. For example, instead of trying to read my mind, try telling me what I said to you this morning."

"When this morning?" I asked.

"Anytime before noon."

"I don't want to," I said.

"You don't *want* to," Sue asked, "or you can't?"

"Okay, I don't want to because I can't. How's that, Miss Smarty Pants?"

"Well, it's honest, anyway," Sue said. "Listen, this is silly. You're never going to read my mind."

"Sounds to me like you're a little afraid I might succeed," I said.

"I'm afraid you might hurt yourself."

Not one to bow to the admonishment of my critics, I charged ahead with the experiment. "Just sit quietly and let me give this a shot," I said.

Looking deep into the sky-blue eyes of the woman I've loved for more than seventeen years, I saw the history of our lives together. In the space of a moment, I pictured the smile that greets me each morning and the friendship I've shared every day. Somewhere back behind her pupils I envisioned every joyous occasion we ever shared. The birth of our children, our first home together, even Scrabble on the living room floor came to life in my lovely wife's eyes.

"I've got it," I said. "I know what you're thinking."

"What?" she asked.

"Sex. You're thinking about sex."

"Remarkable," Sue said. "You're absolutely remarkable!"

"So I'm right?"

"Not even close! You're supposed to read *my* mind," she said, "not your own."

"Okay, then. Pizza! You're thinking about pizza."

"Are you crazy?" Sue asked.

"No, but you know how sex makes me hungry."

"Well, I think we've explored that territory enough for one day," Sue said. "Kreskin will sleep tonight—secure in his job security."

"Come on, wait a minute," I pleaded. "Give me one more try."

"This is ridiculous," Sue said as she got up from the couch to leave.

"No, wait!" I said. "I've got it this time. I know what you're thinking. Give me one more chance!"

"One more," Sue said, "and then I'm going to bed."

"Okay," I said. "I'm sure now. You were thinking how nice it would be if we took Friday off and drove out to that bed-and-breakfast on the coast. You were thinking about how much we'd enjoy having dinner at our favorite restaurant on the boardwalk and taking a stroll on the beach under the moonlight. How's that?"

"Perfect," Sue said. "You read my mind."

I couldn't help but think that my friend Steve was right. There are a few things men shouldn't fool with. Sometimes it is easier to remain ignorant. It is certainly cheaper, anyway.

CELEBRITY COVER-UP

Martha Bolton

$\mathcal{B}$ob Hope is notorious for calling his writers at all hours of the day and night. It was nothing for us to be awakened at midnight, one o'clock, sometimes even two o'clock in the morning. The main reason for this was his frequent travels to different time zones. If he happened to be in Paris or London eating lunch, he figured the whole world was awake too.

On this one particular night he called one of his writers around midnight. The writer's wife answered the phone and heard the all-too-familiar voice on the other end.

Bob asked if her husband was awake. She glanced at her beloved sleeping peacefully next to her and didn't have the heart to wake him up.

"Is he there?" Bob repeated.

Thinking quickly, she answered, "No, he said he was going to be with you tonight."

There was an uncomfortable silence. Bob didn't know what to say, so he just said, "Oh, yeah, here he comes now."

Two Cannibals in Love

Charlene Ann Baumbich

*E*very Halloween I take time to reminisce about George's and my first Halloween as a couple.

With the "I do's" less than two weeks behind us, the invitation arrived. It created quite the excitement for us two love-doves for a couple of reasons: It was the first mail Mr. and Mrs. George Baumbich received; and isn't everything just *wonderful* when you are first married?

We decided to go as cannibals. Yes! We would be Mr. and Mrs. Cannibal. We would take the energy from our wildly soaring love, channel it into unbridled creativity, and be assured of no less than the grand prize at the "Absolutely No One Admitted Without a Costume!" party.

Task number one: Gather a million bones. We would tie them in our hair, hang them around our waists, and arm ourselves with the clublike ones. Although the butchers probably thought we were destitute, we were happy campers after a fruitful hunt.

Task number two: Boil the meat off dem bones. We stood over the boiling cauldron together, holding hands all the while.

Task number three: Decide what we would wear with the bones. We meandered around a fabric shop until happening on the perfect jungle material. It was my moment to dazzle my caveman with my deftness at the sewing machine.

With astonishing flair, I wrapped the material around us and started pinning, like I knew what I was doing. Snip, sew a straight line, snip again. *Voila!* Cannibal costumes. (Who really knows what one's supposed to look like anyway? The only thing I knew for sure, thank goodness, is that they weren't supposed to look tailored.)

Next, we dropped some big bucks at a gag shop: shrunken heads for me to wear as earrings, plastic fangs for our grins, black greasepaint, and a bag of feathers. Feathers adorned the poison dart blowers we crafted out of cardboard tubes that come on hangers from the cleaners. Clever, eh? (Giggles.)

And what would a cannibal be without a spear? Ominous-looking arrows were tooled out of tin foil, then firmly anchored to ruthless broomsticks. Wicked! (Hugs and kisses.)

More miscellaneous doodads were tied, stuck, and pinned about us in a flurry of final touches. I grabbed a couple of my "falls" (fake hairpieces that were big in the '60s), and we laced them with the bones for scalps. Greasepaint war stripes, mixed with menacing hues of sparkling eye shadow, set the final stage for our arm-in-arm gander in the mirror.

We were, without exaggeration, sensational. We were, in no underestimation, authentic. We were, undoubtedly, winners. (Very strange fanged kisses.)

And so we made our way to the car. We strolled ever so slowly to the parking lot from our second-floor apartment, hoping we would run into every tenant in the building for some oohs, aahs, and cheering.

Although the party was only two towns away, the drive seemed to take hours because we were so anxious to make our grand entry. We entertained ourselves and the rest of traffic by making our scary personas obvious while stopped at red lights.

At last we arrived. We paused outside the door for last-minute adjusting, then readied our weapons.

Ding-dong, ding-dong, ding-dong.

As soon as the door was opened wide enough, we leaped in screaming, "Kowabunga!"

"Surprise! Surprise!" echoed back at us. Laughter filled the room.

We slowly lowered our spears and dart blowers. Our eyes tried to drink in what surrounded us: a room full of friends, not one wearing a costume, and all wearing dresses, suits, and ties.

"What's going on?" George quietly asked the host, who was right next to us, doubled over with laughter.

"It's a surprise wedding shower for you guys!" his wife finally eked out.

So there we stood. The best doggone cannibals in the country. We had definitely been tricked—and treated.

FOR 25 YEARS I HATED MY MOP

Janice Crouse

*O*ne day soon after we were married I was mopping the kitchen floor as my husband, Gil, arrived home. When he walked into the kitchen and saw what I was doing he exclaimed, "Oh, yuck. You're using a string mop–that's nasty; you have to get your hands down there and wring that thing out! I'm going to go out right now, Janice, and buy you a sponge mop."

This was at a time in our marriage during which Gil now looks back and admits he was "often wrong, but seldom in doubt." Yet I just stood there looking at him, completely surprised by his outburst and declaration.

I remember thinking, *String mops are nasty? You're kidding. My mother uses a string mop. I've always used string mops. I like string mops. I don't like sponge mops.*

But I didn't say any of that. Gil's feelings seemed so strong on the issue that I didn't think to challenge him. I simply let him go out and buy me a sponge mop. And I used it.

Gil used it too, of course. (He's always been helpful around the house.) Still, I was the one who did most of the mopping. And even though Gil and I differed and compromised on a myriad of issues over the years, the mop issue never resurfaced–until one Saturday morning about four years ago.

I could hear our two college-age children stirring in their rooms at the back of the house. Gil was doing something out in the garage. I was diligently sponge-mopping the kitchen floor when the thought hit me: *I hate sponge mops! I've always hated sponge mops. So why am I mopping my kitchen floor with a sponge mop? I'm an educated, professional person. I consider myself to be an intelligent, independent woman. Yet for almost twenty-five years I've been mopping my kitchen floor with a sponge simply because my husband prefers sponge mops.*

But I'm the one doing the mopping. He's not!

So I threw down the mop, and as the handle clattered on the floor I screamed: "I can't believe it! I just can't believe it!"

The kids came running from their rooms. Gil raced in from the garage. They all wanted to know, "What happened? Are you okay? What's wrong?"

"I can't believe it!" I examined again, this time to an audience. "I can't believe I've been so stupid. For almost twenty-five years I've been mopping floors with a sponge mop just because you [looking at Gil] prefer a sponge mop. When I have always preferred a string mop!"

When I finished this explanatory outburst, my usually bright, empathetic daughter, Charmaine, regarded me with a dumbfounded look that could only be translated as "Huh?"

My analytical son, Gil Jr., stared helplessly at me for a long moment, before he responded (even less supportively than his sister), "Is that all?" Then he looked at Charmaine (and probably rolled his eyes—I couldn't see for sure), shrugged, and headed back to his room. My husband just stood there with his mouth hanging open.

I have to credit Charmaine, though. She stayed in the kitchen with me as my emotions settled. She was still there when I picked up the mop and resumed my work on the floor. So I filled her in on the background story from our early marriage. By the time I'd finished, Gil had discreetly retreated to the garage.

Alone in the house a few hours later, I heard the doorbell ring. I walked to the door and opened it. There stood a delivery person from our local florist shop with a dozen long-stemmed red roses, bound to the handle of a brand-new mop.

I burst out laughing as I accepted the delivery and walked back into the house admiring my unusual bouquet. Then I saw the card and opened it to read in Gil's handwriting: "As long as it's our floors you're mopping, you can use any kind of mop you want." Suddenly I was closer to tears than laughter as I realized the sensitivity of Gil's love and his acceptance of my feelings.

For I had to admit to myself that the message of the bouquet was more symbolic, more representative of our relationship than was that first mop incident back in the early days of our marriage. I felt profoundly grateful to be part of a marriage union that had grown and stretched enough over the years to allow two very different people to become one without sacrificing either of our two strong identities.

When Gil returned home, I expressed my feelings with a greeting that let him know beyond a shadow of a doubt that the price of a dozen roses plus one string mop was one of the sweetest, and smartest, investments he'd ever made.

WILD HARES

Ken Davis

There was a subtle message hidden just beneath the surface of the legalistic theology I knew as a child: *If it's fun, it must not be Christian.* The excitement and laughter generated by a swim party or a pizza feast were not sanctified until they were legitimized by a serious devotional. To skip this step of blessing placed the aforementioned activities squarely in the category of sin.

Since then I've come to believe that God is the author of joy, the fountain from which pure laughter springs.

One Sunday as we prepared for church, my wife, Diane, got what I call a wild hare. A wild hare is a small rabbit that has never been domesticated. Whenever you get a wild hare in a tight spot, it kicks and jumps around for no apparent reason. Occasionally it may even try to bite someone. If you get several wild hares over a short period of time, then it's said that you had a bad hare day.

Diane called the family together and began to rage about kids moving around in church. "I'm sick and tired of seeing teenagers treat church like a rock concert," she ranted. "During the sermon they get up in herds to go to the bathroom, and I'm sick of it."

Evidently she'd been stewing about this for a long time, because this was the wildest hare I'd ever seen. She'd actually given it enough thought to work out a solution. Establishing eye contact, she announced the edict: "This family is not going to be a part of this travesty," she seethed, her face turning a unique shade of red. "I'm making a new rule. Whatever you have to do, you do it before you get to church. Once we're in church, you will sit down and you will not move."

She spat the last three words out one at a time with great emphasis. "Do ... you ... understand?" she demanded, staring wild-eyed, waiting for an answer.

"Yes ma'am," I said. Then she turned to the children and repeated the rule for them.

When we got to church, we were ushered to a seat near the front. I began to squirm. We stood a few minutes later to sing a hymn, and I became acutely aware that I was going to have to break the rule. Of all Sundays for nature to call, it had to be the Sunday of the wild hare. As the congregation sang, I leaned over and whispered to Diane, "I have to go."

She turned quickly and whispered with great hostility, "You will not move. You know the rule."

"I know the rule, and it's a good rule," I said, "but I have to go."

"If you leave," she hissed between clenched teeth, "you're going to set a bad example."

I was doing that little have-to-go dance now. "If I stay, I'm going to set a bad example," I blurted out and exited to the back, trying to walk with some semblance of normalcy. I took care of business and came back quickly. I had no desire to cause any more trouble.

I made it back before the hymn was completed. I quickly slipped into the pew and sat down. I didn't even have to look to know Diane was furious. I could feel hostility and anger radiating from her body. In an effort of reconciliation, I put my arm around her and gave a little hug. I was shocked to feel her pushing me away, digging her elbow into my ribs. Here we were on God's day in God's house, and my wife was elbowing me because I did what had to be done.

I turned to tell her to quit being so angry, only to discover she wasn't my wife. I'd absentmindedly slid into the wrong pew. I was hugging a woman I'd never met while my wife sat directly behind us, watching the whole thing. I'm pretty certain that's where the hostility was radiating from.

The pastor saw the whole thing play out. He tried his best to continue, but he lost the battle and burst into laughter; then the congregation lost it. When the laughter subsided, the pastor wiped the tears from his eyes and proclaimed, "Brothers and sisters, if God can save that man, then God can surely save you."

As I left the church after the service, a very angry woman approached me. "What do you think God thought of that?" she spat. Then she turned on her heel and stomped away.

I was sulking during the drive home, and Diane asked me what was wrong. I somberly repeated the woman's angry words. Diane started laughing. "What *do* you think God thought?" she asked me.

Had God watched from heaven, filled with rage? I think not. Perhaps he saw and called out, "Angels, hurry! Looketh at this idiot! I love that man; I gave him a twisted mind, and look—he's using it!"

High Adventure in the Garage

Charlene Ann Baumbich

$\mathscr{T}$oday I went mountain climbing. Although I have tackled steeper and loftier inclines in my lifetime, I have never encountered one that elicited such emotions.

You see, out of necessity, I climbed the Brown Car. The Brown Car that has been parked—*buried*—in our garage for the last five years. During that time it has metamorphosed into a giant shelf, a shelf like a ship buried at sea and covered with barnacles. Barnacles that turned this once-cherished spiffy new vehicle into a flat-tired, dead-batteried, broken-windshielded, heaped-up sore spot in our marriage.

The reason for my daring climb? To get to the other side. Literally. It was the only way to retrieve the shovel. Good thing George wasn't home. I was blowing fire through my nose by the time I scaled and rappelled the multilayered hazard.

The Brown Car symbolizes procrastination. Its reputation has spread throughout the neighborhood and beyond.

When neighbors are asked when they plan to do something they don't want to do, they respond: "When George sells the brown car." Ah, the blessed comeback that delivers an even deeper message: probably never.

This once beauty is a 1983 Buick LeSabre. Four doors. Six cylinders. Power door locks but no power seats or windows. Okay radio but no tape deck. Automatic transmission with no kick when you punch in. Basic. Stable. The odometer announces that the Brown

Car has seen nearly 100,000 hard-earned miles. It needs new tires and the "Service Engine Soon" light comes on when you start it. Of course, you have to charge the deader-than-dead battery first to see the "Service Engine Soon" light in action.

We bought the Brown Car off the showroom floor, thinking we had "arrived." Wire wheel covers said it all. Yup, we were two *wild thaaangs.* Five years later, however, George received a company vehicle and my dad gave our son Brian his pickup truck. Our other car yielded a more comfortable ride for our midlife backs and so we parked the Brown Car.

And then its insurance ran out. And then its license plates expired. And then its battery went dead. And then, get this, it ran out of gas! Sitting in the garage! George had charged it, turned it over, and revved it up so many times that it ran out of gas. And then the left rear tire went flat. And then something got thrown on the driver's side of the windshield, cracking it.

All this time, George was "getting ready to sell it." For several months he just couldn't find a "For Sale" sign. Once a couple years ago, he actually put an ad in the newspaper. Everyone who called laughed after hearing how many miles it had, especially considering George's price.

New tactic: Wash the car before putting it at the end of the drive bearing the sign he finally found. But nay, the battery was dead again, and he couldn't back it out to wash it.

Tick, tock, tick, tock. Calendar months and years whizzed by; the Brown Car continued to depreciate. George kept mumbling about the thousands it was *really* worth.

In the meantime, the Brown Car took up one half of our two-car garage. It stayed nice and dry in the winter while we scraped ice and jockeyed the rest of our vehicles.

One day, someone actually rang our doorbell and asked to buy it! But George said he had to do this and he had to do that and he had to look up this *and* that to find out what would be a fair price and ... meanwhile, that heaven-sent angel bought another vehicle. Silently, George sighed with relief. I swear, he even smiled at the news.

I've begun to see a pattern in these past years. I've begun to see that the Brown Car is here to stay. It's probably not worth selling.

So instead of whining about its presence, I've rerouted my energy into finding a place to store it. Just like the baby stuff we keep in the attic "just in case." We've had it so long now that we've decided to keep it for our grandchildren. Might as well add the Brown Car to that list of treasures.

Frankly, there'd be a hole in our lives if we no longer had the Brown Car to launch so many lively discussions. Its departure might traumatize those who use it to justify their own procrastinations, including me. The Brown Car, in its own dirt-laden, quiet way, exemplifies the many incomplete projects in my life. Projects that I'm going to get to one day. Projects that have become part of my comfortable chaos. Projects that assure me I have a reason to wake up the next day.

And you know what they say: When you live with someone long enough, you start to become like them. I'm even beginning to ask those "What if?" questions. "What if Brian's truck died?" "What if George had to change jobs?" "What if the other car become disabled?"

Hey! Not to worry! We can always resurrect the Brown Car! It's our security blanket. You know, I believe that's why my husband has found it impossible to let go of that little corner of his world. There's something comforting about just knowing it's there. Just in case.

Just in case we get the urge to indulge in a new experience. Like mountain climbing.

Pulling Strings

Patsy Clairmont

$\mathcal{I}$'m married to a mellow fellow. It's a good thing, because I don't think our house could take two of me. I'm so tightly strung I need the balance of someone who has his feet on the ground.

I can identify with my friend Cindy, who said her husband, Craig, is like a balloon man. He has both feet securely planted. She's like a hot-air balloon, flying off in different directions. Craig watches her until she gets a little too far out, and then he takes hold of the string and pulls Cindy back down to earth.

Even though I'm grateful Les is a mild-mannered man, at times I wish he would show a little more enthusiasm. Recently I purchased a new dress, and I brought it out on a hanger for Les's viewing.

"What do you think?" I prompted.

"That's nice."

"Nice?" I cried.

"Didn't you ask me what I thought of your dress?" he asked, puzzled. "Your dress is nice."

"Les, 'nice' makes me nauseous."

"What do you want from me?"

"I want dramatic; I want dynamic; I want some enthusiasm!" I demanded loudly.

"Patsy, that dress is nice," he said with quiet firmness.

So I took the "nice" dress and stomped back to the closet.

On my way across the room, Les called out, "Patsy, look! Patsy, look!"

I turned and saw my two-hundred-pound husband leaping in the air, arms stretched heavenward, exclaiming, "Wow, what a dress! Wow, what a dress!"

I burst out laughing. My steady, ground-level man was behaving like a helium balloon.

Snore Warzzz

Nancy Kennedy

ecently I read an article about a woman who put a pair of sweatpants over her sleeping husband's head and pulled the drawstring. Horrifying, but understandable: Her husband was snoring.

I was reading the article in bed while my beloved sucked all the air out of the room with his own turbulent throat vibrations. I looked over at my snorting husband and felt a twinge of envy for that desperate wife. She would snooze peacefully, doing twenty-to-life in a nice, quiet prison cell somewhere.

I sighed, poked Barry until he rolled over on his side, then turned out the light and attempted to go to sleep before he flipped over on his back again. I know the routine much too well.

I start: "Barry, do not sleep on your back!"

He pleads: "I won't–I promise."

I reply: "You will and you'll snore."

Sure enough, I'm right. Again.

Barry thinks he's the innocent party, because science and statistics are on his side. When I mentioned the poor woman who was driven to insane criminal action by her husband's incessant buzz saw, Barry reached into his nightstand drawer and produced a news article of his own.

"Look here," he said, handing me the magazine as he snuggled deep into the covers, on his back. "Some science guys did a study and found eight times more men than women snore. You know what that means?"

"Yeah. That eight times as many wives as husbands sleep with their pillows over their heads."

"That means majority rules," he continued. Then he quoted some other science guy who said male snoring is actually a clever defense system our early ancestors used to ward off dangerous predators such as carnivorous cats by mimicking their sounds.

"See," he said, "you should be grateful. I'm protecting your life."

I have to admit Barry's not the only one with annoying bedtime quirks. I wear a retainer at night. It keeps me from grinding my teeth, but not from drooling. Drooling is a trait some folks would find endearing, but unfortunately Barry is not one of them.

He also doesn't like my cold feet on his warm back, although I've pointed out it's biblical. ("If two lie down together, they will keep warm.") He doesn't find my habit of wearing heavy wool socks to bed particularly appealing either, so I lose all the way around.

But at least I don't snore.

Bedtime wasn't always like this. When we were first married we'd laugh over morning breath and chuckle over bed hair. Barry would say, "I like the way your smeared eye makeup makes you look like a raccoon."

And I'd tell him, "Of course I didn't mind your elbow in my ribs all night, and when you accidentally kicked me, I barely screamed at all."

Now, two decades later, being kneed in the back has lost its charm. And while I still find Barry's occasional jabbering in his sleep about catching pop flies somewhat entertaining, I find absolutely no redeeming social value in snoring.

Until just lately, that is. I'm afraid what began as a diatribe against my husband's nightly soft palate serenade has turned into a confessional. An unfortunate shoulder injury is preventing me from sleeping in my favorite position (on my stomach). So I have to sleep on my back. And, well, you get the picture.

(If you don't, Barry will draw you one: "Gee, Hon, not only did you keep the neighbors up last night, but your snoring peeled all the paint off the walls.")

As a result, I no longer consider snoring a moral deficiency or a character weakness. In fact, now I think snoring might be an indicator that all is well with one's soul. Of course, that's only if I fall asleep first. For the times when I don't and Barry's the one who's peeling paint and sucking air, I've got just the remedy—an icy pair of size 7 feet poised and aimed at his warm back.

No Batteries Required

Karen Scalf Linamen

$\mathcal{M}$y computer is wheezing. Would someone please explain this to me?

I realize this is allergy season in some parts of the country, like Texas, where winter doesn't arrive until January and then lasts about as long as an episode of Barney (which, believe me, can feel like an eternity, but in reality only lasts for four hours, three if you don't count the commercials).

But I still don't think that explains the rhythmic wheeze coming from my hard drive.

Then again, what do I know? I am technologically impaired. I not only cannot program the VCR, but I am still figuring out the remote control and I have just recently gotten the hang of programming the microwave.

Maybe my brain is on technology overload. Yeah, that's it. My brain is on overload and, as a result, I have developed a subconscious hostility toward anything that requires a modem, electrical outlet, or battery pack. This would certainly explain why I have such a scary history with things like laptops and cell phones. Oh. You hadn't heard about the laptop?

Let me begin by saying that anytime a woman tells you that she backed over her husband's brand-new laptop computer with her car, you can rest assured there is a perfectly reasonable explanation. I'll let you know when I find one.

Until then, let me just say that my husband was going on a trip, and we were loading his bags into the trunk when the phone rang.

I ran back into the house, and by the time I jumped back in the car and revved the engine, it had sort of slipped my mind that the laptop was still sitting on the driveway behind the left rear tire, and, well . . .

You'll have to use your imagination on the rest of the story because this is a family-friendly book, and I've been asked to keep the profanity and bloodshed to a minimum.

I'm kidding. Actually, my husband was amazingly gracious. Which is why, three weeks later when I ran over my cell phone with the van, I felt perfectly comfortable e-mailing him the news and then leaving town for a week.

If I'd thought he was going to overreact, I would have stayed away much longer.

Chapter Five

Keeping Up (Strange) Appearances

*Half the work that is done in this world is to
make things appear what they are not.*
—E. R. Beadle (1821–1894), American publisher

*Every so often, I like to stick my head out the window,
look up, and smile for a satellite picture.*
—Steven Wright

How we look, what we wear, how we smell—can
these superficial details possibly provoke laughter?
You bet! Because sometimes we act like the most
insignificant things about us—the blemish sprouting
from our nose, the hair growing out of our ears, the
orange juice stain on the seat of our favorite pair of
pants—are signs that the world is about to end. Really,
in thirty years, will anyone care whether your wig fell
off when you were playing tennis with the best-looking
man you ever met? Well, maybe you will, but surely
you won't be able to look back on that moment without a lifetime of laughter to cheer you up.

Beauty for the Beast

Marti Attoun

*M*om greeted me at the door in a dish-towel cape, a dead give-away she was up to some heavy-duty beauty business. Perming, tinting, depilating? I didn't recognize the fumes.

Then I saw the uncapped bottle of Glover's Mange.

"Don't get alarmed," she said as she kneaded the canine goo into her scalp. "It's the only thing I've found that'll cure my itchy head."

Why would I get alarmed? Her hair and hide have survived seventy years of such beastly treatments. When I was a kid, I wasn't alarmed either. I was mortified!

Other mothers moisturized from dainty pastel jars with teeny pearl and teardrop lids. They bought beauty dews by the ounce with sissy scents like honeysuckle and lavender. They dipped, dotted, and dabbed. Mom, meanwhile, treated her skin with the delicacy of barbed wire. Her lotions and potions had earthy names like Corn Huskers Oil and Bag Balm. The instructions read something like: "Smear liberally on Bossy's cracked udders. For best results, scrape algae off shanks before applying."

She didn't buy this miracle stuff from the cosmetics lady at Newman's Department Store, either. She shopped at Carlson's Hardware and Feed.

When she really wanted to pamper herself, Mom sanded her elbows and heels with pumice—a rock, mind you—and bathed in baking soda. She concocted masks of egg white, wheat germ, and honey. Something for her face was always setting up in Pyrex.

As teens do, I secretly compared my mother's dermis (and waistline and wardrobe) to that of my friends' mothers. Mom's pores weathered well, so well that other mothers unfortunately complimented her smooth skin.

"Why, it's no secret, Rosemary. I use Bag Balm," Mom once boomed throughout the produce aisle.

"I'm not familiar with that product," Rosemary said.

"That's because you weren't raised on the farm like me," Mom said.

I hightailed it into the greeting-card aisle as she began to discuss cow's teats, soggy pastures, and such. I prayed she wouldn't share her eye-bag cure: Preparation H.

After years of wishing Mom's beauty secrets would remain so, she suddenly is hotter than Holsteins on kitchen wallpaper.

I should have known that she knew something.

My twelve-year-old daughter just trotted in from Dr. Fly's, a beauty salon, with a bottle of horse shampoo: Mane 'n' Tail. All her luster-haired friends use it, she raved. Just wait till you see Jessie's thick shiny hair. And remember how limp Bethany's hair used to be?

My bored look stopped her mid-gush.

"Your grandmother's been using horse shampoo on her forelock since the original Mr. Ed," I told her. "She buys it by the gallon and dilutes it. I'm sure she'll be happy to share."

"Cool," she said. "Does Granny use Hoofmaker on her nails too?"

I shrugged. "Probably. They're tough as barn wood."

I wonder if the country decorating craze spurred this latest beauty trend. Can we expect to see Cindy Crawford wading through horse plops hawking horse shampoo? What's next: Liz promoting Wild Fescue Perfume? Nancy Kerrigan smearing Bag Balm on her ankles?

On the other hand, it could be that women finally are kicking their heels about dropping a bundle on dainty dews, ritzy replenishers, and moisturizers that enrich manufacturers overnight.

I'm just thrilled that Mom's heavy-duty beauty has gone from tasteless to trendy. Or maybe she was all along and the rest of the world is just now catching up.

Cool.

Nightmare on Perfect Street

Betty Smartt Carter

When our friends Bob and Judy invited us to their tenth anniversary celebration, my husband and I discussed what to get them.

"A nice clock?" he suggested.

"They'd forget to set it."

"A cookbook?"

"Not unless it's *Better Homes and Hot Dogs*. You know how they eat. What about something for the yard?"

He laughed. "These are the people who don't cut their grass until it's blocking the view from their picture window."

For lack of a better idea, we opted to buy Bob and Judy a magazine subscription. I can't remember exactly why we settled on *American Couple,* but it sounded like a safe bet: one of those upbeat family magazines loaded with advice on everything from toning your thighs to building a gazebo.

But when I bought a sample issue to present at their party, the cover worried me a little. Lying on deck chairs in some island paradise, a tanned, blond, gorgeous couple displayed twin sets of dazzling teeth. "They Used to Be Average!" read the copy. "How You, Too, Can Look Perfect and Feel Great."

"Yeah, right," I thought, imagining paunchy Bob getting sunburned in the tropics. Since it was too late to come up with a better gift, I stapled a bow to the man's nose and went to bed.

We enjoyed the anniversary bash, then weeks passed and I realized we hadn't heard from Bob and Judy. So I called Judy to invite them out for dinner.

"That sounds great!" she said in a strangely energetic voice. "Nurturing friendships is part of a healthy emotional lifestyle!"

"Good," I said, a little uncertainly. "How about that new Mexican place?"

"Who needs a restaurant? I can give the four of us a gourmet meal right here at home with just half the fat and for a third the cost!"

I pressed the phone closer to my ear. "Judy, is that you?"

"Our place. Tomorrow night. Six. See you. I'm late for my ab and glute workout."

As I hung up, I felt a bit dazed. The only thing I'd ever known Judy to work out was a way to get her size 14 abs and glutes into a size 12 pair of blue jeans.

The next evening we headed over to Bob and Judy's.

"Wow," my husband said as we pulled up in the driveway. "Look at this yard. There's not a blade of grass out of place."

"And they've painted the house!" I said. "And added a sunroom! How did they find time to do all this?"

We stared at each other, mystified. While my husband headed to the backyard to find Bob, I knocked on the front door, then went inside. The house was ominously neat. Gone were the newspapers heaped on the couch. Gone were the dead plants and the laundry baskets full of dirty clothes.

Bizarre. My heart pounded as I opened the swinging door to the kitchen. But there sat my old pal Judy at the table, sorting piles of uncooked spaghetti noodles.

"Hi!" she said cheerily.

"Oh, thank goodness it's you!" I said, and dropped into a chair. "I was starting to think you guys had been kidnapped by some really tidy aliens. Can I help with dinner?"

"This isn't dinner," Judy told me. "I'm making common household items out of dried pasta. Here—how do you like these manicotti salt and pepper shakers?"

My heart began to pound again. "You don't do crafts, Judy. You can't even glue a fuzzy nose on a finger puppet."

She smiled and put her hand over mine. I noticed that her nails looked unusually long and healthy; her teeth had never been so white. Her bare arms had a firm, buffed look. "Bob and I have embarked on a new life," she said with eerie earnestness. "And it's all thanks to you guys."

"To us?"

"Yes." She reached down beside her chair and hefted a stack of glossy magazines onto the table. *American Couple,* of course. The top issue sported a photo of a rotini chandelier: "Easy Pasta Crafts That Turn Your Home into a Palace."

"When I think of the life we led before!" she said. "How we never cooked with virgin olive oil or made focaccia. How we never firmed up our triceps in just five minutes a day or took three easy steps to having a lawn like the White House. And the worst thing about it is that I was content to just be average. Sad, isn't it?"

I nodded. "Tragic. And this magazine—it changed all that?"

She put her hand over her heart. "We live by it. Every word."

"And you're really happier now?"

Judy's face clouded a little. "Yes, except—well, with all the time we're spending exercising and remodeling the house and doing crafts, there are a few things we don't have time for anymore."

"Such as?"

"Our jobs. We've both quit work in order to devote ourselves to full-time self-improvement."

"B-b-but Judy," I stammered, "how will you make it financially? What good is being perfect if you're starving?"

"Oh, don't worry." She burst into another cheery smile and picked up the newest issue from her stack of magazines. On the cover were our friends, Bob and Judy, posing beside an expensive new grill in their beautifully landscaped backyard. Bob held a spatula in one hand and a platter of portabello mushrooms in the other. I noticed his paunch had disappeared.

"You see?" Judy said. "Who needs a real job when you can make money just by looking perfect in a magazine?" Again she put her hand over mine. "Frankly, Bob and I are so grateful that we'd like to help you get started on your own road to self-improvement. We realize you have a long way to go [she glanced at my nubby fingernails], but it's never too late to start."

Oh, brother. Who has time to live a real life—go to work, raise kids, keep the house clean, fix the plumbing—and also keep their abs firm and their glutes shapely?

"Judy," I said, "I'm glad you're happy, but I think I'll stick with being humdrum and boring."

Just then Bob walked in with my husband. "Honey," said my beloved spouse, waving a copy of *American Couple* in the air, "Bob here's been telling me how I can lower my cholesterol, pay off our mortgage, and promote hair growth without spending a dime or taking precious time from our love life!"

I moaned. We should have given Bob and Judy a cheese board.

I'm Surrounded by Teens with Uncommon Scents

Marti Attoun

I walk into the house and sniff. Yes, Miss Sunflower Extract is home.

These days my eyes mist whenever I'm around my teenage daughter and her friends. It's not mushiness; it's scented and flavored bath gel, deodorant, spritz, spray, shampoo, conditioner, lotions, moisturizing potions, and lip balm, all topped off with perfume. Sometimes I think I'm living in a botanical garden.

It's, eau, too much.

"What in the world *stinks?*" her brother asked the other day when he got into the minivan.

"I gave the botanicals a ride to the mall," I said. "Dewberry, jasmine, and vanilla bean sat in the back."

As if he has any right to complain. One of his pals smells like two-day-old Stetson. The fellow has reached the age of aftershave, but hasn't mastered shower-before.

Not so long ago, teens were seen and heard, not smelled. I remember journeying through teenhood with just a dab of Mom's Estée Lauder Youth Dew on my pulse points for special occasions. In fact, Mom dumped baking soda into the tub water to eliminate odors. She dumped it in the kitchen sink, too, after gutting fish.

Now the trend is to layer the odors on pulse points and every-where else, beginning with the bathwater. Our tub is an oil slick. I don't know what the bath gels do for our skin, but I do know that a glob of juniper rejuvenator sloughed the nonskid seashell decals right off the tub floor. We don't soak in the tub anymore. We ski.

It's quite time-consuming and perplexing, too, for a teen to mix and match all these fragrances. Miss Extract agonized for five minutes in the deodorant aisle about which member of the breeze family to dab on her armpits.

"Oh, great," she said. "I can't remember if I like morning breeze, natural breeze, or spring breeze." When she saw a new one, ocean breeze, she broke out in a sweat.

I tried to help. "Forget ocean breeze. I don't know any CEOs with armpits that smell like seagulls. Give this cool citrus a shot and let's get out of here."

The girl is earth-friendly too. Translation: She prefers to pay double for hair goos and lotions distilled from exotic nut oils and endangered fruits certified to be from the rain forest. "Maybe you would be earth-friendlier if you didn't drain the rain forest of its irreplaceable shampoos and conditioners," I've suggested, but it's like talking to a papaya.

Adding to the aroma overload are celebrities. As soon as anyone is someone, he or she bottles the smell and dribbles it out by the pricey ounce. I have no desire to smell like Michael Jordan, but apparently lots of people do. Liz Claiborne, Calvin Klein, and Ralph Lauren all have signature scents. I suspect that chemists right now are squeezing coconuts and grape seeds to concoct *essence de Sammy Sosa*.

One good thing about this teen aroma is that I can always find my daughter. I simply follow my nose to the roots of the tropical petals mousse.

LIKE DEATH WARMED OVER

Becky Freeman with Ruthie Arnold

I'll never forget my first day back at college after an absence of ten years. I suppose I had secretly hoped I might be mistaken for an eighteen-year-old coed. At the very least, I expected my fellow students to faint when I revealed to them that I was the mother of four children. The actual reaction was more like, "Just four? Any grandkids yet?"

If I seemed elderly to the college kids, they appeared barely pubescent to me. The girls were wearing ponytails and hair ribbons! I might not have passed for Homecoming Queen, but I felt I did look a picture in my sand-colored corduroy skirt, olive jacket, and burnished leather boots. It was an outfit that obviously said, "Back to school! Crisp nip in the air, falling leaves . . ."

Too bad the Texas weather said, "You gotta be kidding!"

I sweltered through my first class, and, just before I passed out from heatstroke, I decided to take a rest room break. Checking my autumn pallet makeup in the mirror, I was transfixed. The face looking back at me was wearing a mustache. Evidently I had wiped the sweat from my newly made up brow, then swiped my hand across my upper lip in an agony of thirst.

"Well," I addressed the coed version of Groucho Marx staring at me from the mirror, "I'll bet *that* impressed the professor."

As I mopped up, I lectured myself. "Wipe that silly mustache off your face! You are finally in college. You are a university student. Now go cash your check at the university bookstore and get yourself a big glass of university iced tea and a collegiate salad at the University S.U.B."

I cashed my check (and sheepishly invested in a few rubber bands and hair ribbons), filled my lunch tray, and poured myself a huge glass of iced tea. The surprise came when I reached for my wallet to pay for my treat and found it empty at the bottom. I had had the money just ten minutes ago, but it was not there. The next surprise came when I found there was no credit to be had in the university cafeteria. I watched as the university lunch ladies took away my tray, then found a quiet corner, sat collegiately down, and cried.

Later that night, Mother called to see how my day went. She seemed to think it was hysterically funny when I told her I had lost my lunch money on my first day of school.

Back on the home front, my memory continued its downward spiral. I became so lax in my responsibilities as tooth fairy that the children were forced to try a variety of techniques to help the old girl out.

One of the children, having despaired of the tooth fairy ever remembering to look under his pillow, tried placing his tooth in a cool cup of water in the middle of the kitchen table where it could not possibly be missed. However, he forgot that Ms. Fairy was nearsighted and that she would also be thirsty at bedtime.

A second toothless child had the bright idea of tying his tooth to a string hanging from the ceiling fan above his parents' bed, thinking perhaps Mom and Dad might have more influence with the important personage they so much wanted to visit them. However, tooth fairy got too warm in the night, and the bicuspid became airborne somewhere in the wee hours of the morning and flew off into never-never land.

The older children began taking their newly shed teeth with them directly to the store where they could whip them out of their pockets while the tooth fairy was nearby with cash in hand. Gabe continued to struggle bravely on, even though he was understandably not quite clear on just how the tooth fairy system was supposed to work.

On a rare day when I had time to make his bed, I lifted his pillow and found, to my surprise (other mothers would probably have felt horror), the tooth-filled jawbone of a long deceased cow.

"Gabriel James!" I bellowed, "What is this filthy thing doing under your pillow?"

I can only describe the grin on his face as cunning.

"How much do you think the tooth fairy will give me for *that?*" he asked.

During this extremely hectic time, my personal appearance also suffered. My Nonnie had an expression to describe people who were not looking their very best. She would say, "They looked like death warmed over." On the morning I had promised to chaperone Zeke's field trip at his school, I woke up with a huge red pimple on the end of my not insignificant schnoz. I thought of my grandmother's expression and decided it was incredibly apt.

"Okay," I told myself. "So you woke up with a little pimple. All right, a *huge* pimple. Why do you, a thirty-something woman, feel thirteen-something again? You will not disgrace your son: you'll be the only one who notices it. You are blowing this tiny imperfection in an otherwise flawless face out of all proportion."

Even so, after inspecting 6,737,294 different specimens of amphibia and reptilia at the Museum of Natural Creatures That Make Mothers Queazy, I was not feeling good about myself.

At Burger Billions for lunch break, I fell into the soggy line at the counter, jostled about in a sea of starving nine-year-olds. I caught a sympathetic glance from another field trip mom. Hoping for comfort, I confessed, "I just feel so ugly today. My hair is a wet mess ..."

A bright-eyed boy named Christopher chimed in, "Yeah, and you've got a great big red mole thing on your nose too!"

That did it! I knew the time had come when I simply had to find some time for myself. As soon as the field trip ground to its merciful end, I dropped the children off at home with their dad and headed for Mary's house. Mary sells a lovely line of cosmetics; she is a professional hairdresser who works from a shop in her home; and she is my best friend. That day I needed all she had to give.

Heading straight for her workstation, I stepped over two toys and one kitten belonging to Mary's children, Michael and Michele, aged nine and six. I dropped into the beauty chair and sighed deeply.

"You know, you're going to think I'm silly, but I've been so self-conscious about this little blemish today."

"Really?" Mary asked in mild surprise. "Why I . . ." She moved in for a closer look, stepped back, frowned, and clicked her tongue. "I don't believe I've ever noticed anything *that* big on your face before."

"Thanks so much," my reply dripped sarcasm. "I didn't mean to offend you with my gross physical deformity. Excuse me while I go to the bathroom to spackle over this volcano on my nose."

In the bathroom, I applied a couple of Band-Aids to the problem, tried to see the humor of it, and returned sheepishly to Mary's chair. Attracted by the Band-Aids, Michael and Michele crawled onto the sofa with the kitten in tow and watched as we discussed what might be a really smashing new hairdo to soothe my battered self-esteem.

"Let's try some color this time, Becky," she suggested. "Something like—Plum Brown. It has nice burgundy highlights to accentuate your red . . . lips," she finished carefully. Then she set to work turning me Plum Brown.

Considering the large size of the yellow gloves she wore, she deftly measured and mixed and stirred.

"Sorry about these big ol' gloves. I had to use kitchen gloves because I'm out of the thin kind." Looking back over my day, it seemed the least of my problems.

At that moment, Kitty decided to make his escape from the sofa and jumped at Mary, attaching himself to her leg with his small but efficient claws. She screamed and planted her dye-smeared gloves into my forehead, leaving three extra large Plum Brown fingerprints, complete with burgundy highlights. In the aftermath, our eyes held.

"Nice touch," I said.

Mary apologized profusely while she applied the dye to my head, jerking and yanking at my hair with the huge plastic gloves.

"I'm not hurting you, am I?" She was really very kind, and through my tears I assured her that it did not hurt quite as much as natural childbirth. I tried to remember my Lamaze breathing. Things seemed to settle down and I began to relax and wonder just how gorgeous I might be when the labor was over. Then Mary said something I found more unsettling than what had already happened to me that day. "Uh-oh," was what she said.

"What do you mean, 'uh-oh'?"

"Oh, nothing." Silence. More pulling. "Becky—you haven't been losing a lot of hair lately, have you?"

"No," I fought the swelling panic in my chest. "Am I losing hair now?"

"A little," Mary answered in a professional, try-not-to-alarm-the-customer voice.

"How much is a little?"

"Well . . . no more than you'd lose with chemotherapy."

From the sofa, Michael and Michele collapsed with glee. "We love it when Becky comes over! This kind of stuff never happens to Mom's other customers. Hey, we could give Becky a T-shirt that says, 'No Hair by Mary.'"

When you've come to the end of your rope, these are the kind of kids who would say, "Tie a knot—and put a noose around your neck."

We managed to salvage what was left of my hair, and I left Mary's house Plum Brown and plumb tuckered out. As I drove wearily into the driveway of our home, Gabriel ran out to meet me and smiled his sweet three-year-old smile. He put both hands on my cheeks and gazed tenderly into my eyes.

"Mommy," he said, "you're fat."

At the moment, Nonnie's expression, "looking like death warmed over," seemed inadequate; "death wormed over" fit much better.

Sometimes I feel overwhelmed by the differences between me and the gorgeous Barbie doll look-alikes I see on TV and in magazines. The message they send is clear: "You are only wanted and desired if you look like me."

Then I get mad. How dare the media lead us to believe our worth depends on how we look? God is such a comfort to my sagging ego. He looks past my less-than-perfect body into my soul, which has had a complete makeover by his forgiveness and love.

Besides, I know a secret. Barbie is hollow inside. I know because Gabe takes her head off regularly. Lord, forgive me for sometimes wanting to do the same thing to real women who wear a size 6.

Yo Quiero No Discount

Martha Bolton

$\mathcal{I}$ always feared it would happen someday, and there it was—in black and white. All I had done was walk into a Taco Bell in east Tennessee and give my order to the teenager behind the counter.

I wasn't trying to cause any trouble, or pick a fight, or be disruptive in any way. I was just trying to get a couple of tacos and a seven-layer burrito. *That's all*. It was lunch. There was no justification for what the clerk did. He should have handed me my order and let me pay for it, and I would have been on my way. A simple transaction. But *noooo*. This guy had to take it one step further. He had to be confrontational. He had to take it upon himself to ruin my otherwise happy and peaceful day. He had to keep going until he pushed my buttons. All right, *his* button—the one on the cash register *that printed out the words "SENIOR DISCOUNT" on my receipt!*

SENIOR DISCOUNT! I almost dropped my tray! The nerve of that acne-faced troublemaker! Had I not been so hungry, I would have taken him on right then and there. I would have put my tray down, told him to meet me outside, then paper-cut him to a pulp with my birth certificate. I may have been over forty, but I was a *long* way from a senior citizen discount!

But I calmed down, decided to turn the other wrinkle—I mean, cheek—and forgive him. It was a simple oversight, after all. I went ahead and gave him the benefit of the doubt. It was the right thing to do. And besides, a ten percent discount is a ten percent discount!

Maybe he had a migraine headache and his vision was temporarily impaired, I reasoned. Or maybe it was Taco Bell's own version of *Candid Camera*. That's what that little video camera above the cash register was all about. Or, what was most likely the case, the young man's finger slipped, causing him to inadvertently hit the senior discount key instead of the coupon key. That had to have been it. Both keys were probably in the same general area. One little slip is all it would have taken.

That would have been the end of it, except I realized I hadn't ordered a drink and had to go back.

"Diet Pepsi, please," I said, watching his every move this time. His finger hit the Diet Pepsi key, then without even getting anywhere near the coupon key, it went straight for the one marked senior discount. He didn't hesitate for a second. He was confident. He was beyond confident. He didn't even bother to ask my age. If you're in doubt about something, you usually ask first, don't you? Like if you're not sure if someone's pregnant or if she's just put on a few pounds, most people ask before throwing a baby shower. It's the same principle.

But apparently this guy had no doubt. He was so confident I deserved a senior discount, he announced it as he handed the receipt to me.

"Here's your drink, ma'am," he said. "And with the senior discount it comes to $1.09."

I didn't have a choice now. I had to stop him before he dug his hole even deeper.

"*Excuse* me," I said, "but I'm not really a senior. I'm not entitled to a discount. In fact, I shouldn't have gotten a discount on my first order, either."

There, I thought to myself, *I've set the record straight. That should make him think twice before giving away Taco Bell's profits to some other undeserving patron.* I smiled, feeling vindicated and proud of myself that I had made the world a safer place for those of us past the forty mark.

"Aw, close enough," he said. "What's a couple of months?"

It had to be the lighting.

Chapter Six

Animal Antics: Weird Humor from the Animal Kingdom

*Did you ever notice when you blow in a dog's face he gets mad at you?
But when you take him in a car he sticks his head out the window!*
—Steve Bluestone

He that lieth down with dogs, shall rise up with fleas.
—Ben Franklin

*Outside of a dog, a man's best friend is a book;
inside of a dog, it is very dark.*
—Groucho Marx

When it comes to humor, the animal kingdom has certainly done its share of tickling our collective funny bone. Maybe dogs are considered "man's best friend" because they keep us in stitches with their crazy and endearing antics. And what about cats? If you have a cat or can borrow one for an hour try this: take a small fishing pole and put something soft, no hooks please, at the end of the line to act as a lure. Then cast the line and see who takes the bait. We dare you not to laugh as you watch your "furry fish" jumping and gyrating like a trophy bass at the end of the line. If you don't have a cat to experiment on, relax. You can still enjoy the antics of a few of the crazy critters whose stories appear in the pages that follow.

HE'S BAAAAAACK!

Ken Davis

$\mathcal{A}$ woman happened to be looking out the window of her home one day. She was horrified to see her German Shepherd shaking the life out of the neighbor's rabbit. Her family had been quarreling with these neighbors; this was certainly going to make matters worse. She grabbed a broom and ran outside, pummeling the pooch until he dropped a rabbit now covered with dog spit—and extremely dead.

After a moment's consideration, the woman lifted the rabbit with the end of the broom and brought it into the house. She dumped its lifeless body into the bathtub and turned on the shower. When the water running off the rabbit was clean, she rolled him over and rinsed the other side.

Now she had a plan. She found her hairdryer and blew the rabbit dry. Using an old comb, she groomed the rabbit until he looked pretty good. Then, when the neighbor wasn't looking, she hopped over the fence, snuck across the backyard, and propped him up in his cage. No way *she* was taking the blame for this thing.

About an hour later, she heard screams coming from the neighbor's yard. She ran outside, pretending she didn't know what was going on. "What's happened?" she asked innocently.

Her neighbor came running to the fence. All the blood had drained from her face. "Our rabbit, our rabbit!" she blubbered. "He died two weeks ago, we buried him—*and now he's back!*"

WHEN IN ROME

Shari MacDonald

A friend of mine told me about a couple she knows who recently got a talking parrot. They positioned its cage in their kitchen, where their two cats often slept.

Now, it was this particular couple's habit to sleep in every Saturday morning. However, the cats would get hungry before their owners were ready to get up, and the animals' incessant crying was impossible to ignore. So the couple would, upon hearing the felines' cries, get up, race to the kitchen and feed them, then go back to bed and shut the door, hoping to catch a few more winks.

On the Saturday morning after the parrot joined the family, the ritual began as usual. The cats started mewing and the couple got up, raced to the kitchen, and threw some cat food in a bowl.

Observing this, the parrot called out, "Hel-*lo?*" as the couple ran back to the bedroom and closed the door.

The following Saturday morning, the hungry cats began to cry once more. On cue, the bedroom door flew open, and the couple ran into the kitchen.

Hungry too, but realizing that English didn't get him anywhere the last time, the crafty parrot ventured hopefully, "Me-*ow?*"

THE PERFECT SONG

Sue Buchanan

$\mathcal{W}$hen I was a teenager I could sing. I sang in a trio that traveled all over West Virginia and beyond. The trio members, Janet, Carlene, and I, along with Susie, who took my place when I went off to college, are still the greatest of friends to this day. One of the highlights of each year is when the four of us get together for a reunion. We laugh! We cry! Sometimes we sing right straight through the hymnbook without stopping! Always we reminisce about the episodes of our youth, our favorite being that of the *great greasy goose*.

We had driven for miles to sing at a youth banquet in a dank, drab, crepe-paper-draped church basement. It should have been a clue that something was amiss when, immediately upon our arrival, we were pulled aside and told to "act naturally no matter what happens, and don't ask questions."

While we were rehearsing, trying to get used to the ancient, out-of-tune, beat-up old piano, we couldn't help noticing a teenage boy sobbing like his heart was broken. Those around him were making an effort, but no one seemed to be able to console him.

There was an air of anticipation as the banquet began. Not necessarily a *positive* air of anticipation, but nevertheless anticipation! We were seated, the blessing was said, and there was a pall-like silence—like in a funeral home when a favorite uncle has died. No one moved a muscle. At last the kitchen door gave a great *whoosh,* and through it came a very determined-looking woman balancing—

on one hand held high in the air as though she was the head chef at the Waldorf Astoria—the biggest platter you've ever seen.

On it was ... the biggest ... the biggest ... what? Turkey? No! Too big for a turkey! Let's just say it was the biggest *bird of unknown origin* we'd ever seen. With great ceremony, the platter was placed on the head table in front of us, and carved right under our noses, for heaven's sake!

The crying got louder—now everybody in the room was crying—but somehow dinner and the program continued as though everyone was in their right mind, which they weren't, of course. Only moments before our trio was introduced someone came forward and gave a lovely speech, thanking the selfless young man, who was now smiling through his tears, for contributing his pet 4-H blue-ribbon goose to the youth dinner! There was a round of applause, a standing ovation, and it was time for us to sing.

"Some glad morning when this life is o'er ...!" The words were barely out of our mouths when we began to pinch each other—we always stood with our arms around each other and pinched if there was a problem. There was—due to the very inappropriate next line of the song—and we were pinching each other senseless! What could we do? It was too late to go back!

"I'll fly away," we sang to a fresh round of tears.

Fortunately, sometimes you can't tell the difference between laughing and crying. Our bodies were shaking convulsively all the way through our first stand and tears were running down our faces like rivers. Just about the time we'd begin to recover, we would glance down at that greasy carcass—which, by the way, stayed on the table till long after the benediction was pronounced—and we would "lose it" again. Afterward everyone thanked us for being so sensitive and caring. Perhaps they thought of our ill-chosen song as a tribute!

Welcome to the Bat Cave

Nate Adams

$\mathcal{I}$ plopped into bed, let out a loud sigh, and peered at the clock radio. I had stayed up too late again—11:40 P.M. on a weeknight. Turning the other way, I saw only the quiet back of my sleeping wife.

It occurred to me that Beth and I hadn't gone to bed at the same time for quite a while. The house we had just moved into needed "a little work," so I was spending most evenings outside while Beth tinkered inside. The arrival of our third little boy just before the move had slowed our progress. When I came in at dark, I usually found additional projects that needed to be completed. Then I'd turn to the office work I hadn't been able to finish between yawns during the day.

I really missed our pre-slumber "talk times." But I was too exhausted for talking. I only had enough energy left to switch off the light ... until my eyes fell on a small black spot where the paneling over our fireplace met the ceiling. I couldn't remember seeing that knothole before.

Just then an insect buzzed past my nose, startling me into an unpleasant memory of the yellow jackets that had just been exterminated from between the first and second floors of our new home. They had entered through a woodpecker's hole to build a nest that the exterminator estimated had contained more than two thousand mean-spirited pests. It had taken four days of treatments to deal with the problem, and tonight's buzzing insect—thankfully just a fly—reminded me that I still needed to plug some woodpecker holes.

Well, I'd worry about that tomorrow. Then I remembered the dark spot on the wall. Was it possible some *other* insect horde was building a nest right in our bedroom? I rolled out of bed and pulled a flashlight from the nightstand. When I shined it up to the dark spot, I saw a strange reflection: two beady little eyes were squinting back at me.

It was a bat. Capping the chimneys was on next week's project list, and pulling the glass fireplace doors open and shut was an occasional pastime of our young sons. At some time during the past twenty-four hours, our bedroom had become a new exit to the bat cave.

My friend Don and his wife had once discovered a bat in their bedroom after they left a window open. Don went after it with a broom, sending the creature into a frenzy surpassed only by that of Don's wife, who ran around the room screaming. Ten minutes after he drove the bat out of the house, a police cruiser pulled up in front. Apparently the neighbors had noticed the bedroom-window silhouette of a man swinging a broom—and the sounds of a woman screaming and Don shouting, "Get out of here, you old bat!" Someone called in a report of domestic violence, and Don spent an embarrassing few minutes explaining that his wife was not the bat in question.

But what about *this* bat? Just then Beth woke up and asked why I was shining a flashlight in the corner of the ceiling. When I told her, she didn't take the news very well. "What are we going to do?" she asked, as she huddled against the opposite wall.

Well, what would *you* do at 11:45 P.M. when you're dead tired, your kids are asleep, and there's a bat hanging from your ceiling? I headed out to the garage, returning with a ladder, my fishing net, a large piece of cardboard, and a Ping-Pong paddle. I was going to try to capture the creature, but in case it got loose and started flying around the room I wanted Beth to have the Ping-Pong paddle ready. She quickly handed the paddle back to me and said if the bat started flying around she'd be locked in the bathroom, praying for my safety.

With that encouragement, I started climbing the ladder, the fishing net in one hand and the cardboard in the other. I positioned the cardboard on the wall just below the bat's head, ready to slide the cardboard underneath the creature after clamping the net down on top of it. I took a deep breath and dropped the net over our visitor.

Then came three blood-curdling screams. The first was from the bat, whose toes I had apparently whacked with the aluminum rim of the fishing net. The second was from me, as I stared into the flaming eyes and bared fangs of the terrifying little creature less than an arm's length away. The third scream, of course, was sort of a supportive, empathetic one from Beth, who managed to stay in the bedroom and even helped steady my climb down the ladder carrying my cardboard-and-fishing-net bat cage. Down the stairs and out the front door, I carefully set my captive and its temporary housing on the front step and fled back inside to watch him wriggle his way to freedom.

My wife's loving embrace rivaled any that Robin Hood received from Maid Marian. With the emergency over Beth and I staggered back to bed. We giggled with each relived moment, eventually talking ourselves to sleep.

In the days that followed, my wife and I didn't work quite as late, or as independently. That little bat helped us value the simple, incredible joys of making memories together and solving problems as a team. And we started setting aside some time for each other before we became too exhausted to talk.

You never know what might happen just as you're switching off the light.

THE POLITE PARROT

Anonymous

$\mathcal{D}$avid received a parrot for his birthday. This parrot was fully grown with a bad attitude and worse vocabulary. Every other word was an expletive. Those that weren't expletives were, to say the least, rude.

David tried hard to change the bird's attitude and was constantly saying polite words, playing soft music, anything he could think of to try and set a good example—but nothing worked. He yelled at the bird and the bird got worse. He shook the bird and the bird got more angry and more rude.

Finally, in a moment of desperation, David put the parrot in the freezer. For a few moments he heard the bird squawking, kicking, and screaming—then suddenly there was quiet.

David was frightened that he might have hurt the bird and quickly opened the freezer door. The parrot calmly stepped out onto David's extended arm and said: "I'm sorry that I might have offended you with my language and actions and I ask your forgiveness. I will endeavor to correct my behavior."

David was astonished at the bird's change in attitude and was about to ask what had made such a dramatic change when the parrot continued: "May I ask what the chicken did?"

Chapter Seven

Body of Laughter

*Most men wear their belts low here, there being so many
outstanding bellies, some big enough to have names of
their own and be formally introduced.*
—Garrison Keillor, *Lake Wobegon Days*

Never eat more than you can lift.
—Miss Piggy

America has two great pastimes and one of them is
not baseball. So what could possibly preempt baseball
when it comes to our affections? Eating, of course. Try
spending a week in Florida during February; you can't
escape the hundreds of thousands of porky Midwesterners that swarm the beaches. What else have these
people been doing all winter but eating themselves
silly? (Please note that we are not trying to say rude
things about Midwesterners. One of us was born and
bred there and is herself in danger of succumbing to
PMS—Porky Midwesterner Syndrome.) After all that
eating it's hard not to wallow in guilt with a capital G.
But just how productive has all that guilt been? Are we
skinnier? Are we healthier? Are we more disciplined?
No way! Maybe laughter about our predicament
would do more to shake us from our obsessions than
guilt ever could. It's not a surefire cure, but a few good
laughs may be just what we need to start us on the road
to recovery.

I Yam What I Yam

Martha Bolton

I should have known better, but it sounded reasonable at the time. Someone suggested to me that a good way to get rid of unsightly cellulite was by using one of those vibrating belts. They even suggested that in addition to using it on the usual body parts, I should try it on my upper arms, since that's where most of my cellulite seemed to be gathering.

So I decided to give it a try. I climbed up onto the platform, strapped the belt around my arms, and leaned into it. It seemed to work fine, shaking my arms as much as they could possibly be shaken. I couldn't see any immediate change, but was sure that I would eventually.

Eventually didn't take very long to arrive. When I woke up the next morning, I looked in the mirror and couldn't believe my eyes. The cellulite was gone! Not entirely gone, though. It was now in a heap down by my elbows! No, that's not a misprint. Apparently, all that shaking had caused my upper arm fat to slide south. Instead of being up north where it belonged, it was now resting comfortably at my elbows. I looked like Popeye.

When I showed my newly acquired abnormality to my doctor, he studied it for several minutes before commenting, "How'd you say you did this again?"

I repeated what I had done and why, and he made some notes in my chart, then called in one of his partners to examine me as well. "How'd you say you did this again?" his partner asked.

I was both embarrassed at my stupidity and depressed at what I had done to my body. I no longer wanted to wear short sleeves, for fear of being accosted by Popeye groupies and hounded for autographs. And forget swimsuits. I looked like a shark had already gotten to me.

My arms stayed like that for two years! Then, one morning, to my amazement, I looked in the mirror and noticed that my upper arm fat had just as mysteriously returned to its rightful position. Without warning, without fanfare, it went home, like the swallows returning to Capistrano. I was back to my normal self, cellulite and all. I still don't know why my unruly fat decided to venture off to regions unknown in the first place. It was some sort of medical oddity. But I'm glad that the whole incident is behind me.

I never did, though, get rid of that craving for spinach.

MOMMYROBICS

Nancy Kennedy

*A*ccording to Newton's theory of gravity, bodies have natural downward motions proportional to their weight. Now, most people have the false notion that he came to this conclusion when an apple fell from a tree and bonked him on the head, but that's just not true. It happened when his wife, about six months after giving birth to their child, turned to him and asked, "Newtie, do you think I'm fat?"

Being a sensitive husband, he answered, "Of course not, dear," though he was really thinking, *Whew! That extra twenty pounds she gained during pregnancy sure did a number on her!*

Then he realized everything that once was firm now was flabby and had fallen to the floor. So he called his discovery "gravity" and suggested his wife do sit-ups to remedy the situation.

Historians disagree on what happened next, but popular theory says Mr. Newton experienced the apple-on-the-head bonking shortly after that. Eyewitnesses reported seeing a woman lurking in the tree above him, but that has never been proven.

History aside, Newton's theory of gravity plagues mothers even to this day. See if you can answer yes to any of these Five Signs It's Time to Exercise:

1. You accidentally slap your child in the face with your arm flab as you towel dry her hair after a bath.
2. When you laugh, you shake like a bowl full of jelly—and you're not Santa.

3. Your child uses your body as a visual aid for his science project on the effects of gravity.
4. The last time you wore your white sweat suit you were mistaken for the Pillsbury Dough Person.
5. When your mother asks what you want for your birthday, you say, "Liposuction."

Now the dilemma: You have a baby attached to one breast and a toddler hanging from your leg. Your preschooler thinks you are his personal pillow and your first-grader just likes holding your hand. You have perhaps thirty-five seconds each day when you're not connected to another human being. You want to exercise, but how? And when? And where? Good news: You can do these exercises during the course of everyday activities.

Twenty-Pound Leg Shakes

Shake that toddler off your leg vigorously. Alternate legs as he switches from one to the other. For added aerobic benefit, breathe deeply and shout, "Off! Off! Get off my leg!"

Sit Uprights

When an ear-piercing wail blasts from the baby monitor on your nightstand, bolt upright. Do this each time, about twenty times a night. Sit uprights can also be done at the sound of a cough, sneeze, crashing fishbowl, or at the sudden intrusion of a preschooler during an intimate moment with your husband.

I Don't Knows

Commonly known as shoulder shrugs. Do these every time you're asked, "Why is grass green?" "Why does that lady have that thing on her lip?" "Do snakes kiss?"

Oh, My Aching Back Bends

Lift your baby from infant seat, carry her to the car, place in car seat. Drive to market. Lift her out of car seat, carry into the market, place in shopping-cart seat. Lift out of shopping-cart seat, place in car seat. Drive to McDonalds. Lift out of car seat, carry inside McDonalds, wait in line, wait for available high chair, place in high chair ...

Fifty-Yard (More or Less) Dashes

Best done in an upscale department store. When your potty-trained toddler unzips his fly in the middle of the lingerie department and announces, "I go pee!" grab him and dash to the ladies' room on the other side of the store.

Two-Hundred-Yard (More or Less) Sprints

Your soapy two-year-old escapes the bathtub when you turn your head to sneeze. By the time someone can say "Gesundheit!" she's out the door and running down the sidewalk to the neighbor's house. Sprint after her.

Deep (in Laundry) Knee Bends

Bend down, pick up a dirty sock, put it in the washer. Bend down, pick up a dirty T-shirt, put it in the washer. Repeat until every article of clothing is washed. You should be finished by the year 2016. Or maybe not.

Running in Circles

Pack three lunches, sign report cards, find the missing math homework, untangle someone's hair, get dressed, come up with book club money, and drag the trash cans to the curb between 7:31 and 7:35 A.M. Run, run, run.

Arm Extensions

Extend arms toward your tired, cranky four-year-old and pull her close. Extend again and pat a discouraged first-grader on the shoulder. Extend again to hug a friend. Finally, extend arms heavenward in praise and thanksgiving to a heavenly Father who loves you, fallen tummy and all.

A Diet Prayer

Victor Buono

Lord, my soul is ripped with riot
Incited by my wicked diet.
"We Are What We Eat," said a wise old man.
And, Lord, if that's true, I'm a garbage can.
I want to rise on Judgment Day, that's plain!
But at my present weight, I'll need a crane.
So grant me strength, that I may not fall
Into the clutches of cholesterol.
May my flesh with carrot-curls be dated,
That my soul may be polyunsaturated.
And show me the light, that I may bear witness
To the President's Council on Physical Fitness.
And at oleomargarine I'll never mutter,
For the road to Hell is spread with butter.
And cream is cursed and cake is awful,
And Satan is hiding in every waffle.
Mephistopheles lurks in provolone;
The Devil is in each slice of baloney.
Beelzebub is a chocolate drop,
And Lucifer is a lollipop.
Give me this day my daily slice,
But cut it thin and toast it twice.
I beg upon my dimpled knees,
Deliver me from jujubes.

And when my days of trial are done,
And my war with malted milk is won,
Let me stand with Heavenly throng,
In a shining robe—size 30 long.
I can do it, Lord, if You'll show to me,
The virtues of lettuce and celery.
If You'll teach me the evil of mayonnaise,
Of pasta à la Milannaise, potatoes à la Lyonnaise
And crisp-fried chicken from the South.
Lord, if You love me, shut my mouth.

Counting Fat Grams

Chonda Pierce

$\mathcal{T}$he only thing worse than being on a diet is being around someone who is on a diet.

Now, I don't want to seem insensitive. After all, my high school nickname was Tweetie Bird, partly because of my high-pitched, squeaky voice and partly because of my skinny, knobby-kneed legs. So I know insensitivity when I hear it.

I never used to have to worry about my weight, but Mother says I have to think about diets now. Something about corn chips and being *almost* forty, but I don't know.

Anyway, what I'm talking about here is the career dieter. My mother has tried everything from Weight Watcher's to Slim Fast, from Dial-a-Meal to Melt-a-Meal—complete with some contraption that melts your food down to pill form. Don't ask. It's another one of those late-night Ronco deals for three easy payments of just $14.95 each.

Mike Smith has been my manager for about three years. He's an average-sized man over fifty—well over fifty. Most of our years together, he's been on a diet of some sort. Amazingly, he's lost nearly 113 pounds, but he's gained 112. On this roller coaster ride, he's eaten and not eaten all sorts of things. He tried the popcorn-only diet. No matter how good that stuff smells, after one bag I never want to see it again. The cup-a-day diet. That one wasn't so bad because you could eat anything you could fit into a cup. Once I watched Mike cram a double-cheeseburger and a large order of fries into a coffee mug.

The weekend David and I planned to go off to a cabin on the river with Mike and his wife, Jan, was the same weekend Mike began his no-fat-grams diet. On the five-hour drive Mike rode along, sipping his bottled water without complaints. He swirled the clear liquid in the bottle and said with a satisfied grin, "Not a single fat gram!"

"Good for you, Mike. I'm proud of you," I said, and I really meant it.

The cabin was in central Kentucky at the end of a long, dirt road—no telephone, no TV—but a fine fishing river about four hundred yards away at the end of a grassy field.

"This is great," David said, as he unloaded two big grocery sacks of snacks and burgers.

"Yeah," Mike chimed in, "we'll burn off some fat grams walking down to the river."

"Maybe we'll catch some fish too," David said.

"You know, a two-pound catfish has only four fat grams," Mike said.

"Really? I didn't know that," David said. Mike was teaching us all.

Rather than walk, David and Mike *drove* the van to the river while Jan and I started supper: hamburgers and potato chips. The men came back without any catfish so we threw a couple of extra burgers on the grill.

"I'll just have a salad," Mike told me, as I flipped the red meat over to brown.

"Are you sure?" I asked.

Mike frowned and nodded. "Yeah, I think it's best. Just one burger has eighty grams of fat. You add mayonnaise, and that's another twelve. What kind of bread is that, wheat? No? Then tack on another six."

David walked up, fanning away the smoke from the burgers. His cheek poked out like a squirrel's. That's how he ate sunflower seeds. "Hey, Mike, want some seeds?"

Mike's face clouded with fear. "Oh, my goodness, let me see that." He snatched the open pack of seeds from David. After studying the package, Mike announced, "Twenty-six fat grams per pack! My goodness, why don't you just go ahead and put a gun to your head?!"

"It's just sunflower seeds, Mike," David said and spit an empty shell off the porch. "We'll play badminton later and burn it all off."

Mike continued to stare in shock at David's fat-gram-filled cheeks. Then, shaking his head, Mike walked away visibly upset.

That evening we played rummy. All was quiet when suddenly Mike announced, "You know, one Pecan Shortbread cookie has almost five grams of fat."

David whistled sharply.

I looked around the table. No Pecan Shortbread cookies in sight.

Without looking away from his cards, Mike announced, "Even a Fig Newton—full of fruit, mind you—has almost two per cookie." He discarded and concentrated on his hand as he regrouped his cards.

Jan seemed to ignore him, playing sixes and nines and discarding out. She took a bite from her bag of Cheese Doodles to celebrate. The snack was still in the bag so Mike turned the package to read the label. "Wow, would you look at this!" He held the bag with one hand and stabbed at the numbers with his other. "Nine grams per serving, seven servings in a bag. That's sixty-three grams of fat in this one bag!"

"Okay, whose deal?" I said, and for a brief moment we all tried to forget about fat grams.

Later that night, I discovered that out in the middle of nowhere, in the woods, in Kentucky, it can get pretty dark and pretty scary. Noises are out there that either are drowned out in the city by other sounds or occur only out in the woods in the middle of nowhere.

It was late, very late, and everyone had gone to bed. And was it ever dark. I awoke for some reason; I thought I'd heard something. David was breathing, but that wasn't it. A scratching sound was coming from the kitchen, the kind of sound a mouse makes while gnawing through plastic. I held my breath and tried to remember where all the furniture was. If I had to jump out of bed, I certainly didn't want to crash into a rocking chair.

Scratch, scratch.

"David, did you hear that?" I whispered.

He didn't budge.

Scratch, scratch.

I gripped the covers and pulled them up tightly to my chin.

Finally, Mike's voice scared away my fear of rodents. "Can you believe this?" he said, his voice coming from the kitchen. "Just one Nutty Buddy bar has sixteen grams of fat. Oh, and look at these barbecue chips. One serving has—"

Then Jan, no longer quiet, no longer understanding, went off like a fire alarm—a fat-gram alarm. "LISTEN HERE, FAT-GRAM BOY, IF I HEAR ONE MORE WORD ABOUT FAT GRAMS, YOU'RE WALKING HOME. HOW MANY FAT GRAMS DO YOU THINK YOU'LL BURN OFF THEN?!"

David sat up. In the dark I imagined his eyes bugging out, his mouth forming a little *O*.

For a long time there was only silence, no more scratching. After a while, the chirping of the crickets returned, and David eased his head back to his pillow. But before I fell asleep, I thought about what I had heard and wondered if, after that, Mike would even dare to *dream* about fat grams.

The next morning, I fried some eggs, and Jan laid some strips of fresh bacon in the skillet. Mike had brought along a cantaloupe for himself. No one said anything about what had happened the night before.

Finally breaking the eerie silence, Mike announced, "Give me two eggs and some of that bacon."

All eyes turned to him.

"Do you know how many fat grams are in that meal?" David asked.

"Yep!" Mike answered. "But I'm not doing that anymore." He dragged two greasy strips of fat from the stack to his plate. And we ate like pigs. When he finished, Mike pushed back from the table and dabbed his mouth with a napkin.

David was preparing himself a biscuit and some grape jelly when Mike cut a disbelieving glance his way. He whistled sharply. "Do you know how many *calories* are in that?"

We all ignored him.

"Do you know that you can gain two calories by licking a little bitty postage stamp?"

Fortunately for all of us, this story ends well: Mike went on to lose lots of weight (I think he did it by counting carbohydrates);

Jan got a new pressure cooker (that was during the phase in which Mike was laying off fried foods); and I got a chapter for my book.

We can count fat grams, we can count calories, or we can count peanut butter and jelly sandwiches. There's nothing wrong with counting, and I'm all for being healthy, but I don't want to be silly about it.

Now, I know Mike isn't the only one who has ever been concerned about his appearance—even I am sometimes. So when I get to feeling blue about the outside of me and seriously consider counting something (like bites of chocolate), I think about God's view of me. "For you created my inmost being; you knit me together in my mother's womb. I praise you because I am fearfully and wonderfully made; your works are wonderful, I know that full well. My frame was not hidden from you when I was made in the secret place" (Psalm 139:13–15).

I love knowing that I am "fearfully and wonderfully made." We *all* are—even you, Mike. So why not tell the Lord about your fat grams and the calories on a postage stamp? Because the rest of us are sick of hearing about it!

Chapter Eight

Parenting, the Funniest Job of All

Parents are the bones on which children cut their teeth.
—Peter Ustinov

When I was born, I was so surprised
I couldn't talk for a year and a half.
—Gracie Allen

Children seldom misquote you. In fact, they usually
repeat word for word what you shouldn't have said.
—Unknown

Being a parent has got to be one of the toughest yet greatest jobs ever invented. Part of what makes it so incredible is all the fringe benefits: you don't have to worry about going bald because you've already pulled out all your hair, you get to say the exact same things to your kids that your mother said to you, and you have the pleasure of stifling all those belly laughs that threaten to erupt just as you're trying to discipline a mischievous child. Well go ahead, nobody's looking now. Sit down in your favorite easy chair and let the laughter roll.

LAMENTATIONS OF THE FATHER

Ian Frazier

Laws Concerning Food

Of the beasts of the field, and of the fishes of the sea, and of all foods that are acceptable in my sight you may eat, but not in the living room. Of the hoofed animals, broiled or ground into burgers, you may eat, but not in the living room. Of the cereal grains, of the corn and of the wheat and of the oats, and of all the cereals that are of bright color and unknown provenance you may eat, but not in the living room.

Of the quiescently frozen dessert and of all frozen after-meal treats you may eat, but absolutely not in the living room. Of the juices and other beverages, yes, even of those in sippy-cups, you may drink, but not in the living room, neither may you carry such therein. Indeed, when you reach the place where the living room carpet begins, of any food or beverage there you may not eat, neither may you drink.

But if you are sick and are lying down and watching something, then may you eat in the living room.

Laws When at the Table

And if you are seated in your high chair, or in a chair such as a greater person might use, keep your legs and feet below you as they were. Neither raise up your knees, nor place your feet upon the table, for that is an abomination to me. Yes, even when you have an interesting bandage to show, your feet upon the table are an abomination, and worthy of rebuke. Drink your milk as it is given you, neither use on it any utensils, nor fork, nor knife, nor spoon, for that is not what they are for; if you will dip your blocks in the milk, and lick it off, you will be sent away.

When you have drunk, let the empty cup then remain upon the table, and do not bite it upon its edge and by your teeth hold it to your face in order to make noises in it sounding like a duck; for you will be sent away.

When you chew your food, keep your mouth closed until you have swallowed, and do not open it to show your brother or your sister what is within; I say to you, do not so, even if your brother or your sister has done the same to you. Eat your food only; do not eat that which is not food; neither seize the table between your jaws, nor use the raiment of the table to wipe your lips. I say again to you, do not touch it, but leave it as it is.

And though your stick of carrot does indeed resemble a marker, draw not with it upon the table, even in pretend, for we do not do that, that is why. And though the pieces of broccoli are very like small trees, do not stand them upright to make a forest, because we do not do that, that is why. Sit just as I have told you, and do not lean to one side or the other, nor slide down until you are nearly slid away. Heed me; for if you sit like that, your hair will go into the syrup. And now behold, even as I have said, it has come to pass.

Laws Pertaining to Dessert

For we judge between the plate that is unclean and the plate that is clean, saying first, if the plate is clean, then you shall have dessert. But of the unclean plate, the laws are these: If you have eaten most of your meat, and two bites of your peas with each bite consisting of not less than three peas each, or in total six peas, eaten where I can see, and you have also eaten enough of your potatoes to fill two forks, both forkfuls eaten where I can see, then you shall have dessert. But if you eat a lesser number of peas, and yet you eat the potatoes, still you shall not have dessert; and if you eat the peas, yet leave the potatoes uneaten, you shall not have dessert, no, not even a small portion thereof. And if you try to deceive by moving the potatoes or peas around with a fork, that it may appear you have eaten what you have not, you will fall into iniquity. And I will know, and you shall have no dessert.

On Screaming

Do not scream; for it is as if you scream all the time. If you are given a plate on which two foods you do not wish to touch each other are touching each other, your voice rises up even to the ceiling, while you point to the offense with the finger of your right hand; but I say to you, scream not, only remonstrate gently with the server, that the server may correct the fault.

Likewise, if you receive a portion of fish from which every piece of herbal seasoning has not been scraped off, and the herbal seasoning is loathsome to you, and steeped in vileness, again I say, refrain from screaming. Though the vileness overwhelm you and cause you a faint unto death, make not that sound from within your throat, neither cover your face, nor press your fingers to your nose. For even now I have made the fish as it should be; behold, I eat of it myself, yet do not die.

Concerning Face and Hands

Cast your countenance upward to the light, and lift your eyes to the hills, that I may more easily wash you off. For the stains are upon you; even to the back of your head, there is rice thereon. And in the breast pocket of your garment, and upon the tie of your shoe, rice and other fragments are distributed in a manner wonderful to see. Only hold yourself still; hold still, I say. Give each finger in its turn for my examination thereof, and also each thumb. Lo, how iniquitous they appear. What I do is as it must be; and you shall not go hence until I have done.

Various Other Laws, Statutes, and Ordinances

Bite not, lest you be cast into quiet time. Neither drink of your own bathwater, nor of bathwater of any kind; nor rub your feet on bread, even if it be in the package, nor rub yourself against cars, nor against any building; nor eat sand.

Leave the cat alone, for what has the cat done, that you should so afflict it with tape? And hum not that humming in your nose as I read, nor stand between the light and the book. Indeed, you will drive me to madness. Nor forget what I said about the tape.

Complaints and Lamentations

O my children, you are disobedient. For when I tell you what you must do, you argue and dispute hotly even to the littlest detail; and when I do not accede, you cry out, and hit and kick. Yes, and even sometimes do you spit, and shout "stupid-head" and other blasphemies, and hit and kick the wall and the molding thereof when you are sent to the corner. And though the law teaches that no one shall be sent to the corner for more minutes than he has years of age, yet I would leave you there all day, so mighty am I in anger. But upon being sent to the corner you ask straightaway, "Can I come out?" and I reply, "No, you may not come out." And again you ask, and again I give the same reply. But when you ask a third time, then you may come out.

Hear me, O my children, for the bills they kill me. I pay and pay again, even to the twelfth time in a year, and yet again they mount higher than before. For our health, that we may be covered, I give six hundred and twenty talents twelve times in a year; but even this covers not the fifteen hundred deductible for each member of the family within a calendar year. And yet for ordinary visits we still are not covered, nor for many medicines, nor for the teeth within our mouths. Guess not at what rage is in my mind, for surely you cannot know.

For I will come to you at the first of the month and at the fifteenth of the month with the bills and a great whining and moan. And when the month of taxes comes, I will decry the wrong and unfairness of it, and mourn with wine and ashtrays, and rend my receipts. And you shall remember that I am that I am: before, after, and until you are twenty-one. Hear me then, and avoid me in my wrath, O children of me.

Deck the Halls with Poison Ivy

G. Ron Darbee

"Jingle bells—
Batman smells—
Robin laid an ..."

"Whoa, whoa, whoa!" I yelled, interrupting the impromptu songfest taking place on our living room floor. "What's gotten into you guys?" I addressed my children with the stern parental look I had practiced in order to communicate such moments of dissatisfaction.

"What?" Ron asked, oblivious as to the nature of their infraction. Two years his sister's senior, at age eight, Ron had already assumed his role as the pair's self-appointed spokesman.

"What?" I mimicked, "You're off-key, that's what. Now try it again, this time in the key of C ... or B ... or something sharp or flat. Never mind, just listen. It goes like this:

"Jingle bells—
Batman smells ..."

My wife, Susan, a wonderful woman with an unfortunate knack for bad timing, chose this moment to walk in the front door. Unaware of my penchant for music and my gift of near-perfect pitch, she appeared surprised—dare I say awestruck—and remained motionless, mouth agape, taking in the spectacle before her.

"*You're* teaching them those songs?" Sue has never been a music aficionada and displays a total lack of appreciation for the classics.

"I don't suppose you'd believe me if I said they were teaching me?" I asked.

"Nope."

"Just as well. I couldn't say that anyway," I said. "It was purely a philosophical question. But I do want to go on record as saying your suspicious nature and accusatory tone pain me deeply."

"So noted," Sue said.

The children, having inherited bad timing from their mother, saw the following lull in our conversation as an appropriate opening for their melodic rendition of "Randolph the Red-Faced Cowboy."

"You're killing me here, you know that?" I said, glaring at my young prodigies, to which little Benedict Arnold and his sister Mata Hari responded by rolling on the floor and giggling gleefully in the face of their father's plight.

"And what other songs has Daddy taught you?" Sue asked.

"I really doubt you'd be interested," I interrupted. I had guessed wrong, and Sue insisted on hearing their entire repertoire.

They were a fountain of information, my two little turncoats, and they spewed forth a virtual stream of familiar, if not traditional, holiday titles. I spent the next few minutes explaining that "Grandma Got Run Over by a Reindeer" was in no way directed toward my in-laws, and that, yes, I loved her mother and wished her no harm—be it at the hands (or hooves) of fawn or foe. Sue wasn't really angry, just stunned, a state of mind that has become the hallmark of our life together.

"Can't you teach them something a bit more constructive?" Sue asked, once the kids had scampered off to seek other entertainment.

"I suppose I could try," I said, "but it goes against my better nature. I'm Dad, remember? I get to play the role of the overgrown, happy-go-lucky playmate, the fun guy."

"And what does that make me?" Sue asked.

"Uh-uh, nope—not even gonna answer that one," I said, shaking my head from side to side. "You know it's unfair to ask questions that don't have correct answers." Sue laughed and threw a handful of clean laundry in my direction that had been sitting on the couch, waiting for the folding fairy to make an appearance. Normally, I would make a few sock balls and return her fire, but my present standing considered, I opted to fold and sort, a visible, if silent, demonstration of my repentance.

"You know," Sue said, folding an undershirt into thirds, "a group from the church is going caroling next week. If you want, you could teach the kids a few songs they could really use."

"Caroling?" I asked.

"Yes, caroling," she said. "What's wrong with that?"

"Look outside, Dorothy," I said, "we're not in Kansas anymore." Sue and I, both cold-climate natives, had moved to California a number of years earlier.

"What does that have to do with anything?" she asked.

"It has everything to do with it," I said. "You can't go around spreading Yuletide joy in shorts and a T-shirt. For crying out loud! You put a few cups of hot wassail in those kids, and they'll be passing out with heatstroke."

"Where is it written that you can't sing Christmas songs unless it's twenty degrees outside?" Sue asked.

"I think it's a union thing," I said. "Anyway, it just wouldn't be the same."

Despite my logical and well-presented arguments to the contrary, Sue remained intent on joining the carolers, and I reluctantly took on the responsibility of teaching the kids a few traditional Christmas tunes. We started off with "Silent Night, Holy Night," moved into "The Little Drummer Boy" and, by the end of day four, wrapped up with a favorite of mine: "Away in a Manger." In the process, I learned that young children possess an incredible capacity for memorization and absolutely no concept of melody or rhythm. Thankfully, kids are cute enough to get credit for the presentation without being judged for musical quality. I considered the endeavor a complete success.

So confident was I, in fact, that I called the kids into the kitchen and invited Sue to enjoy a special sneak preview of the Darbee Family Carolers. Pulling a pair of chairs off to one side of the room, we cleared a space in the center and sat back to enjoy the show: Sue as a spectator, me as the proud and satisfied father/coach.

"What should we sing first?" Melissa asked, anxious to display her newfound talents.

"Anything you want, sweetheart," Sue said.

"Just pick your favorite," I added. "Show Mommy how much you've learned." I leaned back in my chair, arms folded, nose slightly tilted in the air, sporting the look of a man who has performed admirably, and achieved a measure of greatness—in short, a man ready for a major fall.

"Jingle bells—

Batman smells—

Robin laid an . . ."

"Now wait just a minute!" I yelled. "That's not what we've been practicing." Not to be deterred by the reaction of one dissatisfied fan, however, Ron and Melissa continued through to the end of the song's chorus.

"Don't be upset with them," Sue said, applauding Melissa's curtsy and Ron's bow. "It was a special request."

"You?" I questioned. "*You* put them up to this?"

"Sure," Sue said. "Why not? You don't have to be Dad to be the fun guy, you know. Moms can be playful too. Let me see," she continued, "if I'm the fun one, that would make you . . ."

"The other fun one," I said. "Merry Christmas, Sue."

"Merry Christmas, sweetheart."

Surprise, Surprise!

Barbara Johnson

*O*ur youngest son, Barney, was planning a surprise party for his wife, Shannon, at a hotel in San Diego, and he invited Bill and me to join the fun. On a lark, we decided to take the train, and we invited my friend Lynda along.

After our train arrived, we jostled our carry-on bags into the train station, expecting Barney to be waiting for us on the platform. All the other passengers scurried around as we stood there, scanning the crowd for Barney's handsome face. But he wasn't there.

We shuffled our things over to the bench to wait. Gradually, the large waiting area emptied, and we were alone. I dug through my purse for a quarter and the number of the hotel where we were supposed to stay. The only pay phone in sight was way off in the corner, and as Lynda and I walked toward it, a disheveled man leaning against the wall raised his head and watched us.

From beneath a tattered baseball cap, his long, scraggly, black hair fell over his eyes and hung in tangles. His stained and wrinkled trousers were four sizes too big. One part of his ragged shirttail hung outside his sagging waistband while the rest was loosely stuffed inside. His canvas shoes were as holey as Swiss cheese. Little clouds of smoke rose out of the cigarette that dangled from his mouth.

My heart lurched a little at the unexpected sight, and Lynda must have been startled by the man's appearance too, because she reached for my arm and said, "Barb …" as she made a frightened face.

"Just imagine," I told her, patting her hand reassuringly, "that poor man is someone's kid."

I made the call, only to find Barney wasn't at the hotel. "I guess we'll just have to wait. He probably got stopped for another traffic ticket."

As soon as I sat on the bench, the disheveled man slowly ambled toward us.

"Barb, he's coming toward us!" Lynda gasped, scooting closer to me on the bench.

"No, he's not," I hissed back, turning my head and pretending to look the other way while noting his every move out of the corner of my eye.

"He is! He's gonna rob us!" Lynda's lips didn't move, but her words were distinct.

The man's hands were in his pockets, and he was staring at us as he drew nearer.

I began to shuffle through my purse, trying to decide whether to offer him a couple dollars—or a breath mint. Bill, engrossed in a magazine, was oblivious to the unfolding drama. I elbowed him, causing him to turn to me impatiently. "What?" he said too loudly.

The man was now less than ten feet away from us, and my heart was pounding. Lynda squirmed next to me on the bench, and the three of us sat there huddled together, watching the ragged man come nearer. Suddenly he spoke.

"Hi, Mom!"

Mom? If I wore dentures, they would have clattered to the floor. I stared at the man, who stood so close to me now I could look up under the bill of the baseball cap and peer into those twinkling dark eyes, those suddenly familiar eyes ...

"Barney, it's you! What on earth ... ?"

Now he was laughing so hard he couldn't talk. Wordlessly, he lifted off the cap—and the long, scraggly, black hair came off with it, a wig attached to the cap. The cigarette was fake too; it emitted clouds of powder rather than smoke whenever Barney puffed on it. With a smile as wide as the Mississippi, he hitched up his enormous trousers while pulling me into his arms for a hug. Still feeling a little bewildered, I suddenly regretted all those tricks I had played on my family during our boys' growing up years. Now, I realized, it was payback time.

Since that moment, I have developed a new empathy for how poor old Isaac must have felt when his conniving son Jacob showed up at Isaac's bedside disguised as his older brother, Esau. And I have a new understanding of the Scripture passage that says, "Can a mother forget her little child and not have love for her own son? Yet even if that should be, I will not forget you" (Isaiah 49:15 LB).

Even when we're so low down and hard up our own mothers wouldn't recognize us, God sees through our disguises. He looks into our hearts and calls us his own.

Picky, Picky

Nancy Kennedy

I recently read *Tales of a Fourth Grade Nothing,* in which a kid named Fudge eats a turtle. Obviously, he's not what you'd call a picky eater. While I'm not sure I'd want my daughters to snack on a reptile, it might be a welcome relief from having to plan meals around a child who doesn't like rice, prefers white meat only, and whose sandwich absolutely must have the mustard next to the cheese and the mayonnaise next to the lettuce. Plus she sniffs every morsel of food before she'll eat it, asking, "Is chicken supposed to smell like this?"

Her sister eats peanut butter sandwiches without jelly and jelly sandwiches without peanut butter, but never peanut butter and jelly together–and no crusts, ever! Mostly, though, she likes anything that rhymes with "eat-za" or can be served from a drive-through window.

I take some comfort in knowing that I'm not alone in the battle against picky eating. I know a mom who breaks out in hives whenever she takes her three daughters to a fast food restaurant. She orders three cheeseburgers: one without ketchup, one without mustard, and one without ketchup, mustard, onions, pickles, bun, or meat. The hives come with the counter clerk's usual response: "Lady, are you nuts?" But this woman has a child who will only eat cheese, and fast food restaurants won't sell her just a slice so she's learned to order cheeseburgers sans everything but the cheese.

Take it from my friend Patty, there's nothing too far-fetched when it comes to getting kids to eat. Afraid she'd be labeled a failure as a mother because her kids wouldn't eat broccoli or peas, one night she told them: "Kids, after you went to sleep last night I found a jar of fairy dust–and here it is!" She held up a jar of finely ground parmesan cheese. "This does something wonderful. It makes anything you eat taste delicious."

At dinner that evening she let the kids sprinkle fairy dust all over their lasagna (which was full of zucchini and other green things) saying, "Not only will this taste wonderful, but it will make you stronger and taller! You'll be able to lift heavy toys and put them away, and you'll be able to reach a little higher than before so you can get a drink of water without calling for me or Daddy."

Patty's ploy actually worked–until her daughter caught her refilling the fairy jar with store-bought parmesan. Now she's back to sneaking green stuff into gingerbread. (Note: It was the mother of a picky eater who invented carrot cake.)

Mothers throughout the ages have fretted over their children's eating habits. I ran into a group of such moms at the mall food court. They were wandering around in a daze saying to their small children, "What about a bagel? How about some chicken?"

As I watched, I wrote down some of the picky eater wisdom I've acquired over the years.

Sometimes you can get kids to eat healthy yet "yucky" food by using favorite character names: Barney Bran Flake Cereal, Big Bird Scrambled Eggs, Little Mermaid Split Pea Soup. Sometimes. The nose of a baby who eats only strained carrots and mashed sweet potatoes will eventually turn orange. Pleading, begging, and threatening may get a forkful of lima beans into a child's mouth, but only a miracle can keep him from spitting them out and shoving them under his plate. A toddler who won't eat anything from the table will eat the same food after it has been dropped on the floor. Sometimes when a child insists, "If I eat that, I'll throw up!" she isn't being overdramatic. Pay particular attention when tomato juice is involved.

Although getting your children to eat may seem like a hopeless situation, it really isn't. If kids get hungry enough, they'll eat. (Just keep the dog biscuits out of reach. Trust me on this one.) Not only that, mothers of picky eaters can take comfort in the fact that there is ultimate justice in the world. Many of our pickiest eaters grow up to beget pickies of their own, and then they're the ones faced with a child who refuses to eat what's served.

If you doubt that, just ask your mom.

The Great Toaster Tart Conspiracy

Randy Frame

*W*hen most people are asked to identify the biggest threats to their marriages, they come up with things like poor communication, money, and contrasting lifestyles. But based on what I experienced recently, I'd have to put the dreaded Toaster Tart at the top of my list.

In a two-week period, my family experienced no fewer than six conflicts of all varieties: parent-versus-child, child-versus-child, and, of course, the familiar parent-versus-parent-via-child. And all of these focused on the same thing—that tasty, rectangular, fruit-filled breakfast treat.

Sure, they look innocent enough. But I'm convinced they have hidden motives: They're out to destroy my marriage—and yours, too, if you're not careful.

It all began when I took my three kids to the grocery store. My first mistake was that I failed to avoid the Toaster Tart aisle. And once you go down that aisle, it's all over. Toaster Tarts attract kids' attention like a magnet; then they plant the subliminal message: "Buy me! Fuss and whine until I'm in your grocery cart!"

And so the negotiating begins. Me: "If you kids promise to behave the whole time we're shopping, I'll get you some Toaster Tarts." That was my second mistake. I could hear the Toaster Tarts whispering to one another: "Phase One of our plan has succeeded."

Phase Two began while the grocery bags were being unpacked at home. My wife wasn't impressed by my ability to make good decisions at the grocery store. The discussion quickly degenerated into suggestions that I am impulsive and undisciplined. "No," I explained, "I'm merely spontaneous and liberated."

Then I pointed out that, according to the nutritional information on the side of the box, Toaster Tarts are in the same class as the fruit bars my wife buys. (In appealing to "facts," I made my third mistake.)

"This is not about facts," came my wife's reply. "This is about principle." Jeron informed me that, when she does the shopping, the Toaster Tart becomes the arena in which the parent-child battle for control is waged. And if parents give in on that battle, we might as well surrender the war.

How did I respond to the tension? I ate a Toaster Tart. Or maybe more than one—it's all a blur now. Anyway, that was my fourth mistake. My wife wondered aloud whether I got the pastries for the kids or for myself.

A week later it was time for me to return to the scene of the crime. Toaster Tarts didn't number among the thirty things on the grocery list. Nevertheless, I debated all the way to the store: to buy or not to buy? One of the children—our seven-year-old—made the decision easy for me by falling asleep in the car on the way. She wasn't happy about being awakened. It was 5:30 and I had to be somewhere at 6:30. Nothing I had to say could calm her down until, in a moment of desperation, out came the magic words: "I'll get you Toaster Tarts."

The storm subsided, but quickly resumed inside the store when Children B and C couldn't agree on cherry or cinnamon. Easy solution. I got both (mistakes number five and six).

Once I got home, my wife and I threw the fruity pastries somewhat off track when we refused to repeat the scene of the previous week. We chalked it up to agreeing to disagree. But did that stop the Toaster Tarts? Nooooooo. They simply went to work on the children, planting subtle doubts and concerns about parental fairness.

To wit, on Saturday morning Kids A and B had two Toaster Tarts apiece. Kid C decided to save one for later on. Then it was Sunday morning and Kid B was lobbying for another breakfast pastry. I threw down the gauntlet: "No, young lady. You had two yesterday!" I offered her ten possibilities for breakfast, but she held out for a Toaster Tart.

I drew my battle line for control. But what about Kid C? She pointed out that, unlike her sisters, she only had one yesterday. So I gave her a tart, telling her not to eat it in front of A and B (mistake number seven). Kid C promptly showed her Toaster Tart to Kid B, who made the strategic decision to work on Mom instead.

My wife, unaware of who had what yesterday, gave in to B. The next thing I knew, Kid B was tapping on my shoulder. "Yoo-hoo," she said. Then she produced the pastry from behind her back and waved it in my face.

I couldn't believe this was happening. My wife failed to support me in the battle, and the Toaster Tarts—I'm certain of it—were thinking, "This is too easy."

As I marched toward the kitchen to talk to my wife, headed straight for mistake number eight, it finally hit me: This is exactly what the blasted Toaster Tarts want me to do! I paused to think about what had just happened. My child—my own flesh and blood—would not have shoved a fruit-filled pastry in my face. The only other option was . . . my kid had been taken over by a Toaster Tart! They were trying to wreck my family life.

I refused to let it happen.

Instead of marching into the kitchen to confront my wife, I went back to the living room. And when I did, I could almost hear a collective sigh of disappointment coming from the worldwide Toaster Tart community. The battle was over, and I had emerged victorious.

Oh, one other thing. Once you've faced a frontal assault from Toaster Tarts, those boring fruit bars my wife buys start looking pretty good.

Chapter Nine

Real Men Do Laugh

What Women Want: To be loved, to be listened to, to be desired,
to be respected, to be needed, to be trusted, and sometimes,
just to be held.
What Men Want: Tickets for the World Series.
—Dave Barry

Everybody knows that real men don't cry and that they certainly don't eat cheesecake. But if you think they don't know how to laugh, then you've never met a real man. Of course, men come in all shapes, sizes, colors, and flavors, but the ones women (and men for that matter) enjoy most are the ones who know that if life is worth living, it's also worth laughing about.

Dental Advice

Mark Lowry

The best Christmas gift I've ever gotten in my life was a set of horrible, ugly, protruding teeth. The wrong teeth are in the wrong places, facing all the wrong directions, and the front tooth—which is about four shades yellower than the others—has a huge cavity at the gum line. My brother owned a dental lab for a while and made them for me. And when I put them in my mouth, it just changes my whole personality.

I was ecstatic when I unwrapped them.

See, I'd been waiting for them before I made my first appointment with my new dentist. I'd spent lots of time in dental offices. I got all my teeth capped. They asked, "How white do you want 'em?" I said, "White as they come! I want Chiclets!"

So I wanted to start this new dental relationship off right. I popped the teeth in and headed out. (On my way, I stopped by the Waffle House. The manager took one look at me in my ugly false teeth and asked if I could cook.)

The dentist's office was packed when I burst through the door. Two little kids were playing on the floor, a mother was sitting on the couch reading to a toddler, and two teenagers with braces and acne were talking in the back corner.

I was in the right place—and I was ready, wearing my upper plate of cavity-infested, plaque-encrusted fake teeth.

Walking over to the counter, I announced loudly (if garbled): "Hey, I'm Mark Lowry! I've got a 10:30 appointment!"

146

The way that nurse threw that clipboard at me, you'd think body contact caused tooth decay. She said, "You're going to have to fill this out."

I gave her a big, ugly, toothy smile. "I'll be happy to, ma'am."

A hush filled the waiting room. Little kids were running to their mothers, and everyone was looking at my teeth. I went over and sat by the lady reading to her little kid. "I don't know why they make me fill this out," I told her. "I come in here every week."

Nurse after nurse after nurse kept peeking in at me. I'd look up and smile my biggest truck-stop grin. "How ya'll doing?"

One kid couldn't stand it anymore. I was way too interesting to view from afar. He came over and stared straight into my mouth.

"This is what happens when you don't floss, kid," I told him.

Finally, I took out the teeth and announced, "This is just a joke. My brother made these for me."

Laughing, the receptionist said, "Leave them in for the dentist!"

I popped them back in, and she took me ahead of everybody. (Waiting Room Tip: This is how you can get ahead of everybody else at the dentist.) She set me back in the examining chair, stuck a bib around me, and told me she'd send the dentist right in.

When the dentist came, he took one look at me and lost all his oral faculties. You'd have thought I'd shot him with a stun gun.

I grinned big and wide. "Hi, Doc, I've been flossing. I use rope, small chain, anything I can find, but Doc—" I spread my lips as wide as I could, "—I think I may have a cavity or two."

He stammered, "Well . . . we can help you, we can help you."

He washed his hands and washed them and washed them. And washed them and washed them. I started to think the guy was headed for the linoleum.

So I took the teeth out. "It's just a joke, Doctor."

He fell back against the wall and shook his head. "Man," he groaned, "all I could think about was that I had to put my hands into that mouth."

Everybody ought to get a set of teeth like mine. Because if you eat at Shoney's and tell them you found them in the salad bar, they'll give you a free salad.

It works every time.

How to Have a Relationship with a Guy

Dave Barry

$\mathcal{C}$ontrary to what many women believe, it's fairly easy to develop a long-term, stable, intimate, and mutually fulfilling relationship with a guy. Of course this guy has to be a Labrador retriever. With human guys, it's extremely difficult. This is because guys don't really grasp what women mean by the term *relationship*.

Let's say a guy named Roger is attracted to a woman named Elaine. He asks her out to a movie; she accepts; they have a pretty good time. A few nights later he asks her out to dinner, and again they enjoy themselves. They continue to see each other regularly, and after a while neither one of them is seeing anybody else.

And then, one evening when they're driving home, a thought occurs to Elaine, and, without really thinking, she says it aloud: "Do you realize that, as of tonight, we've been seeing each other for exactly six months?"

And then there is silence in the car. To Elaine, it seems like a very loud silence. She thinks to herself: Geez, I wonder if it bothers him that I said that. Maybe he's been feeling confined by our relationship; maybe he thinks I'm trying to push him into some kind of obligation that he doesn't want, or isn't sure of.

And Roger is thinking: Gosh. *Six months.*

And Elaine is thinking: But hey, *I'm* not so sure I want this kind of relationship, either. Sometimes I wish *I* had a little more space, so I'd have time to think about whether I really want us to keep going the way we are, moving steadily toward ... I mean, where *are* we going? Are we just going to keep seeing each other at this level of intimacy? Are we heading toward *marriage?* Toward *children?* Toward a *lifetime* together? Am I ready for that level of commitment? Do I really even *know* this person?

And Roger is thinking: . . . so that means it was . . . let's see . . . *February* when we started going out, which was right after I had the car at the dealer's, which means . . . lemme check the odometer . . . *Whoa!* I am *way* overdue for an oil change here.

And Elaine is thinking: He's upset. I can see it on his face. Maybe I'm reading this completely wrong. Maybe he wants *more* from our relationship, *more* intimacy, *more* commitment; maybe he has sensed—even before *I* sensed it—that I was feeling some reservations. Yes, I bet that's it. That's why he's so reluctant to say anything about his own feelings. He's afraid of being rejected.

And Roger is thinking: And I'm gonna have them look at the transmission again. I don't care *what* those morons say, it's still not shifting right. And they better not try to blame it on the cold weather this time. *What* cold weather? It's 87 degrees out, and this thing is shifting like a *garbage truck,* and I paid those incompetent thieves *six hundred dollars.*

And Elaine is thinking: He's angry. And I don't blame him. I'd be angry too. I feel so *guilty,* putting him through this, but I can't help the way I feel. I'm just not *sure.*

And Roger is thinking: They'll probably say it's only a ninety-day warranty. That's exactly what they're gonna say, the scumbags.

And Elaine is thinking: Maybe I'm just too idealistic, waiting for a knight to come riding up on his white horse, when I'm sitting right next to a perfectly good person, a person I enjoy being with, a person I truly do care about, a person who seems to truly care about me. A person who is in pain because of my self-centered, schoolgirl, romantic fantasy.

And Roger is thinking: Warranty? They want a warranty? *I'll* give them a darn warranty. I'll take their warranty and stick it where . . .

"Roger," Elaine says aloud.

"What?" says Roger, startled.

"Please don't torture yourself like this," she says, her eyes beginning to brim with tears. "Maybe I should never have . . . Oh, I feel so . . . " *(She breaks down, sobbing.)*

"What?" says Roger.

"I'm such a fool," Elaine sobs. "I mean, I know there's no knight. I really know that. It's silly. There's no knight, and there's no horse."

"There's no horse?" says Roger.

"You think I'm a fool, don't you?" Elaine says.

"No!" says Roger, glad to finally know the correct answer.

"It's just that. . . . It's that I . . . I need some time," Elaine says.

(There is a fifteen-second pause while Roger, thinking as fast as he can, tries to come up with a safe response. Finally he comes up with one that he thinks might work.) "Yes," he says.

(Elaine, deeply moved, touches his hand.)

"Oh, Roger, do you really feel that way?" she says.

" What way?" says Roger.

" That way about time," says Elaine.

" Oh," says Roger. "Yes."

(Elaine turns to face him and gazes deeply into his eyes, causing him to become very nervous about what she might say next, especially if it involves a horse. At last she speaks.)

"Thank you, Roger," she says.

"Thank *you*," says Roger.

Then he takes her home, and she lies on her bed, a conflicted, tortured soul, and weeps until dawn, whereas when Roger gets back to his place, he opens a bag of Doritos, turns on the TV, and immediately becomes deeply involved in a rerun of a tennis match between two Czechoslovakians he's never heard of. A tiny voice in the far recesses of his mind tells him that something major was going on back there in the car, but he is pretty sure there is no way he would ever understand *what,* and so he figures it's better if he doesn't think about it.

The next day Elaine will call her closest friend, or perhaps two of them, and they will talk about this situation for six straight hours. In painstaking detail, they will analyze everything she said and everything he said, going over it time and time again, exploring every word, expression, and gesture for nuances of meaning, considering every possible ramification. They will continue to discuss this subject, off and on, for weeks, maybe months, never reaching any definite conclusions, but never getting bored with it, either.

Meanwhile, Roger, while playing racquetball one day with a mutual friend of his and Elaine's, will pause just before serving, frown, and say: "Norm, did Elaine ever own a horse?"

Airplane Babies

Mark Lowry

I was flying not too long ago on a full flight. It was packed. I have to fly so much, I wish I could just be faxed over. Especially now that the cheap fares make it easy for everyone to fly. Before that, I could have several seats open around me, so I could relax. You know what I mean—I could loosen my belt and explode. But now, people are in these seats and don't leave me any room to expand.

And sometimes those people have something worse than airline food. Worse than narrow, bottom-busting airline seats. Worse than carry-on trunks.

They have babies.

I was flying in a window seat on a long flight, and I was praying I'd have an empty seat next to me. At the last minute, the old gentleman sitting on the aisle had been bumped up to first class. I thought, "That's great! I'm going to have both of these seats to myself. I'll get to raise those armrests, grab the pillows and blankets, then lie down and enjoy myself."

But I was not so fortunate. I looked up the aisle and saw *them* coming: a young mother and her six-month-old child.

And they were heading straight toward me.

Plop. They settled in. And worse, the baby was going to fly in the seat by me.

I don't have anything against children. I'm single, never married, and I don't have offspring. If you're going to stay single, never get married, and you want to be in the ministry, you really shouldn't be having children.

So I'm not used to kids. I like my nephews and my nieces, but I don't want every other kid around me, because I don't know what to do with them.

And I had no idea what to do with this baby beside me. She sucked on anything she could get in her mouth. She was sucking on the seat belt for a while. Then she got bored with that, saw me, decided I looked edible, and began sucking on my arm. The mother thought it was cute. The hairs on my arm looked like they had been moussed before we got off the ground. I felt like a salt block. I didn't think she was sucking that hard until I noticed two of my tattoos were missing.

Then the mother began to talk to me. She was one of these friendly types who talks nonstop. You know, a circular breather. So I just put my book down. I figured I was going to have to talk.

"What do you do for a living?" she asked me. I hate that question, because I have no idea what I do for a living.

I said, "Well, I tell stories about my life from a Christian perspective. I write Christian songs, I sing in a gospel quartet, and I just travel around doing my little thing."

She said, "Oh, that's nice!"

Then, about halfway through the flight, she said to me, "Do you mind if I change her diaper right here? It's only a wet one."

I felt like saying, "Do you mind if I throw up right here? It's only a wet one."

What could I tell her? I'd already told her I was a Christian, so I couldn't tell her what I really thought.

She opened a Pampers box, and I fought the urge to say, "Looky there, you don't have to change her diaper! It says right on the box, up to twenty-six pounds. We can weigh her and keep flying!"

Oh, but no, she wouldn't have it. She opened that diaper, and *surprise! surprise! surprise!* It wasn't just a wet one.

The oxygen masks fell out of the ceiling. I thought they were going to have to raise that wall back up in Germany. It looked like that kid had eaten a whole bottle of Dijon mustard. The guy behind me leaned over and said, "Pardon me, but do you have any Grey Poupon?"

My dad would say, "Mark, you need to learn to watch what you say."

Dad, if you knew what I was editing out, you'd be proud.

Mr. Mom

James R. Judge, M.D.

It seemed like a perfectly reasonable thing to do. Me taking care of our three daughters while my wife went out of town for a week. When Cindy questioned whether she should be gone so long, I tried to calm her fears. "I'm a doctor, for goodness sake. I think I can handle this."

My daughters, ages thirteen, eleven, and eight, greeted the news with relative exuberance. I'm sure the vision of Mom ("the enforcer") gone and Dad ("the easy touch") in charge filled their heads with exciting possibilities.

Cindy did her usual thorough job of creating a flawless, hour-by-hour schedule for us to follow in her absence. She also left two meals in the freezer and called Grandma and Grandpa to come in to cook two more. I had the distinct feeling that my capabilities were being questioned, and my dad machismo kicked in. I'd show her what a man can accomplish. Not only would I run the errands, do the chauffeuring, work fifty-plus hours, and make the meals, I'd also get our bedroom painted and new curtains put up before Cindy got back home.

Monday

The morning after Cindy left town, I got up early, had half an hour of quiet time, exercised for thirty minutes, and took a shower. Then I was ready for some domestic action. I decided to let our two junior high girls sleep an extra twenty minutes while I made the lunches.

I'll stop here for a quick confession. When something isn't in the refrigerator, there's a good chance I don't have a clue where to find it. Around the house, I mostly do "man stuff"—repairs, painting, wiring. So that morning, trying to fix three school lunches, I hunted in cupboards I hadn't opened since moving into this house, and I'm talking years here.

So fifteen minutes behind schedule, I bounded up the stairs to wake the girls. Their sleepy "good morning, Daddy dearest" looks soon dissolved when they realized it was thirty minutes later than it was supposed to be. How was I to know that thirty minutes made the difference between a good hair day and a disaster? They grabbed their lunches and exploded out the door.

On my lunch hour, I decided to run to the store to pick up a few things. Twenty minutes and $101.93 later, I was tweaked with a slight sense of guilt as the clerk filled four bags with items that weren't necessarily on my original list. (How the gummy trolls got there, I don't know.)

The evening was a blur of Domino's pizza (it's got all four basic food groups), algebra, scraping off old wallpaper in the bedroom, and a chapter of *Mandie*. I crashed into bed about 1:00 A.M. and fell asleep wondering whether I should lower the bar—maybe just strive for survival rather than excellence.

Tuesday

I woke a little earlier, had a fifteen-minute quiet time, and spent fifteen minutes on the exercise bike. The girls were up early, the sun was shining, and the birds were singing. Then the phone rang. It was Cindy's parents. A storm had been predicted, so they were leaving early. They'd arrive in an hour and a half.

I tried to keep down my rising panic. I had planned on coming home at lunch to clean up before they got here. Cindy's compulsive need for things to be clean was only a dim reflection of her mother's compulsive need. Lemon Pledge, don't fail me now!

I called the office and canceled my first hour of appointments, then engaged in a session of aerobic housecleaning. I don't know how efficient the vacuuming was, but at least it left those telltale marks in the carpet. Then I was off to work, looking so haggard my nurse gave me one look and said, "Oh, that's right. Cindy's out of town."

When I walked in the door that evening I was greeted by the wonderful smell of home cooking and Grandma and Grandpa's happy faces. The evening meal was fabulous, but the reprieve lasted only one day. Grandma and Grandpa left the next day.

Wednesday

I woke up. I thought about a quiet time, but exercise never entered my mind. I was making lunches when I noticed I'd forgotten to get bread. So I prepared bagel sandwiches and threw in an extra bag of gummy trolls in hopes the girls wouldn't notice the bagels. (They noticed.)

At the office, my small talk with mothers took a decidedly different turn. I asked single moms what they did to make things run better at home. I wanted to fix these gals a cup of coffee and let them sit back and relax because, doggone it, they deserved it!

After work I drove one daughter to a piano lesson and another to youth group. I picked up the first child from piano and then another from a friend's house. Then I went back to get the third daughter from youth group, helped with three levels of math, and stayed up till 1:30 A.M. painting the bedroom ceiling.

Thursday

The girls woke me up. I painted the rest of the bedroom. I can't remember anything else.

Friday

Only one more day until Cindy's return! I wanted to do a dance right there in the kitchen. Instead, I wrote out all the jobs that still needed to be done, carefully placing a child's name next to each job.

What was I thinking? It was Friday, which meant each of the girls had a social agenda requiring its own personal secretary. Cindy had warned me of this with a cryptic notation on her original schedule: "Friday night—check with girls." Suffice it to say that no one even looked at my little task list. The evening brought sleepovers, snacks to buy, school dances, multiple sets of girlfriends running in and out. Before it was over I was reduced to running to the store to buy panty hose. The girl at the checkout handed me my bag and asked, "Wife out of town?"

Saturday

There can be no more beautiful sight on this earth than a wife returning home from seven days away. Cindy looked so calm, so collected, so capable. I hugged her and assured her that everything had gone just fine. I was so happy to see her I didn't want to spoil the moment.

She needed time to adjust. Anyway, I knew the truth would come out soon enough.

Chapter Ten

Hey, Moms Are Fun Too!

Giving birth is like taking your lower lip and
forcing it over your head.
–Carol Burnett

If evolution really works, how come mothers only have two hands?
–Milton Berle

Some moms feel they've been permanently cast in the role of the bad guy, always having to spout out orders about the most trivial matters:

1. "Never ever feed your brother's goldfish to the kitty. I mean it!"
2. "Wait a minute . . . that's not the potty!!"
3. "You're going to sit here until next Tuesday unless you take at least one bite of broccoli!!!"
4. "I don't care what her mother said she could wear, you're not wearing that to the bathroom, let alone to the dance!!!!"

Some of us (we know who we are) live in a permanent state of overemphasis, speaking as though our kids won't hear us unless we talk in exclamation points. But give us a break. Moms have a tough job. We may not always know the best thing to say or do for our children, but we do know that one of the very best things we can do for ourselves and for them is to keep our sense of humor intact, guarding it as one of God's precious gifts.

Help! I've Got TMS!

Nancy Kennedy

*A*sk any mother, "What's your idea of ultimate pleasure?" and before she can get out her first yawn she'll reply, "Sleep with a capital Zzzzzzz . . ."

The irony is, while moms esteem sleep as the Holy Grail of motherhood and hold it up with a borderline-worshipful state of desire, to kids it's a necessary evil that must be fought against valiantly. As a result, they're the number one cause of the dreaded TMS (Tired Mother Syndrome), which has afflicted mothers universally down through the ages.

Although researchers at the Centers for Disease Control and Prevention in Atlanta have tried (unsuccessfully) for years to document it—they've yet to find a TMS sufferer who could stay awake long enough to answer their questions—they've pinpointed two warning signs:

Brain Scrambling

This is a direct result of a woman not spending enough quality time with her pillow. I know a mother of five girls. (She has terminal TMS.) Recently I saw her sitting in her car in the library parking lot coloring in a Bugs Bunny coloring book. When I asked her what she was doing, she answered, "Cooking dinner."

Now, she's an intelligent woman. She fully understood that she was not cooking dinner but was actually waiting for her oldest child to check out a library book. Because of Brain Scrambling it came out, "Cooking dinner."

Pew Slumbering

This is a potentially embarrassing sign. I remember my first episode. I'd been up all night with a teething baby, wondering about the world record for the longest consecutive number of sleepless nights—and whether I'd surpassed it. The next morning I walked into church and flopped down on a pew. As the pastor stood to welcome the congregation, my head fell backward and I let out a resounding snort.

Now, I don't usually make a habit of snoring. However, I firmly believe that if you're going to do something, you should do it with all your might. So in front of God and everybody I snored at the top of my lungs, in harmony with the choir as they sang, "O for a Thousand Tongues." Eventually someone tipped me over, which stopped my snoring, allowing me—and everyone around me—to enjoy the rest of the service. I don't remember the sermon, but I do remember it being the most refreshing service I'd ever attended.

I assumed (mistakenly) that I'd get to sleep once the kids got older, that TMS is a temporary condition—a common misconception among TMS sufferers. You tell yourself from day one, "As soon as she sleeps through the night I'll get some sleep." When that day comes, three years later, you and your husband celebrate. Nine months later you're up all night once again. So what's the answer? Author Melissa Fay Greene once wrote that she's developed a motto: When presented with a multiple-choice situation in which sleep is one of the options, choose sleep.

When sleep isn't an option, however, I propose another one: reciting Psalm 121:3–4, "... he who watches over you will not slumber; indeed, he who watches over Israel will neither slumber nor sleep." I hear God's whispers most clearly in the quiet hours of the night as I recall his words: "Come to me, all you who are weary and burdened, and I will give you rest" (Matthew 11:28). "Cast all your anxiety on him because he cares for you" (1 Peter 5:7).

So next time you're up before dawn nursing a baby, chasing monsters from the closet, or changing sheets, remember that the God of the universe is also awake, and you're in the best company.

Mama's On Hold

Mark Lowry

My mama was always standing up for God. She could witness to a statue and lead it to Christ.

I can remember Mama going to the supermarket, witnessing to the cashier lady and having her on her knees while the line was winding around the milk department, past the Ding-Dongs and the Twinkies, and back again.

I used to say, "Mama, this place is open twenty-four hours a day! You can come back at three in the morning and lead the whole place to Christ. But the line's backing up."

By the way, Mama had a surefire way of handling obscene phone callers. She witnessed to them. The moment she picked up the phone, the guy on the other end didn't have a chance.

"Hello . . . ?" she'd say. "I beg your *pardon?* Young man! Did you know that Jesus Christ suffered, bled, and died on the cross so you could have eternal life? Did you know he was buried in a borrowed tomb and rose again on the third day? Did you know he could set you free from this phone perversion? Get on your knees right now. I said, GET ON YOUR KNEES RIGHT NOW and repeat this prayer after me: Say, 'Dear Lord, come into my life, forgive me of my SINS!'. . . Hello?"

Most of them hung up on Mama, but a few of them got saved and became deacons.

Mama even witnessed to Madalyn Murray O'Hair when I was a little kid.

It happened when I was about eight, and I'll never forget it. Madalyn Murray O'Hair was at the time the world's best-known atheist. Madalyn could wipe out anybody in a debate. I heard her debate Dr. W. A. Criswell one night in 1975, and she cleaned his clock because he was such a gentleman. He would allow that woman to interrupt him and get him off his train of thought, then he'd lose track of what he was talking about.

Well, the difference between Mama and Dr. Criswell is that Mama is not a gentleman. You can't interrupt Mama. Mama doesn't have to breathe. Mama can go for days on one breath.

My brother and I were down the hall in our room, listening on the radio to Madalyn running over everyone who called in.

I thought, "Oh, lady, have fun. Mama's on hold."

Finally, the commentator said, "Beverly–" that's Mama. "Beverly, you're on the air."

Have you ever seen the moment at an auto race when the starting guy waves that flag and the cars vroom into action?

That was Mama.

VROOOOM. The flag was down, and Mama was off to the races. Madalyn kept saying, "Ma'am . . . ma'am . . . ma'am . . . what church do you go to?"

But Mama went vrooming right on. VROOOM, VROOOOOOOOM!

Madalyn kept trying to interrupt: "Ma'am . . . what church do you go–?"

Mama: VROOOOOOOOOM!

"Ma'am, ma'am! What church–?"

Mama: VROOOOOOOOOOOOOOOOM!

While down the hall my brother and I were yelling, "Get her, Mama!"

Well, Mama gave her the whole Bible. She started in Genesis, and she went straight through to the maps.

Finally, the last thing Mama said was the only thing I remember her saying. But I'll never forget it.

She said, loud and proud, "You asked me how I know he LIVES? He lives within my HEART!"

There was dead silence on the radio for a solid five seconds. Finally, the commentator spoke up, mumbling like he was crawling out from underneath the table.

He said, "Uhm, ma'am, would you please tell her what church you go to?"

When Mama hung up, we heard Madalyn say, "That woman is very intelligent, but she's dangerous."

I thought, *Madalyn, if you only knew.*

Hello

Patsy Clairmont

$\mathcal{O}$ur son Marty was about to return home from the Air Force. He had been stationed in Guam, and we hadn't seen him for eighteen months.

The night before his flight was to arrive, Les and I were at the mall, and I headed for the Party Center store. I found cone-shaped hats with gala fringe spewing out the top, horns arrayed in sparkling glitter, and multicolored confetti shaped like stars.

This is going to be one fun reunion, I thought, as I headed for the checkout counter.

"What are you doing?" I heard a voice ask behind me. I turned; Les was standing there with his eyebrows bumping together in puzzlement.

It seemed obvious to me what I was doing, but I humored him. "I'm getting supplies for our celebration."

"Just where do you think you're going to use them?" The words sounded more like a threat than a question.

"At the airport tomorrow, of course," I responded uneasily.

"What airport?" he questioned. "Not the same airport I'm going to. If you're taking that stuff, you'll have to go to a different airport by yourself."

I couldn't believe my ears. But I decided at such a happy time we shouldn't be hassling over horns and hats, so I put the party favors back.

When we arrived at Marty's gate, two of his friends were already waiting. We sat chatting excitedly; then I mentioned that ol'

Mr. Party Pooper wouldn't let me buy the delightful hats, horns, and confetti.

In unison the two young men turned to my husband and said, "Thank you!"

Before I could respond, an airline representative announced the plane had touched down.

I learned that day that mothers don't need party paraphernalia to celebrate. I didn't need hats or horns because I had hands and a mouth. I started leaping in the air, trying to get a glimpse of Marty deplaning. My hands came together like clanging cymbals, over and over sounding out my joy. I began to laugh and whoop out words for the world to hear, "My son is home, my son is home!"

Then I was in his arms baptizing his uniform in a mother's relief.

At this point I'm not sure where Les and Marty's friends were ... hmmm, now that I think about it, they seemed to have faded back in the crowd.

And Her Husband Thought *He* Had a Stressful Job

Phil Callaway

The wife of an army colonel had endured an all-night flight across the Atlantic to meet her husband at his latest military assignment. She arrived at Rhein-Main Air Base in Germany with nine good reasons to be exhausted. As she exited the plane all nine of them followed her—not a one over the age of eleven.

Collecting their many suitcases, the entourage filed noisily into the cramped customs area. A young official stared at them in wide-eyed disbelief.

"Ma'am," he said, "do all these children belong to you?"

"Yes, sir," she said with a sigh. "They're all mine."

"Well, how about this luggage. Is it all yours?"

"Yes, sir," she said with a nod. "It's mine too."

"Ma'am," he continued, "do you have in your possession any weapons, contraband, or illegal drugs?"

"Sir," she calmly replied, "if I had any of those items I would have used them by now."

FREE AT LAST?

Pamela Shires Sneddon

*A*nother first day of school has arrived. But this year, it's different. As I give a kiss to five-year-old Katie, the youngest of my nine children, I realize that this is the first time in twenty-five years I won't have a child at home.

Almost before I finish waving good-bye to Katie, I'm stopped by another parent. "What are you going to do now that all your kids are in school?" she asks.

What am I going to do? Is she kidding? I know exactly what I'm going to do: all those things that have been on hold for the past twenty-five years. I'm going to clean closets, write a book, make slipcovers for the couch, learn to sail. But first, I'm just going to sit. Sit and listen to the silence. Sit and have a leisurely cup of coffee. Sit and think. Sit and have a quiet time with God that's actually quiet. I can't wait.

I step into my hushed and empty house, ready to savor this new experience of solitude. It's a short savor, however. The phone rings: "I forgot my lunch, Mom," says the piping voice of my eight-year-old.

Okay, I think. I can do this. One quick trip to school and I'll be back.

Sure enough, one quick trip and I'm back. I reach for my favorite coffee cup. I notice the answering machine light is blinking. I push the button.

"Mom," says a voice slightly less piping than the last one. "I forgot the check! I have to turn it in now or I can't go on the band trip!"

Okay, I can do this. One slightly longer trip to the junior high, that's all.

What's that? You're thinking that I should tell them, "Tough luck, you forgot it, you pay the consequences," right? I should do that, I know. And I will, too, the next call I get.

When I return home, I pour my coffee, walk into the living room, my steps echoing strangely. I sink into the couch, pull out the shoe my twelve-year-old couldn't find this morning, and put my feet up on the coffee table. I lean my head back against the cushions and study the spider spinning a lavishly webbed creation from the beam above me. It's so pleasant to watch someone else working that it takes me a moment to realize that the phone is ringing again.

"Pam," says an adult voice, "we need you."

Oh no. This is even worse than the I-forgot-my-lunch call. Worse than the I-fell-in-the-mud-and-I-need-clean-clothes call. This is that dreaded summons: The Field Trip Driver call. I'm an easy target since I possess the most envied item an elementary school parent can own: a car with eight seat belts. And it doesn't help that I'm not mentally prepared for this phone call. I haven't had time to come up with any excuses for why I can't possible drive to the symphony.

The symphony! Memories of last year's symphony trip flash against the frontal lobes of my brain. I pretend I'm the answering machine, but fail to make the *beep* noise correctly. My friend laughs heartlessly. I argue a sudden onset of flu, heart palpitations, extreme dizziness. No use. My friend is calling from a hospital bed. They're releasing her early so she can drive one group of kids, but she still needs me to drive seven ten-year-old boys.

"You're the only one with enough seat belts," she reminds me.

I have one request: "Please don't give me the twins. Remember what they did to the last field trip driver?"

My friend reminds me that is why she is in the hospital. She also reminds me that the twins are my sons.

Fine. I'll do the field trip. After all, it will only be two hours or so out of my day. Fifteen minutes of symphonic armpit noises in the car on the way there, twenty minutes of jumping and punching in line as we wait to get in, an hour of trying to keep ten-year-olds in their seats without giving the appearance of being in any way responsible for them. Maybe no one will swallow a jawbreaker this time.

And now I'm driving and I'm driving—it seems as though I've been driving forever. I glance in the rearview mirror.

"Charlie Baker, get your head back in the car, don't lean out like that! Sam, grab Charlie, please. Bobby, I can see you. Wait a minute, I can't see Ryan. Where's Ryan? Oh no! I forgot Ryan! Wait, I need to think. When did we last see Ryan? Was it before he dropped the sour balls during the flute solo or was it when the lady on crutches got knocked over? Russ, are you sitting on Ryan? Let Ryan up. I'm pulling this car over until you let Ryan up!"

Suddenly, the whole car is shouting, "Let Ryan up! Let Ryan up!"

I come to with a start, my head stuck between the sofa cushions. I've been asleep! It's all been a dream, a dream that couldn't possible come true. At least, not until later in the school year, and there's still time to sell the car.

It takes a few minutes for my heart rate to drop, to realize that I'm still alone in my silent house. The telephone is quiet. There are no messages on the answering machine. The very walls, dented as they are by soccer balls and heads, reflect tranquility (at least they would if tranquility didn't have to travel through so many layers of dirt).

There's so much I can do now. I can think long thoughts. I can form complete sentences. I can try to match thirty-five different styles of white athletic socks. I can go out to lunch.

Lunch out? Is it possible at last? Yes, it can happen! I put on some real clothes, leaving my sweats to stand alone in the closet. The dog barks wildly as I prepare to head out the door.

Don't answer that phone. Don't answer that phone. Don't answer—

"Mrs. Sneddon, this is the school secretary. Your child is throwing up in the office."

Chapter Eleven

Seize the Moment . . . for Laughter

The human race has one really effective weapon,
and that is laughter.
−Mark Twain

Laughter is like changing a baby's diaper. It doesn't permanently
solve any problems, but it makes things more acceptable for a while.
−Unknown

Some people are gluttons for laughter. They don't simply wait for the next stray joke to come along; instead, they make laughter a way of life. They seize even the most mundane moments, hoping that maybe, just maybe, something hilarious is lurking right around the corner. If you feel too timid to culti-vate such a lifestyle, at least cultivate a few friends whose zany behaviors you can enjoy vicariously. But watch out, you might just get sucked in. Before you know it, you may become the Ethel to their Lucy.

I Dare You

Luci Swindoll

*M*ore often than not I wish I had taken a camera along to capture some of the zany antics of Marilyn and me. Then maybe people would believe they really happened. However, the story I am about to relate is one of those rare occasions that I will be forever grateful no camera was available to record.

I had been living in southern California for about a year when I received a call from a former Mobil Oil supervisor in Dallas; he was going to be vacationing in my area and would like to take me to dinner. I was thrilled with the prospect. Bill was a man I had dated a few times in Texas, and I always enjoyed his company ... not to mention his tall, handsome looks and stylish grooming. He was great fun to be with and a gentleman.

During the afternoon of the day Bill and I were to go out, I was riding along in Marilyn's car on the way to my house after we picked up her daughter from school. When I mentioned my *big evening,* she asked what I was planning to wear. "Well, I don't know ... I really haven't thought about it. What do you think?" She liked the pantsuit I had on and suggested I wear that, but we both noticed a little spot on the front of the jacket; it really needed cleaning before it could be worn again. Marilyn said, "Oh well, you'll find something else, I'm sure," and turned on my street to drop me off.

"Wait a minute, Mar," I said. "Take me to the cleaners. I want to wear *this,* and if I don't get it there right now I can't have one-hour service." She stopped the car, looked at me, and inquired, "What will you wear home, Luci? You don't *have* to wear that outfit tonight, you know."

"Oh yes, I do. Please . . . just drive me to the cleaners and I'll take this off in the car and go home in my underwear. You'll take it in for me, won't you, and protect me from being seen?"

Immediately, I began to undress—jacket, blouse, slacks—as Marilyn headed for the cleaners. I hunkered down in my panties and bra while sweet little eleven-year-old Beth just stared at me in horror from the backseat. "Don't worry, honey," I assured her, "your mother won't let me be seen in my underwear. It's all right."

When we got to the cleaners' parking lot, I offered a silent prayer of thanks when I saw there was no one else there. Marilyn took my clothes, opened the door, and left it *wide open* as she proceeded into the cleaners to request one-hour service on my behalf. I scrambled to hide behind my purse, a box of Kleenex, and the steering wheel as another car pulled in and Beth slithered to the floorboard for cover.

When Marilyn got back in the car I choked on a half-hysterical giggle. "Marilyn . . . *how could you* leave that door open? What if a church member had driven up, or somebody who craved my body? What would I have done?"

In mock innocence she said, "I left the door open? How careless of me."

All the way home, we laughed ourselves silly: she, from an upright position behind the steering wheel; I, hunched over with my head in my purse; and Beth, muttering from the backseat floorboard, "I don't believe this . . . I just don't believe it."

From inside my house, Marilyn brought me an old beat-up housecoat that I wouldn't wear to dump the garbage, much less in front of my apartment. But what could I do? I threw the robe on and marched up my walkway like that housecoat was what I always wore to pick up Beth from school. Even now, in the recesses of my mind, I can still hear Marilyn's cackling laughter as she sped away, and see Beth's head through the back window, shaking from side to side in perpetual incredulity.

Is there a moral to this crazy story? I think there is—an important one. Some of us are so set in concrete, we can't remember when we last laughed. Or created anything to laugh *at*. Everything is terribly serious. Heavy. Solemn. I'm not saying there's no place for this kind of attitude . . . but *every minute of the day?* Where is the joy? Where is the zaniness?

I dare you to do something today that will make you giggle. Invent it yourself. Bend a little. Dare to embrace something a bit risky and wild. And don't put it off until tomorrow. How do you know tomorrow will ever get here?

Did I See That?

Marilyn Meberg

When Luci Swindoll left her native Texas to move to California nearly twenty-five years ago, there were numerous little culture shocks she experienced as she attempted to absorb the "peculiar" California customs. One of those peculiarities was that our freeways are often littered with chairs, couch cushions, stray clothing, and various other abandoned treasures. Luci maintained that in Texas we would never see junk like that strewn about the freeways.

We would frequently be zipping (that's when I drove) the freeway only to have our conversation interrupted numerous times with Luci-statements like:

"Can you believe that . . . three Tupperware bowls in the middle of the fast lane?" (I don't know how she could know they were Tupperware.)

"How do people lose shoes on the freeway? Does someone simply toss them out? And why only one shoe . . . I don't think I've seen a pair."

"Oh, Mar, look at that little yellow stuffed gorilla. I wonder why it's yellow . . . don't you think it would make more sense if it were brown? I can imagine some little kid feels awful about now. Maybe the mother tossed it out. I don't think I could drive with a yellow gorilla . . ."

One afternoon we were driving back from Los Angeles at a fairly good clip and I noticed a green couch off the edge of the freeway not far ahead of us. Luci and I were involved in a pretty heady conversation, which I didn't want to interrupt, so without announcement, I

173

switched lanes and pulled off the freeway several feet away from the couch. With unexpressed but mutual understanding, we both got out of the car, walked to the couch, sat down, and continued our conversation.

You should have seen the whiplash responses of people as they hurtled past. They couldn't believe they had just seen two women chatting animatedly on a discarded couch by the side of the freeway.

Later as we pulled back into traffic still laughing, Luci said, "You know, Mar, I wouldn't have missed that for the world!"

"Neither would I, Luci. And just think, if we'd been in Texas, we wouldn't have had a place to sit!"

GARTH AND PAT

Chonda Pierce

*A*nd, oh, by the way," Bob Whitaker, my friend and manager of the Grand Ole Opry, called to remind me, "your appearance with Garth Brooks will be on live TV. See you then."

On live TV? With Garth Brooks? This would mean that during my five-minute performance the Opry would be filled to capacity with more than five thousand Garth fans—waiting for the ditzy blond to get off the stage so they could see the real star. They would chant, "Garth! Garth! Garth!" as I tried valiantly but hopelessly to tell my stories! The estimated forty million viewers watching the live program at home would all, of course, run to the bathroom during my portion, a little aggravated by the comedian who was taking up precious airtime. And only a very small handful of my family would be huddled around a television set somewhere asking one another, "What did she say? Her name's not Garth! Why do they keep calling her Garth?" I called my mother—as usual. She was so excited! She went on and on about what an outstanding opportunity this would be for me: the exposure, the blessing, the thrill of working with this entertainment icon. "Oh, honey, this is wonderful!" she said. "But now tell me, who exactly *is* Garth Brooks?" Once again, without even realizing it, my mother had placed into perspective the things I needed to concentrate on and the things I shouldn't worry about.

I arrived at the Opry at my appropriate call time. Backstage was like a photographer's convention. This could mean only one thing: Mr. Brooks was in the building. I stopped in the makeup room, sat in a chair, and challenged the ladies to make me look like a star. In the middle of a "coifing" the door opened, and without fanfare a young couple stepped into the room. The lady found a seat, and the man walked over to the chair beside me. He very calmly and politely slipped off his black cowboy hat, nodded, and introduced himself to me and the makeup ladies. We were all stunned, frozen—my hair not quite done. Garth Brooks! *I should think of something really witty and clever to say,* I thought. I should be aggressive and hand him my tape. I should borrow a few million dollars! But we just sat quietly in our makeup chairs as the room slowly filled with flashbulbs of autograph seekers (granted, one of those cameras was my own) and recording industry folks.

After a quick interview on the preview show, "Backstage at the Grand Ole Opry," I slipped into my designated spot in the wings to wait for Johnny Russell to introduce me to the eager crowd. There was no entourage in my corner except for my husband and a few close friends. No flashbulbs, no autograph seekers. I made my way to center stage, took a deep breath, and started with a few stories. Amazingly enough, there were no "Garth" chants as I'd envisioned. They were politely attentive, and I think I even remember a chuckle or two (my husband used the word "guffaw" to describe their response). I said good night, and Johnny Russell called me back out for a second bow when I noticed the quiet figure taking his place in preparation for his time in the spotlight. I passed through the crowd and mustered up enough nerve to shake his hand as he went by. I don't know if he ever saw my performance, but his kind smile seemed to tell me that everything was fine, that he'd been in those intimidating places, when your stomach is in knots and you think the world is not listening to what you have to say. He patted me on the back and stopped for a picture. I've never seen him again.

A few weeks later, a nearby television station, TBN, telephoned and invited me to appear on their *Gospel America* show. I recognized the host's name. I had seen him on a few gospel programs in the past. I loved his daughter's singing voice. And his films were cute. The show would be prerecorded, and there wouldn't be a live audience at all. I accepted and phoned Mother, as usual, to tell her the news. I almost dropped the phone as she screamed with excitement on the other end. She knew exactly who the host was and insisted that I take her along. "This is truly a blessing," she said, "and he can sing rings around that Garth fella!" She couldn't wait for the chance to get his autograph. She started naming movie titles and singing songs to me on the phone. She went on and on about how handsome he was and about how "cool" his white patent leather shoes were. It was the perfect opportunity to ask, "Mom, now tell me—exactly who is Pat Boone?"

You Drive Me Crazy

Marilyn Meberg

𝒩o one has ever accused me of lacking a sense of adventure—a sense of dignity perhaps—but not a sense of life's crazy possibilities.

Since my early twenties I have wanted a Fiat convertible. Prior to falling in love with Ken Meberg, I envisioned myself an old-maid schoolteacher living in sunny, southern California, tearing madly through the beach cities in a Fiat convertible. I exchanged that fantasy for the more sedate image of being a married school-teacher living in sunny, southern California, driving sanely through the beach cities in a Ford Falcon. A few years ago, in the midst of my unpredictable midlife years, Ken bought me a gorgeous, blue Fiat convertible. I absolutely loved it! I'd go zipping about in this little machine—my hair flying in all directions—feeling as though I owned the road. I experienced an indescribable sense of eupho-ria—a touch of reckless abandon—in this little car.

One Saturday afternoon preceding the beginning of winter semester, my daughter Beth and I drove over to Biola University, where I taught, so I could put my class syllabuses on the secretary's desk for typing and then distribution to classes Monday morning. I needed to get into my office, but the building was locked on the outside. That meant I had to walk all the way over to the adminis-tration building and pick up a master key. I grumbled and snorted my way over there, asked for a key to the building, was told I had to leave my driver's license, agreed to those peculiar terms, made my way back to my office, left the syllabuses, and was irritated that

I had to walk all the way back to administration to return the key. Beth had come with me because she had a four o'clock appointment several miles from the university. With all the time involved in tromping across campus for a key, we were in danger of missing her deadline.

The Biola buildings are connected by a network of sidewalks that crisscross all over the campus. As I walked these various sidewalks during a typical class day, I often mused about the width of the walks and whether or not my Fiat would fit on them—idle ponderings characteristic of a partially vacant mind, nothing more.

As I walked to the car (my Fiat) to tell Beth that I still had to get the key back to administration and that I feared we would be late for her appointment, a most compelling idea dropped into my head. I looked about the campus. It was nearly four o'clock on a Saturday afternoon, not a sign of life anywhere. The promise of anonymity and sweet fulfillment fueled the idea in my mind. I jumped in the car, backed up carefully, assured myself that Beth and I were the only living creatures within a radius of five miles, and pulled onto the first sidewalk leading to my destination. We were a perfect fit. Just as I was settling into the deliciousness of it all, I heard a jarringly loud honk. I couldn't believe it; there behind me, not on the sidewalk but sitting self-righteously on the road leading to the sidewalk, was a campus security squad car. Where on earth had he come from?

I had almost completed my goal of reaching the steps of the administration building; my presence was now known, my wrongdoing irreversible. Under those circumstances, why stop? So I continued jauntily on my way. The squad car then joined me on the sidewalk. (I was gratified to note in my side mirror that his tires hung over the sides of the walk—it was not a tidy fit at all.) Beth had slipped to the floor of the car in humiliation as the security car's siren and red light came on in response to my heedlessness. Apparently, I had stretched my delinquency to the limit. It seemed wise to stop.

To assure the young security man that I was not a fugitive, I hopped out of the car and met him as he got out of his. He stared at me for a moment and then quietly asked, "What are you doing?"

I went blank—I didn't really have an answer. I stared vacantly at him. "Why are you driving on the sidewalk? Did you hear me honk? Why didn't you stop?" I didn't have a sensible answer to any of his questions. Looking into his puzzled but warm brown eyes, I ventured, "Well, you probably can't understand this, but you see, I'm in midlife crisis. I get these nearly uncontrollable urges from time to time." He looked at me curiously. "Where were you going?" "Well, actually, I was on my way to the administration building to pick up my driver's license."

I told the officer that I knew my behavior was puzzling as well as reprehensible, that I deserved a citation, and that I would willingly accept one. I had been mentally comforting myself that at least he didn't know who I was. I would take the reprimand and the citation I deserved and quietly leave. He continued to look at me searchingly and finally said, "You're Marilyn Meberg, aren't you? You teach in the English department here—isn't that right?" My heart sank.

He suggested then that I turn around (only I could turn around on the sidewalk—his car was too fat), retrace my steps, park, walk to administration, return the key, and secure my driver's license. An indulgent young man (a Biola graduate student), he did not give me a citation. He did not even give me the scolding I deserved. But he undoubtedly had misgivings about whether I would make it safely through midlife crisis. (I told this incident at a retreat one weekend, and a woman mailed me a bumper sticker, which I put on my car. It reads: "If you don't like the way I drive, stay off the sidewalk.")

PLAYFUL PEOPLE

Marilyn Meberg

$\mathcal{I}$ love playful people! People who aren't too sophisticated or too proper to engage in zany antics draw me like a two-year-old to mud. Ken Meberg was such a person.

One of my favorite exchanges of play with him revolved around an Ajax sticker—you know, the one that covers those little holes in the top of the cleanser can.

That sticker caught my attention one night as I was cleaning the sink. Removing the sticker, I thought it really hadn't seen the last of its usefulness. It was so sturdy and full of "stickum," it seemed a waste to just toss it in the trash.

Carrying it into the bedroom, I took a guess as to which pair of slacks Ken would wear to work the next day and then placed the sticker on the inside pant leg just low enough so he wouldn't be protected by an undergarment but high enough so any overt hand movement in the direction of the sticker would appear indelicate.

According to my expectations, the next day Ken wore the slacks I had "stickered" but said absolutely nothing about it when he came home. I was dying of curiosity, especially since I knew he was chairing a meeting that required him to stand in front of people most of the day. But I contained myself and didn't ask.

After he had changed his clothes and was in the backyard with our son, Jeff, I tore into the bedroom and checked his slacks. The sticker was gone.

Several weeks later I was speaking at a luncheon and became increasingly aware of scraping irritation in my right armpit. No amount of subtle movement seemed to bring relief, but to scratch or claw at my underarm seemed ill-advised since I was surrounded by rather classy ladies who probably had never yielded to a scratch impulse in their lives. Later, at home, I discovered the strategically placed Ajax sticker in the underarm portion of my silk blouse.

This game went on for weeks with neither of us knowing where or when the sticker would appear. My favorite appearance occurred when a policeman stopped Ken for going through a yellow light that turned red while he was in the intersection. When Ken showed his driver's license to the policeman, he laughed and said, "You really must hate your DMV photo."

"Well, not really . . ."

"Then why is your face covered up with some sort of sticker?"

Several days later Ken walked into the kitchen holding the limp sticker by one corner and with mock seriousness announced that the sticker had died; it had no more "stickum." Only then did we settle into a raucous description of our individual experiences with the sticker.

Sometimes I think we responsible adults assume that being playful might be interpreted as being childish, maybe even silly. Admittedly, nothing is more tragic than an adult who fails to gain the maturity and wisdom necessary to live a productive life. But equally tragic are adults who forget how to vent their play instincts.

As in all arenas of successful living, we attempt to work toward a balance. The Danish philosopher Kierkegaard maintains that what we want to remember in living is that "we all possess a childlike quality, but we do not want to be possessed with that quality." To give heedless expression to our childlike impulses is no more desirable than totally to suppress them. The mature person is able to recognize the distinction between the two worlds and choose which world is appropriate for the moment.

Jesus said it's impossible to enter the kingdom unless we become as little children (Mark 10:15). He seemed to place a high premium on that childlike quality. The most profound truth in the universe is that God loves us; yet many miss that truth because of its simplicity. When Jesus said, "I praise you, Father, Lord of heaven and earth, because you have hidden these things from the wise and learned, and revealed them to little children" (Matthew 11:25), he reminds us of how preferable it is at times to be childlike.

Chapter Twelve

Hee, Hee, Hee ... All the Way Home

Home is the place where, when you have to go there,
they have to take you in.
—Robert Frost, "The Death of the Hired Man"

Cleaning your house while your kids are still growing is like
shoveling the walk before it stops snowing.
—Phyllis Diller

May the forces of evil become confused on the way to your house.
—George Carlin

Humor is ubiquitous. That's a fancy way of saying you can't escape it because it's everywhere. Sometimes the funniest things happen not across the country but inside the kitchen, where clouds of billowing smoke create a never-to-be-forgotten dessert, or in a playroom artfully transformed by the perfect homemaker into a Central Park look-alike. Regardless of your tastes in architecture—Queen Anne, Colonial, Classical, Modern, or 1950s Tract House Chic—you can find plenty to laugh about wherever you live.

Hey, Good Lookin', Whatcha Got Burnin'?

Becky Freeman

For a creative person, it's amazing how badly I've failed in the art of cuisine. My worst handicap in the cooking arena is that I tend to burn everything. One morning, when our son Zeke was about five years old, I handed him a perfectly browned piece of toast. Then I watched in fascination as he grabbed a dinner knife, walked robotically to the trash can, and began scraping at the toast.

"Zeke!" I exclaimed. "Guess *what?* Mommy didn't burn the toast today—you don't have to scrape it!"

He looked up at me with startled brown eyes and said in surprise, "Oh! I thought we always had to whittle toast." Bless his heart. He thought the normal routine for toast-eating children everywhere was to burn a piece of bread, scrape it, then eat it.

As my children grew older, they began to realize that other families are different in several ways from our own. Not all families, for example, use the smoke alarm as their dinner bell.

When Zach was a teenager, he strolled into the kitchen one afternoon, where I'd just burnt a cobbler so badly that it had bubbled up, blackened, and hardened into a peculiar sculpture. (Later we all agreed it looked a lot like Ross Perot's ears.) As Zach casually observed the smoke billowing from the oven, heard the smoke alarm blaring, and noted the sweat dripping from my brow, he paused to give me a hug, then cheerfully announced, "Mmmm-mmm-mmm. Smells like Mom's home cooking!"

I used to worry that my kids would go to someone's barbecue and pig out on the charcoal instead of the meat.

Not only do I have a tendency to burn food, but I just can't seem to get the hang of stocking the refrigerator. Scott opened the door to the fridge one day and said, "Becky, I have to hand it to you—you are the Condiment Queen. We have French's mustard, hot mustard, sweet-and-sour mustard, and relish mustard. And there's no shortage of mayonnaise either—regular, light, Hellman's, Miracle Whip, and no-fat. But there's not a single slice of lunch meat or bread anywhere in the house to put the spreads *on*."

"Yes, well . . . ," I started to explain, but Scott was still talking to himself, fiddling with the endless rows of bottles in the door.

"Oh, look!" He held up three red containers for my observation. "Do we ever have ketchup—Heinz, Del Monte, and Sam's Choice! And if it's relish I wanted, I could pick from hot, sweet, sour, chow-chow, and Cajun spice. But lo, I see nary a hot dog or even a lone bun in here. There are ninety-seven bottles of salad dressing, but if there's a shred of lettuce or slice of tomato to make a salad to put under all that dressing, I'm not finding it."

"I can explain . . ."

"There are little midget pickles, giant pickles, olives—black and green—and seven jars of jelly, jam, and preserves. Becky," he paused for effect, as he turned to face me. "I just want to know one thing. Why do you buy all these condiments?!?"

I shrugged my shoulders. "To make sauces."

"Yes but, honey," he asked incredulously, "to go on *what?*"

"I don't know," I stammered. "Pickles and olives?"

Needless to say, Scott and I went out for burgers.

People often ask me how I do all I do. How do I write, speak, enjoy my kids and husband and friends, and also keep up with cooking and cleaning? To tell you the truth, something had to go. I can't do it all. In our home, baking, dusting, and mending are foreign terms to my children. But when you think about it, isn't it good times with our family that we're most hungry for? It's the fun we have as we gather together to ask the Lord's blessing that they'll remember, whether that blessing is over a roast and hot gravy or a take-home sack of spicy tacos.

Besides, my future daughters-in-law will someday have me to thank for the fact that their husbands will never whine, "This homemade apple pie just doesn't taste like my mom's."

Unless, that is, her pies come out of the oven in cinders, to the symphony of smoke alarms.

Young Love Turns Daughter into Teen Cleaning Machine

Marti Attoun

The front door is freshly squeegeed. Towel bars are loaded with clean, matching towels; countertops are unloaded. Dumbstruck by our teenage daughter's cleaning blitz, her father and I listen to our last-minute instructions.

"Mom, whatever you do, just don't talk. I'll *die* if he hears your hick accent. And, Dad, please, I *beg* you, go change that ratty shirt."

Tonight we meet the boyfriend.

I won't tell our daughter that this romance has the shelf life of a bagel. I don't dare, when my windfall laundress is attacking the Himalayas of dirty clothes in the basement.

"What if he wants to play Ping-Pong down here?" she shrieks. "I'll be humiliated if he sees these nasty piles!"

Her father rolls his eyes. I roll her the bleach.

"And, Dad, don't you *dare* sing one of your silly songs. I'd be mortified."

Dad, oh so wicked, immediately belts out, "What shall we do with the drunken sailor?" Little brother giggles.

"Oh, *no*. What's that smell?" Our daughter sniffs shoe soles, the refrigerator, her brothers, the trash can. "Mom, something stinks. Help me track it down." I, the Sherlock of household odors, open the broken dishwasher, where foul water puddles. Daughter gasps and shoots it with Lysol.

Dad relaxes now in an upgraded shirt in front of the TV with his stocking feet on the coffee table, which suddenly is swept bare of the usual newspapers and magazines. He pulls three feet of dental floss from its canister and begins to saw on a back molar.

Daughter's scream rattles the faux chandelier. At first I think it's the smoke alarm. "Why don't you go ahead and clip your toenails too, Dad? Go ahead and *wreck* my life entirely. And dig out the harmonica and serenade the entire county while you're at it."

Little brother chuckles between slurps of chicken noodle soup and goldfish crackers right from the saucepan.

"Oh, my gosh. Mom, make him use a bowl tonight, *please!*" I hand him a bowl—and a napkin. Tonight's special.

Suddenly, she stops and surveys me head to toe. It's my moment of truth.

"How many years have you had those jeans?" she asks pointedly. My long-term memory fails me. "They're way too short, Mom. And do something with that hair. It's as flat as a raft."

I tug on my jeans. I poof my hair.

And I remember. When I introduced my first boyfriend to my mother, she greeted him with, "Nice to meet you, Jim. Where do you go to church?" I prayed that the brown shag carpet would swallow me like Jonah. A new boyfriend always inspired my brother-in-law to twang his guitar à la Woody Guthrie, even though his voice is à la Alvin and the Chipmunks. My older sister informed one date that I used mustache bleach. I laugh now as I recall the guy sneaking a peek all night at my upper lip.

"That laugh is *so* loud and goofy, Mom." My daughter emits a four-syllable sigh.

The doorbell rings. The two titter.

"I'd like you to meet my family," my daughter says so sweetly, and we all play along with her game.

Someday, she'll even mean it. I remember that too.

HOUSEHOLD SKULLDUGGERY

Renae Bottom

$\mathcal{I}$ apologize to the rest of you if archaeologists in the distant future ever stumble onto my home in an excavation site. Such a discovery could inspire these scholars to write book-length studies claiming that all family groups from our culture shared the same peculiar habits.

"Why," the future archaeologists would wonder, "did inhabitants of late twentieth-century North America hide old birthday cards in their underwear drawers? And why did they stuff bags of outdated newspapers in their closets?"

Digging a little further, they would unearth a decade's worth of scenic wall calendars from behind the microwave. Then they'd locate the ticket stubs and programs from family outings stuck between place mats in the linen closet.

In case *you're* wondering, the answer is simple: It was vital to do these things to preserve the peaceful coexistence of the particular North Americans who resided at my address. That's because my home is ruled by the housekeeping equivalent of Jekyll and Hyde.

My husband, Mark, is a highly organized neat freak, the Jekyll role in our domestic partnership. When he walks through the living room, magazines jump up off the floor and arrange themselves tastefully (by issue date) on the coffee table. Encyclopedias re-alphabetize themselves. Dust balls roll out from under the sofa and march single file to the trash can.

Then there's me, a bit absentminded and downright comfortable with clutter. Just call me Hyde. When I walk through the room, magazines hurl themselves off end tables (kamikaze style) onto the carpet. Dirty socks leap from the laundry basket and scurry underneath the recliner.

Mark loves vacant countertops and uncluttered desks. Any item not specifically required for sustaining life in the next fifteen minutes he deems unnecessary and throws away.

I live to be organized too, but not today. I plan to be organized tomorrow. I have never encountered an "unnecessary item" in my life. Any objects that wander in the front door, from broken-handled brooms to single-bladed scissors, appear to me somehow useful. And I get nervous when my countertops are showing.

How have two such opposite-minded people managed sixteen years of happy marriage? It has a lot to do with deep, abiding love and the calculated use of clutter concealment. I simply hide all my important stuff where Mark can't find it.

Hence the underwear drawer full of old birthday cards (which I will one day organize in a scrapbook); the closets full of newspapers (containing articles I will one day clip and organize in a scrapbook); the scenic wall calendars (full of attractive pictures I will one day mount on construction paper and organize in a scrapbook); and a linen closet full of family outing keepsakes (which I will one day sort and—you know the rest).

Before you judge me too harshly, consider how you might feel if you found yourself chasing the end of your garden hose across the lawn because your obsessively organized mate was around the corner rolling it up before you could finish dousing the petunias. Or how might you react if the clean clothes you laid out in the morning were routinely rounded up and placed in the laundry hamper before you could even get out of the shower?

And I'm not alone in this game. Mark carries out his own secret maneuvers. For instance, if a nice sturdy box finds its way into our home while I'm out (the kind of box Mark knows I will fill with more vital stuff), he breaks it down and hides it behind the trash bin in the garage.

Little does he know, I have a counterplan. If I intercept a sturdy box while Mark is gone, I seal it with clear tape, label it (as though it actually contained something), and stack it in the basement. That way, Mark doesn't suspect it's empty and just waiting to be filled with more stuff.

The really frightening part is that our children have begun copying our behavior. Lately, when I've opened the piano bench to stash some cereal box tops (I'm saving up for a *Hits from the Seventies* CD), I've encountered preschool craft items and crayon drawings that I didn't hide there. Our five-year-old son had a simple answer: "I didn't want Dad to throw them away."

And my daughter, eleven years old and savvy to her mother's Hyde-like habits, is careful to keep her library books secured in her room, where they can't be carried off to one of my infamous piles never to be seen again.

But I'm not the only parent who makes her nervous. She's equally careful to keep her homework off the kitchen counter, where her father may collect it in one of his frequent "clean sweeps" through the area and throw it away before she has a chance to hand it in.

I doubt that archaeologists excavating our home will ever understand how domestic cohabitation spawned elaborate household rituals like math papers hidden under cookbooks, completely empty boxes sealed and stacked in the basement, and preschool craft items stuffed in the piano bench. But there's nothing I can do about it. We're happy—now that we've learned to live together in an atmosphere of peace and good-natured skullduggery.

HOME BEAUTIFUL

Marsha Crockett

I used to think only a few people really possessed the gift of creative decorating. I was equally certain I wasn't one of them. After all, my kitchen cabinets hold more plastic action-figure cups than lovely goblets. I've been known to let my children and husband turn the living room into an exercise room. My bedroom is not a haven of rest or an oasis of love (unless you get a thrill from stepping over the stacks of file folders, magazines, and a basket of unfolded clothes next to my computer).

On the other hand, my neighbor, Sally, seems to have a natural ability for creating beauty. For a long time, I explained away her beautifully spotless house on the fact that she stayed home and had only one child. I chuckled at the ease of her life. *My house would look like that too, if I didn't have two children and a job!* I told myself.

But then Sally opened a day care in her home and had six kids in her house every day. This I had to see! So measuring cup in hand, I headed to Sally's in no time flat to borrow some sugar. That's when I got my first clue about what to expect: Hanging on her front door was a cute little blackboard with a "Memo to Parents." On it was neatly written: "Today's Lunch—homemade vegetable soup, orange slice smiles, and whole wheat crackers. Today's Snack—peanut-butter-and-jelly stars"!?

I guess Sally saw me coming up the walk because she opened the door before I could close my mouth.

"Cute sign," I commented. "I just need a cup of sugar. I'm making . . . uh, clown-shaped snickerdoodle cookies for the girls."

"Oh, some special occasion?" she asked, as if she really had made these things before.

"No, just one of those fun things we like to do now and then."

I looked around. I heard children laughing—but didn't see them or any mess in the house. "What happened to the kids?"

"They're in the playroom. You're welcome to go see what I did in there."

I went down the hall with a sense of foreboding and looked in. It wasn't a room, it was a park. Sally had actually painted an outdoor motif on the walls, complete with sky, puffy clouds, grass, and trees. Little white park benches perched against two walls, with a rack full of books in between. Next to the silk tree sat a picnic table covered in a red-and-white checked plastic tablecloth. Jars of Play-Doh stood at attention in the center.

"It's beautiful in here, Sally. But I bet the kids can really make a mess of it, huh?"

"Oh, they know the rules: 'Put away before you play,'" she replied.

I couldn't take it any more, so I asked her for some sugar, thanked her, and headed toward my front door—the one with the leaves stuck in the spiderwebs at the corner of the doorjamb. I went inside and looked around at my home, the one with crooked curtains, four pairs of shoes in the living room, and a red stain on the dining room carpet. The girls were playing with Lincoln Logs and Barbies . . . in the kitchen.

With a deep sigh I said to my husband, "Honey, I think I'll move in with Sally."

"No, you can't," he said with a teasing grin. "Who would clean up this mess?"

After living next to Sally for eleven years, I'm finally learning I can't be Sally, or Martha Stewart, or anyone else for that matter. I agree with author Primo Levi, who wrote, "I live in my house as I live inside my skin; I know more beautiful, more ample, more sturdy, and more picturesque skins; but it would seem to me unnatural to exchange them for mine." I think maybe I do have what it takes to create beauty. It's just that I have to be more comfortable with my own style, my own likes and dislikes in my home.

This realization called for celebration. So I poured red punch into four plastic Batman cups. My family and I raised our glasses and toasted who we are in Christ, and I reveled in the miracle of this "home beautiful."

THE FASHION PLATE ON MY FRONT YARD

Marti Attoun

*E*veryone talks about the hidden costs of owning a house or a car, but no one mentions the hidden costs of owning a pink plastic flamingo. You plunk down fifteen dollars for the "tacky chic" yard bird, stake him in the hostas, and figure that you're home free.

Don't say I didn't warn you. A seamstress in San Antonio is making a mint stitching up flamingo clothes. You know how these trends creep to the rest of the country. At first we chuckle. Then one day, we look at our flamingo standing in his birthday plumes out in the front yard and we think, "Man, he'd look good in a pair of Capri pants and a little sun visor."

Before long, we're buying active wear for our flamingo, maybe a crop top and shorts for hot summer days and a cardigan for breezy nights. Perhaps something glittery and edgy for evening wear, or a bolero jacket to show off those pecs?

Unless you live out in the sticks, your flamingo is obligated to keep up with the Joneses' flamingo who, by the way, is right now standing in the kids' wading pool, looking like a bloated watermelon in that ridiculous Speedo.

I told Mom about this wacky seamstress sewing flamingo fashions, and she got really excited, although there isn't a single flamingo among her yard froufrou.

"I wonder if we could get that woman's phone number," she said. "You know, I've been trying for years to find someone who can sew for me. I'd love to get a pair of pants that fit right in the straddle."

Gee, I hadn't even considered that angle. Anyone who can custom fit a flamingo must be the next Gucci. We're talking measures of 16–16–16 with an inseam of 56. A cucumber on stilts. Talk about a body-design challenge.

"I don't know, Ma. I bet those pants hang like curtains on that bird," I told her, "which is the same complaint you have with your white polyesters."

See, it's already happening. I'm talking about a flamingo wearing pants as if it's a sensible thing. And it's a complete fashion blunder. With a gut like that and pipe-cleaner legs, a flamingo has no business wearing pants. A simple loose dress, maybe.

And who has time to dress a flamingo? I already know what will happen if you give a flamingo his own closet. Next, he'll want foot cream, sunblock, and a subscription to *Vogue*.

There's no end to the hidden costs of owning such a tacky bird. Take it from the daughter of a concrete goose owner.

Chapter Thirteen

A Woman's Place Is . . . Laughing

Laugh and the world laughs with you.
Cry and you cry with your girlfriends.
—Laurie Kuslansky

My license plate says PMS. Nobody cuts me off.
—Wendy Liebman

Remember the Wicked Witch of the West in *The Wizard of Oz?* She was such a pain until Dorothy's little dog, Toto, knocked over a bucket of water and did her in. That's all it took—a little H_2O and she melted away forever. That's what laughter can do to many of the troubles that plague our lives. PMS, obstinate kids, feelings of inadequacy—big deal! Try dousing your frustrations—even the nonstop kind—with a splash of laughter and see if it doesn't make all the difference.

PMS: Psychotic Mood Swings

Kathy Peel

$\mathcal{I}t$ had been a stressful day—or so I rationalized. On the way to the veterinarian, our Labrador retriever decided to make a large deposit on the backseat . . . the aroma of which caused James to throw up in the front seat. After the vet turned down my request to board them both, I went straight to a full-service car wash and hid in the rest room. (I was afraid the attendants would ask for hazardous-duty pay before touching my car.)

Then my banker called to say, "Let's do lunch!" *How special,* I thought. I just love personal attention. But this guy turned out to be no fun *at all.* He didn't find it one bit amusing that I tried to pay our mortgage with my credit card to earn a free trip to Florida. "Just think of it as creative accounting," I explained. He didn't smile. And I was insulted when he asked if I was on a budget. "Of course I'm on a budget," I snapped. "I never spend more than I can borrow against our life insurance."

Wednesday went from bad to worse, and so did my personality. The problem was—Wednesday lasted all week. Harrison Ford could have walked through the door, and I would have found something negative to say. By Friday my family was ready to lock me in the closet and slip my meals under the door. Bill, fearing for his life, gently asked me, "Honey, do you think you could be experiencing a touch of PMS?" I burst into tears. "How dare you accuse me of something so . . . so *average.* Every other woman in America has PMS. You know how I hate to be like everybody else. What a cruel thing to say!" At this point he knew he couldn't win.

The next week I was totally embarrassed by my behavior. Thankfully, Bill is a gracious guy. Trying to find humor in the situation, he wrote The PMS Rules and taped a copy to our bedroom door. The rules are more accurate than I care to confess.

The PMS Rules

1. The female always makes the rules.
2. The female has the right to change the rules at any time without prior notification.
3. The female is never wrong.
4. If the female is wrong, it is not her fault and the male must apologize to the female immediately for any complicity on his part, actual or imaginary.
5. The female has the right to plead not guilty for an action by reason of temporary insanity from PMS, and claim immunity from any consequences.
6. The male, on the other hand, must never suggest that PMS has in any way influenced the behavior of the female.
7. The male must avoid bringing up anything controversial that needs rational discussion during an "attack."
8. The male must memorize the verse "This too shall pass," but never repeat it aloud in the presence of the female.
9. Should by some cruel twist of fate the male have a bad day, he must at all costs suppress his emotions. (Ulcers are better than fingernail lacerations.)
10. If there is any disagreement about the interpretation of these rules, see rule one.

I've never met a woman who prided herself in being selfish, cantankerous, and hard to live with. None of us wants her epitaph to read: "May she rest in peace; now we'll finally have some." As I thought one day about how I wanted my family and friends to describe me when I die, I wrote my own epitaph.

Here Lies Kathy Peel

Kathy Peel was the most incredible woman we've ever known. In everything she did, she pursued excellence and always delivered more than she promised. She was extremely disciplined and lived a life worth emulating. She brought God's beauty to everything she touched—whether a relationship, a room, or an event. She had a way of pushing people gently to do their best. She laughed a lot and brought joy to the lives of many.

When Bill read this, he laughed hysterically. After I promised he'd be singing more than a few stanzas of "Can't Touch This" for the next week, he got the message I was really serious. Although it's lofty, and there are far more days than not when the epitaph I wrote sounds like someone else's, I read it regularly. I frequently fall on my face in defeat, making myself and everyone around me miserable.

During those fallen-down times, I must stop and ask, Who am I really? Am I as unlovely as I think? Am I a victim, powerless to do anything about my moods? Am I a failure? Am I really as empty as I feel?

Oftentimes during that infamous time of the month, I feel anything but lovely. But God tells me that he loves me and accepts me as I am with all my flaws. "For I am convinced that nothing can ever separate us from his love. Death can't, and life can't. The angels won't, and all the powers of hell itself cannot keep God's love away. Our fears for today, our worries about tomorrow, or where we are—high above the sky, or in the deepest ocean—nothing will ever be able to separate us from the love of God demonstrated by our Lord Jesus Christ when he died for us" (Romans 8:38–39 LB). I am loved!

MIXED BLESSINGS

Anonymous

My wife invited some people to dinner. At the table, she turned to our six-year-old daughter and said, "Would you like to say the blessing?"

"I wouldn't know what to say," she replied.

"Just say what you hear Mommy say," my wife said.

Our daughter bowed her head and said, "Dear Lord, why on earth did I invite all these people to dinner?"

A Fun Day Composting with Martha Stewart

Chonda Pierce

It happened again last night: I dreamed about Martha Stewart. This time she showed up wearing a denim shirt—unbuttoned, of course—over a pink T-shirt. She was standing on my back deck, waving, smiling, motioning for me to come outside. So I cinched up my terry cloth robe, slipped on my bunny slippers, and stepped cautiously out into the early morning of my dream.

I know, undoubtedly, that right now some shrink is out there writing on his scratch pad, *"Chonda seems to have an obsession with Martha Stewart, allowing her to perpetuate this ongoing struggle she has with feeling inadequate as a homemaker."*

To that I say, "Hogwash!" Comedians have been picking on Martha for years. Just because she shows up at my house and finds me in my terry cloth robe tied together with one of David's old neckties doesn't mean a thing! Anyway, back to my dream.

"Welcome," she said, even though we were at my house. "Have you ever wondered what to do with all your yard clippings and the organic materials that come from your kitchen?"

"Not really," I answered.

"Well," she continued, ignoring me. "I'm going to show you how they can be a valuable addition to your garden as a rich food source for your plants. Follow me."

And I did, even though this was my home. We walked off the deck to the rear of my backyard where three square, wooden bins had been constructed.

"Where did those come from?" I asked Martha. She turned sideways and traced a hand along the top edge of one of the planks. "These locally milled and planed boards have been pressure treated with a biodegradable retardant that will not harm the environment or small animals. They are perfect for creating our own compost, as we shall see today."

That answered several of my questions, especially the big one: What are you doing here?

"We'll begin with some clippings I took from your apple espalier located on your south lawn."

"I have an apple espalier? Just what is an apple espalier?" I asked.

Martha wagged a finger at me. "Yes, indeed, you have a beautiful espalier. And if you had awakened before 7:00 A.M., you could have seen me plant, build, and prune it for you."

"But I don't even have a south lawn," I added.

She thought for only a moment before saying, "Then maybe I built it in your neighbor's yard. At any rate," she went on, not seeming to be the least bit discouraged by this revelation, "I have some fresh clippings, and we will deposit these in bin number one." And she did, saying, "That's good. Now, bins number two and three are much older and much more advanced in their decomposition stages."

"Much older? How long have you been out here?" I asked.

"How long have you been asleep?" Martha asked with a grin. "Now, this whole endeavor is very important for the life of your plants. So if you'd like to help, we will get started. Maybe we can finish before you awaken. After all, this is your dream."

So, for the remainder of my dream, Martha Stewart and I made compost, I in my terry cloth robe, she in her Martha Stewart outfit. I borrowed her cute, plastic wheelbarrow to haul compost from my kitchen. (In real life, my organic material would have consisted of old crusty edges of pizza slices, mushy leftover Cheerios, and a few burnt corners of some blueberry Pop-Tarts. But since this was only a dream, I rolled out wheelbarrows full of leftover zucchini slices, avocado peelings, and bits of Earl Grey tea leaves.)

My neighbor came over and thanked me for her new apple espalier. "It looks just like something Martha Stewart would make," she said.

"She did."

"Then that explains it." She looked at my wheelbarrow and me and asked, "What are you doing?"

I told her, and she said she would help. She produced her own wheelbarrow, and together we began to haul mounds of coffee grounds, eggshells, and rotten vegetables from our kitchens to bin number two. We would shovel it in and then go back to our kitchens for more.

We worked hard and long, and I could imagine all my plants (and my neighbor's) thanking me for the nice meal they would receive because of our efforts. By the end of our workday, we had completely filled bin number two. As a matter of fact, it was mounded so high it spilled over the edges, feeding the grass that bordered the bin.

My neighbor and I stood leaning on our shovel handles and admired our work—the almost artistic mound that eggshells, peelings, and coffee grounds could make. It was heaped up higher than our heads. The breeze stirred and blew the smell of fresh compost in my face. I recalled fond memories of late nights at the Waffle House.

"Where's Martha?" my neighbor asked, interrupting my dream within a dream.

I shrugged. "Don't know. Haven't seen her for awhile." The breeze moved again, and I took a deep whiff. "Listen, I haven't had breakfast yet. Would you like to join me for some eggs and coffee?"

"Sounds good." So we parked our wheelbarrows and left for breakfast, believing the heap of compost was more than capable of decomposing without our supervision.

We ate in my kitchen that overlooked my backyard. As we ate, I noticed something rather odd about my new mountain of compost. From this angle—farther away now so I could get a better perspective, and enhanced by the mottled sunlight that filtered through the apple espalier—my compost heap looked a lot like Martha Stewart. A compost statue of Martha Stewart, if you will. At first the thought of burying Martha beneath all that compost alarmed me. But then again, like Martha had said, it was *my* dream.

Maybe my subconscious obsession with Martha Stewart is due to my house being in such disarray recently. I don't know if this reoccurring dream is a sign that I fear I will never become a perfect, Martha-Stewart housewife, or perhaps I feel like lately I've been living in the second bin. Whatever the subliminal message my brain is sending me, I must admit, I woke up in a pretty good mood after that dream. Perhaps it was God's humorous way of putting all my failings as a housewife into perspective: Just toss them out with the compost!

Go ahead and check out books from the library about apple espaliers if you want to (if that will make you feel better). But we may never measure up to a domestic standard that someone else (who just so happens to have her own TV show, magazine, books, and columns about domestic excellence) has set for us. The best thing to do is to take a deep breath and know there are worse things than not having compost—you could *be* the compost.

NEVER UNDERESTIMATE THE POWER OF AN IMPERFECT WOMAN

Karen Scalf Linamen

Several months ago my four-year-old walked into my office and announced, "I'm ready to go to the party."

Indeed, Kacie was supposed to attend a birthday party in a couple hours. I looked at her. She was wearing her Princess Barbie Nightgown.

"Kacie, you can't wear that to a birthday party. That's a nightgown."

"Mom, it's a nightgown at *night*. Today it's a dress. I'm wearing this to the party." Immediately I thought back to my childhood. When I was growing up, there were rules about these sort of things. People understood the meaning of the word *etiquette*. We not only didn't wear pajamas to birthday parties, we didn't even wear our play clothes. We wore *party dresses,* for crying out loud. We had standards. We had manners. This is what made America great.

All this was running through my head as I evaluated Kacie's request.

"This is what I want to wear," Kacie repeated.

"Alright," I said. "But the Pokemon slippers have got to go."

I've got *some* standards, after all.

In my defense let me remind you that I'm nearly forty, not to mention the fact that Kacie is my second child. We forty-year-old women simply do not have the energy to raise our second, third, or fourth children as diligently as we raised our firstborns back when big hair and leggings were in style.

So Kacie wore the Princess Barbie Nightgown. I did, however, take extra pains adorning her hair with pink ribbons, and I made her wear frilly socks and Sunday shoes.

After all, I didn't want the other women to think of my daughter as a poor, neglected child whose mother would pack her off to a party in pajamas.

No way. I wanted them to realize this was a *beloved* and *well-cared-for* child whose mother would pack her off to a party in pajamas.

There *is* a difference.

Look, I came to grips several years ago with the fact that I'm not Superwoman.

That was always my dream. I wanted to be Superwoman. When it came to homemaking, marriage, being a friend, and especially raising my kids, I wanted "perfection" to be my middle name.

Unfortunately, I soon discovered that I'm hard pressed to outrun a speeding toddler much less a speeding bullet. And leaping tall buildings in a single bound isn't even in the realm of reality—not after I sprained my ankle trying to hop over a sprawling Barbie metropolis my kids erected in my kitchen one rainy afternoon.

So I'm not Superwoman.

How can I be so sure?

Not only would a real superwoman refrain from sending her child to a birthday party in Barbie pajamas, she also would never be rushing to get ready for an important job interview, nick her leg shaving, and have to walk out the door wearing a Muppet Babies Band Aid under her hose.

Furthermore, a real superwoman would never hang up on her editor while shouting the phrase, "I HAVE TO GO! THE BABY'S IN THE TOILET!" and she *certainly* would not be growing eleven different strains of penicillin in her refrigerator.

I used to want people to think I was perfect.

Now I'm relieved when they realize I'm not.

Frequently folks write reviews of my books, and one review in particular made me want to hug the writer when she referred to my tendency to use the smoke alarm interchangeably with the oven timer and then went on to observe: "This woman is a non-threatening teacher. We are convinced that she needs help, but since we do too, we will accept any pearls she has to offer."

Have you ever looked at your life and thought, "Gee, I'd love to be a positive influence in someone's life, but my own life feels too flawed/chaotic/imperfect/unorganized or broken for me to have anything worthwhile to offer"?

Yeah, me too.

But I'm wondering if you and I don't have it all backwards. Maybe our struggles and imperfections don't *disqualify* us from reaching out to others after all. Maybe they are, indeed, the very things that give us not just credibility but compassion as well.

For example, I have a couple friends who have experienced depression, as I have. When I feel myself slipping back into the abyss that claimed my life for several years, these are the women I turn to. Do they have all the answers? No way. Sometimes they still struggle too! But I know they've walked a similar path, and that whatever answers they have gleaned will be shared with me in a heartbeat.

But the real reason I turn to these friends isn't for their solutions. It's for the passion I see in their faces when they look me in the eyes and say, "I know you're tired. But please hang on. You can get through this."

The truth is, accountability and encouragement coming from someone who appears to have her own life completely "together" can feel stifling and obtrusive.

But accountability and encouragement coming from a friend who has scars and wounds of her own is both humbling and empowering.

Am I Superwoman? No way.

Are you Superwoman? I don't think I'm going out on a limb here by saying, "Fat chance."

Isn't that great? That means you and I have the credentials to encourage, inspire, entertain, educate, mentor, train, teach, laugh with, walk with, and cry with each other all the way through this crazy ride called life.

Which means we can relax. In fact, wouldn't it be great to get together some evening, maybe at a favorite restaurant, and linger over coffee and pie as we laugh and talk? We could leave our facades at home and talk about our shortcomings, and how God manages to use us to bless others in spite of ourselves, and how he uses other imperfect folks to bless us.

In fact, you pick the restaurant and I'll meet you there. You shouldn't have any trouble recognizing me.

I'll be the one in my pajamas.

THAT OLD SEW-AND-SEW

Marilyn Meberg

$\mathcal{W}$hen I was in the seventh grade, I had an experience in my sewing class which, if my person were evaluated on the basis of my performance, I would score a zero! I had come into the class optimistically expecting to master the art of sewing within the first few weeks. My confidence was reinforced by the teacher's promise that we could all become expert seamstresses by the end of the semester.

The first week of class was entitled "Knowing Our Machine." I soon discovered my machine had no desire to be known. In fact, it had no interest in a relationship whatsoever! I watched intently as our teacher demonstrated the intricate maze the thread had to follow from the spool to the needle. Every time I thought I had successfully completed each step and pressed the lever to begin the magical process of sewing, the thread would be slurped up by some unknown force and flail wildly about on the spool.

Threading the machine was not the only difficulty I experienced. To the left of the needle there is a little trapdoor where the bobbin lives. On the third day of class, for some inexplicable reason, my bobbin chose to fling itself out upon the floor and go racing across the room. The thread was bright red and left a telltale path to my machine. At this point my classmates gleefully assumed my ineptitude would provide them innumerable laughs throughout the semester. The teacher, however, did not appear to relish that prospect. As she loomed over my machine with errant bobbin in hand, she said in carefully controlled tones, "Apparently we don't know our machine."

The project for the class was to make a pair of pajamas. I chose a flannel fabric with little pink rosebuds. Perhaps you are aware that repeated ripping and sewing causes the threads in the fabric to separate and the design to become indistinguishable. It soon became impossible to discern if there were rosebuds, windmills, or frogs in the design.

As the semester progressed and I did not, I was in serious danger of failing. I was horrified—I had never failed a class before. I needed much more help than I felt free to ask for, because by now the teacher had adopted a certain stance toward me which was very disconcerting. She had the most peculiar response any time she saw me heading toward her desk with my fragile pajamas extended before me. She would begin to take in air, and the longer I remained at her desk the more she inhaled. There were times when I was sure she doubled in size, nearly filling her end of the room. Not only was I inhibited by this response, I was also unable to distinguish what she said as the sucked-in air whistled slightly through her clenched teeth. I would usually flee from her desk in defeat and relief as the audible expulsion of breath signaled that she had once again survived her massive inhalations.

The day before the class was over I was still working to finish my pajamas. Shortly before the bell rang, I triumphantly put in the final stitch. I gingerly took the pajamas up to the teacher for her final inspection. To my dismay, through clenched teeth she ordered me to "Try them on." I did not think the fabric could withstand the pressure of my body. She was adamant, however, so I complied. I could not believe my eyes. I had sewn the left leg into the right arm and the right arm into the left leg. I tried every possible way to scrunch up my body so that maybe I could get by with them as they were, but one would have had to have been far more deformed than I to pass them off as a good fit.

My friend Jane, when she recovered from hysterics, promised to help me take out each wrong stitch with a straight pin after school and then pin the leg and the arm into their proper places. All I would have to do the next day was put in the final stitches. It seemed simple enough. The next day I settled down with my machine and began to sew very carefully. Within twenty minutes

I had finished. I leaped jubilantly to my feet with the intention of rushing up to my teacher to show her my now completed project. In my haste, I neglected to pull the lever up to release the needle from the cloth. My sudden movement of jumping up without first releasing the pajamas knocked the machine off balance. As I stepped back from the falling machine, I realized I had inadvertently sewn my skirt into the pajama top so that I could not free myself from the material or the fall. I flew over the top of the machine as if I were on the end of a whip. I sprawled on the floor in final surrender to that piece of equipment which had sought to defeat me all semester. My wonderful friends shrieked in hysterics; for once, the teacher did not begin her usual inhalations; she merely put her head down on her desk. Finally Jane cut me loose with giant pinking shears.

I soon began to laugh about my experience. My dad told me some weeks after the class was over that though he and Mom felt sorry for me as I muddled my way through sewing, they also had to exercise tremendous self-control as I would daily apprise them of my hard-to-believe errors. On several occasions they laughed uncontrollably when they were alone. Mom told me that she had never been able to grasp the details of sewing, absolutely abhorred the class she had to take in high school, and hoped never to see a sewing machine again. We began to laugh about the incidences from our respective classes, until finally, one of our standing family jokes was to include a request for a sewing machine on our Christmas list each year.

One of my dad's favorite lines, even now, is to admire something I'm wearing and then with mock seriousness ask, "Did you make that yourself?"

Chapter Fourteen

Life Is Unpredictable, but God Is Good

Sheer joy is God's and this demands companionship.
—Thomas Aquinas

When the devil starts messing, God starts blessing.
—R. W. Schambach

Delicate humor is the crowning virtue of the saints.
—Evelyn Underhill

We don't usually think of God as having a sense of humor. But why not? He created us, after all. And human beings must certainly offer an endless supply of laughs; that is, when we aren't causing an endless supply of grief. Whatever God's motive for making mercurial creatures like us, one thing we know for certain: No matter how much life changes, God is always the same—always loving, always merciful, always forgiving. And if that one fact about God doesn't make you break out in a great big grin, then we can't imagine what will!

GOD'S TIMING

Brennan Manning

The mind-boggling figure of twelve to fifteen billion years—the estimated life of our universe—reminds me of a wonderful story in the Yiddish tradition. One day Israel Schwartz asked God, "Yahweh, is it true that for you a thousand years is just a minute?"

Yahweh answered, "Yes, Izzy, that is true."

Izzy had a second question: "And Yahweh, is it true that for you a million dollars is just a penny?"

Yahweh replied, "Yes, Izzy, that is also true."

Extending his right hand with palm upturned, Izzy Schwartz said, "Yahweh, give me a penny."

And Yahweh said, "Certainly. It'll take only a minute."

I Could Lose Myself in Thought, but Then Again, It's Such Unfamiliar Territory

Sue Buchanan

*W*e have enough trouble goin' on today without worrying about tomorrow. My mother once said that she had been a worrier all her life, but that not one single thing she'd worried about had come true. She suggested that a lot of times worrying is really an outgrowth of boredom. In her wise way, she suggested that keeping your mind busy and productive was a good antidote to worry, that "an idle mind is the Devil's workshop."

It's true for me. I can go a little crazy, obsessing about the most insignificant things. Knowing my own weakness, however, I've developed a few little tricks to keep myself on track, telling myself there really is no excuse for being bored. I say that even if you are broke and have no friends, you can "people watch," and it can keep you busy for days on end.

Once I was with friends at a flea market in Texas and got bored with shopping. I told them I'd meet them later–that I was going to write a book on what men think about while their wives shop, and I needed to do research. They bought it, and I struck out on my own.

All the men I talked to were more than willing to cooperate. Of course, I told them I was writing a book! I got short answers: "I think I'm fixin' to go crazy." And I got long answers: "Well, I'm a deer hunter. I'm thinkin' 'bout when I go deer huntin'–makin' a mental list of supplies 'n' stuff. Yer five *hunert* miles from home and ya gotta take food 'n' ever'thing." He began to list "everything" and my eyes glazed over–bedding, salt, flour, catsup, containers, soap, bug spray, pills if you get sick, etc. "Yer sixtysome miles from the near'st phone so ya cain't fergit nothin'. 'Course, ya gotta take yer gun 'n' yer *amanition*" . . . and on and on.

Some of the men I talked to felt it was a give-and-take situation: "I can't complain 'cause she went to the drag races with me last night." Or, "She said she'd make it up to me tonight. *(Blush!)* What I mean is she's gonna fix me a big ol' chicken dinner."

"C'mere and sit down," said one old-timer. "See that step over there? I've been sittin' here since noon. Watch. Every third person trips on it." Sure enough!

There were philosophical answers: "I'm sittin' here thinkin' women are real intelligent. You have to watch 'em to figure that out. Sometimes you just need to be quiet and watch to appreciate them." Another philosopher said, "I watch everybody and try to figure out their feelings. People can be real funny looking, but everybody has feelings—regardless."

I decided to stop my research when a big old country boy pulled me down beside him, took my hand in his, and whispered in my ear: "I was just sitting here wishing a good-lookin' blonde-haired woman would come by and tell me she was writing a book and ask me what I was thinking."

What's in a Name?

Thelma Wells

*H*ave you ever been driving along and seen something that caused you to do a double take? *What . . . ? What was that?* That's the way it was for me when I visited Ghana.

It started when I noticed a sign on a taxi in front of us: "Jesus Cares Taxi." *Okay,* I thought. *You're right. He does care. That's nice that the cab owner recognizes that.* But as I looked out the window to my right, I saw another sign. Then I noticed other vans and vehicles passing us with all kinds of Christian wording and Scriptures written on them.

That's odd, I thought. *We don't do anything like this in America. Why do they do this?* I realize that our cultures are very, very different. But whoever heard of writing stuff like that all over cars and buildings? *Can't they think of something better to name their businesses?* I wondered. *Are they fanatics, or what? Has someone ordered them to do this?*

I saw so many signs that I started writing them down. My personal mission became to record as many of these signs as possible. But I saw so many words and phrases that expressed people's praise and thanksgiving to God that my hand grew tired of writing before I'd recorded a fraction of what I witnessed.

As we drove through downtown Accra, the capital of Ghana, I saw still more signs. I finally asked our World Vision host, Agnes, why the people did this.

"Christians in Ghana love the Lord and want everyone to know it," she replied. "This is our way of spreading the gospel. We want to carry the message of the saving power of Jesus Christ everywhere we go. We want to praise him in all we do, and we want people to know that we bless the Lord at all times. Some people believe that if they name their businesses after the Lord, they will be successful. Also, others display these signs as evidence that they denounce other religions, because God is greater."

The ride from Accra to Kumaski to Atebubu to Coast Cape was a challenge. Picture me riding along, bumping and bouncing up and down over the dirt roads and jungle terrain, frantically recording all the signs I saw on shacks, dumpsters, modest businesses, and cars. Would you dare name your business one of these sixty names I saw in Ghana, even though you love the Lord?

1. Nant Nante Yie (Walk Well with the Lord)
2. Nhyira Nka Boafo (Blessed Be My Helper)
3. Blessed Beauty Shop
4. Garden of Eden Sports Shop
5. Mustard Seed Prayer Center
6. Oh! Yes Jesus (bus)
7. Salon De Hope
8. Baby Jesus Nursery School
9. God Is Able Fashion Center
10. End Times Professional Studio
11. Peace Art Store
12. Nso Ya (Nothing is too difficult for God. When you get him, you are satisfied!)
13. Jesus of the Deep Forest Books
14. God's Time = Mere (The Best Time)
15. Pentecost Fire (taxi)
16. Oh Jesus! (taxi)
17. Emmanuel (a common name and used on many businesses and vehicles)
18. God Is So Good (retail store)
19. Ays Fa Firi Wo (Father Forgive Them)
20. Divine Love Art Centre
21. The Merciful Lion Photographs (photos on tombstones)
22. Thank U Jesus (retail store)
23. God Is So Wonderful Fashions
24. Prince of Peace Snacks

25. The Name of the Lord Is a Strong Tower New Hope Farm
26. El Shaddai (Lord God Almighty) Center
27. Adonai (age to age you're still the same by the power of your name) Complex
28. King Jesus Cares Nursery
29. Peace and Love Shop
30. All Hail the Power of Jesus' Name (business)
31. Blessed Assurance (business)
32. All Creation Praise Jehovah (truck)
33. Jesus Saves Pharmacy
34. In God's Time Electrical Repair
35. Jesus Never Fails (truck)
36. God Is Able International
37. God's Will Coke-a-Cola
38. Nothing but the Blood Barber Shop
39. Calvary Blood Tonic
40. Zion Car Wash Shop
41. My Dawn Restaurant
42. Father Into Thy Hands I Commit My Spirit (truck)
43. Who Is Free Fashions
44. Victory Electrical Works
45. Father Abraham Construction, Ltd.
46. Heavenly Fashion and Bridal Design
47. Savior Plumbing Works
48. Dr. Jesus Bread Stand
49. Follow Me to Jesus (truck)
50. God First Beauty Shop
51. God Never Fails Building Supply
52. Peace and Love Electrical
53. New Generation Plumbing
54. Clap for Jesus Coke-a-Cola
55. Heaven's Snacks
56. Almighty Plywood and Nails
57. Christ Is My Redeemer Beauty Shop
58. Have Faith Drug Store
59. Providence (business)
60. God Is Good Haircuts

Ain't these names outlandish? What if this caught on in America? What if Burger King changed its name to "The Lord's Supper Burgers"? What if the Hyatt changed its name to the "Heavenly Rest with Jesus Hotel"? Imagine an automatic door or gate company called "The Pearly Gates Are Open Door Company." What if a home builder named his company "You've Got a Mansion Just over the Hilltop"? Would we think they were a little bit nuts? Probably.

Outlandish as these commercial expressions may be, we Americans ought to be so bold. Remember the apostle Paul's words: "I am not ashamed of the gospel, because it is the power of God for the salvation of everyone who believes" (Romans 1:16).

AND EDITH WITH THEM

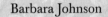

Barbara Johnson

Do you ever feel like you miss the point when it comes to God's love? The greatest love story ever told, the Bible, tells us repeatedly that his gracious love is a free gift from a devoted father to a beloved child, an endless supply of everything we need to be secure and happy. And yet ... we miss the point. Like Jesus' devoted friend Martha, who found it so difficult simply to *accept* and *enjoy* his free and boundless love, we often scurry around in our endless activities *for* God and miss his ever-present love *for* us.

Not so with Edith. She got it, right from God's heart to hers.

Edith was a little girl who was an orphan on the streets of London after World War II. She would often sneak into the backs of public buildings to get warm, and one Sunday evening she slipped into the back of a church and listened to the sermon. How excited she was at what she heard!

As the congregation was filing out, shaking hands with the minister, the little girl rushed up to him and said, "Oh sir, sir, I'm so excited! I didn't know my name was in the Bible!"

The minister wracked his brain to recall mentioning a female's name in the text of his sermon, but he came up blank. Not wanting to hurt the little girl's feelings, he asked, "Well, honey, what *is* your name?"

"My name is Edith."

He was really confused now, and he *really* didn't want to hurt her feelings, but he had to admit that the name "Edith" does not occur in Scripture.

"But it does!" Edith said. "I heard you say it clearly tonight: 'Jesus receiveth sinners and Edith with them.'"

The minister chuckled as he reached out to stroke Edith's cheek. He had been preaching on Luke 15:2, where the Pharisees and religious teachers were complaining about how Jesus, the self-proclaimed holy man, spent time with sinners and "eateth" with them. (God forbid!) Little Edith may have misunderstood the word, but she certainly got the point! She heard the truth for her, for you, for me: The boundless love of God reaches out toward each and every one of us.

MISSING IN ACTION

Patsy Clairmont

Do you know what I'm tired of? Of course you don't, but I asked that so I could tell you. I have to tell someone because it's pressing down on my threadbare nerves. I'm tired of looking for things. There, I said it. I spend a great deal of energy—mental and physical—looking for lost, misplaced, and hidden stuff. I find the hunt frustrating, even maddening, and frequently unnecessary.

Take my glasses. You might as well; someone does every time I set them down. I often have to solicit my family's help in searching the premises for my bifocals. My family thinks I should hire my own posse because of the frequency with which I need help rounding up my belongings. I'm afraid they're right.

Keys, purse, and vital papers elude me. I know they can't walk off, but I have wondered if the Tidy Bowl Brother who constantly taps inside my clock has something to do with my ongoing dilemma. Maybe he has a trapdoor, and he and his brother rifle through my belongings and then scurry off to hide my stuff. All right, all right. I know it's my absentminded personality, not the Tidy Bowl Brother.

Here's what I think would help me and others prone to lostness—Velcro. More specifically, Velcro bodies. Think about it. Instead of laying down my glasses, I'd just press them on the outside of my upper arm. Then, when I needed them, I'd have them. The same with my keys. I could press my car key on one earlobe and the house key on the other. Practical, handy, and within an arm's reach at any given moment.

Of course, the Velcro thing could get tricky when people shook hands or, worse yet, hugged. Getting shed of the other person might be touchy if not painful. And what if we Velcroed our glasses onto someone else without realizing it?

Oh, never mind. Back to the drawing board.

Velcro couldn't help me with my directions anyway. First off, I lose numbers. They just slip through my brain like money through my fingers. Second, I don't have a working grip on north, south, east, and west. And third, I'm a tad off center, and when under pressure, I can't remember my right from my left. Now, on a calm day, that's not a problem. But when I'm searching for, say, a specific street and traffic is heavy, I've been known to turn into one-way traffic—all headed toward me!

Nothing is worse than not knowing where you are. I remember flying into an airport in southern California and waiting for someone to pick me up. No one came. To make matters worse, I didn't know the names of the people who were supposed to tend to me. After an extended wait, the skycaps took note of my ongoing presence and became concerned. They even stopped anyone who drove slowly past the outdoor luggage retrieval and asked them if they were looking for me. How embarrassing.

It turned out my driver was at another airport waiting for me. The skycaps were flipping coins to see who would adopt me, when finally I was paged. My driver, relieved to find me, said she would be there as soon as she could. So, after another hour, when she pulled up, the skycaps cheered her arrival. They ran my luggage to her car and wouldn't accept a tip. Their lost lamb had found her shepherdess.

Gratefully we do have a Shepherd—and he's not waiting at the wrong airport. He is the Good Shepherd who will seek out the stray lambs and bring them back to the safety of the fold. He promises he will never leave us or forsake us. He is one who sticks closer than a brother (or Velcro).

A Mirror Image

Marilyn Meberg

*A*s an only child, I never experienced the mirroring that often comes with having a sibling—you know, that catching a body gesture or tone of voice that wasn't mine but still looked or sounded a lot like mine. My childhood fantasy was to have an identical twin. In fact, I used to pretend I had a twin; in my imagination we talked alike, looked alike, and behaved alike.

I don't know the source of my desire for a twin other than the sense of isolation I occasionally felt as an only child in small rural communities. I wonder if in some way I thought an identical twin would validate my existence, assure me that "Yes, you are who you are and yes, you are there." (This sounds a bit neurotic, Marilyn ...)

I thought I'd outgrown my "mirror-neurosis" until I met my Aunt Wilda for the first time about six years ago. She is my father's "baby sister." We don't look anything alike, but what startled me into a kind of primal recognition was her approach to life. As we were having dinner together in my home, Aunt Wilda, at my request, began to tell some of her early life experiences.

Her unbridled enthusiasm, zest for minor mischief, as well as preference for the fast-paced life stirred in me a sense of having met my twin. What cinched that sense was her admission of her driving record. With twinkling Irish blue eyes she told me she was not proud of the fact that she continually got speeding tickets; but, she said, "Marilyn, how in the world do people manage to stay within the speed limit ... it's simply too slow!" Responding with a hug of instant kinship, I began to share my own driving history and penchant for speeding.

Her response to my string of confessions was to pronounce, "There's no hope for you, Marilyn. Let me show you why." She then told me how, shortly before Christmas one year, she had been pulled over by a policeman just outside her hometown of Toronto, Canada. He checked her license and insurance papers, then asked if she knew how fast she'd been going. Her response was, "Well, not as fast as I'd like . . . there are simply too many cars on the road!"

"Mrs. Johnson, I see by our computerized printout that you have quite a record of speeding tickets."

"Yes, I do, but that's not because I want them."

"What are the chances of your simply driving more slowly?"

"Probably not good."

"May I ask how old you are, Mrs. Johnson?"

"Eighty-two."

"I suppose it wouldn't do much good if I gave you a ticket then, would it?"

"I doubt it."

He patted her shoulder, told her to take care of herself, and said he hoped he would never have occasion to stop her again. She cheerfully replied, "I wouldn't mind that a bit. You are a lovely young man."

Concluding her story, she explained, "So you see, Marilyn, some things never change. You simply have 'speed genes'; you were probably born with them!"

I do not for one moment condone speeding and then excusing it by claiming, "I can't help it; it runs in the family." My point here is that there is sometimes an almost mysterious sense of the "ah-ha" when we meet people that seem to so perfectly mirror portions of ourselves. That experience provides a companionable feeling of oneness and kinship.

What is even more mysterious and provides an even greater sense of the "ah-ha" is the fact that we have been created in God's image. Jesus, who said "if you have seen me you have seen the Father," experienced every feeling, every nuance of emotion, every temptation on this earth that you and I do. If this truth is a reality to us, we can't help but be humbled by his graciousness in continually working to conform us to his image. What an awesome privilege that in our rebellious state he loves us and welcomes us always as part of the family—not because of what we do, but because of what he did on the cross.

When we look into the mirror, may we see more and more of him.

Is It Love... or Is It the Flu?

Sheila Walsh

*B*arry and I had been dating for over a year, and tonight we were going to one of our favorite Laguna Beach restaurants. Italian. Inside my size 6 or 8 body (depending on the time of the month, new Ben and Jerry's ice cream flavors, the situation in Bosnia, etc.), there is a robust Italian woman longing to get out.

I knew Barry would pick me up around 7:00, so I had just enough time to finish an essay for my C. S. Lewis class at Fuller Seminary. I was in no great rush. We were far beyond the trying-to-look-perfect-on-every-date stage. (That lasted about four dates for me ... too much work.)

Next time I looked at the clock I saw it was almost 7:00. I changed out of my jeans and put on a dress. I'm not much of a dress woman. My favorite uniform is blue jeans, a white shirt, and no shoes. If I do wear shoes, then they usually have four-inch heels. I believe it goes back to my primal fear of God calling me to be a missionary in lands with great hairy beasties. In my subconscious mind I determined that if God was scanning the earth looking for good missionary stock, he would say, "Well, we can't send her. Look at her shoes!" So although dresses are not my thing (I have fat knees—honestly!), I made some concessions for Barry.

At seven on the dot the doorbell rang. I opened the door, still struggling to get into shoe number two, and took a good look at my boyfriend.

"You don't look well," I said. "Are you feeling all right?"

"Yes! Sure! I'm fine," he replied, pacing the apartment like a woman with a wallet full of cash the day before Nordstrom's big sale.

"We don't have to go out," I said. "I could cook something, and we could watch a movie."

"No! I mean . . . I'm fine. Really, I'm fine. Let's go."

It usually took fifteen minutes to drive from my apartment to downtown Laguna, but on a busy Friday night all bets were off. Barry seemed to be getting worse as we waited in traffic. I felt his forehead.

"You're hot," I said. "I think you might have the flu. It's going around, you know."

"Really, I promise I don't have the flu. I might throw up, but don't worry . . . I don't have the flu."

We finally found a parking spot and made our way into the bustling restaurant. Those innocents without reservations had no hope, but Barry had planned ahead. We were shown to our table and I remember thinking as I watched him sweat, *I wonder if he wants to break up with me? If he does, then I'm definitely having the tiramisu. Two of them!*

The waiter gave us our menus. I set mine down on the table for a moment, enjoying the boisterous Italian atmosphere.

"Aren't you going to order?" Barry barked.

"Man, you're cranky tonight," I said. "Here, have some bread. Your blood sugar must be off."

He glared at me. Finally, to avoid an international incident, I picked up my menu to look for the most fattening item. Cranky men do not deserve thin girlfriends.

I couldn't understand the menu at first. There wasn't a cream sauce in sight. Then I realized that it wasn't a menu at all, but a typed-out proposal.

I love you with all my heart. Will you marry me?

I stared at the words for a moment. Then I looked up and found myself staring into a television camera.

"Am I on *Candid Camera?*" I asked.

"Well, answer him!"

The voice came from behind me. It was my best friend, Marlene. I suddenly realized that the restaurant was full of our friends, all waiting for my answer.

I turned back to look at Barry, but he wasn't there. He was on his knees beside me holding out the most beautiful ring imaginable. There was a moment of silence. All eyes were on us.

"Yes," I answered. "Of course I will marry you." Everyone cheered and clapped.

Later that evening as Barry was dropping me off at my apartment I asked him, "What would you have done if I'd said no? I mean, you had a camera crew; all our friends were watching. It could have been mortifying!"

"You are worth the risk," he said simply as he kissed me good night.

I often think about that when I meet women across the country. One thing we all have in common is a deep desire for love that says, "You are worthwhile. You are priceless. You are worth risking for." We have a deep well that we long to have filled with significance and a sense of belonging. We want to be cherished.

I don't know how romantic your life is or how many sweet moments and memories you have tucked into the satin pockets of your heart. But I know this: You are adored and cherished by God. Human romance is wonderful, but it comes and goes. God's passionate love for us never wanes. It's not affected by whether we are size 6 or 26. And the outlandish lengths to which God will go to prove his love are beyond any scheme a human being—even one as willing to risk as my husband—could dream up.

"This is how God showed his love among us: He sent his one and only Son into the world that we might live through him. This is love: not that we loved God, but that he loved us and sent his Son as an atoning sacrifice for our sins" (1 John 4:9–10).

I'd say that's a pretty outlandish plan. What a risk he took! I mean, we could have all said, "No, thanks." And many have.

I'm so glad I said yes to God's invitation to everlasting love. How about you?

I'm Alive!

Charlene Ann Baumbich

$\mathcal{W}$hen I check in to drive for senior citizen hot meals, I pick up a map, individual cards concerning special instructions for clients, and, of course, the food.

The directives may vary. "Don't knock, go right in." "Enter on the west side and leave the food on the counter." "Hard of hearing." "Two sacks instead of one." Sometimes, in the more condensed apartments, I might be told, "If she's not home, knock on 235."

One day I received a new route. As I sat in my car studying the cards so I wouldn't miss important cues, one card stood out. It had a huge asterisk and the message, "He is ninety-eight." That's all I needed to dream up various scenarios, the most obvious being that I would be the lucky one to try and deliver meatloaf and mashed potatoes to someone who expired in the night.

When I pulled into the circle drive in front of his home, I was given a peek into his personality. There were lawn ornaments everywhere. Animals, signs, posters, shiny things . . . It was like a little wonderland, and I smiled. I opened the hot container, grabbed the oven mitt, selected one of the foil-covered dishes, and sat it on the car roof. Then I got into the cooler and picked out the paper bag with his name on it. My hands were full by the time I got to the door, but I found a way to knock.

And then I waited.

And then I knocked a little harder.

And then I waited.

And then my heart started racing. I tried to discern my next course of action. Look in the windows? Get to a pay phone (before my car phone days) and call 911? Start screaming for help? Call the hot meals facility?

Just before hyperventilating, I heard a rustling noise and the door began to open. Eke open, ever so slowly. At last a small man appeared with a twinkle in his eyes.

"I'm alive!" he bellowed, as loudly as frailty can manage.

"And no one is happier about that than me," I assured him.

He collected the food from my hands and thanked me. I found myself wishing this was the last stop on my route because I would have liked to chat for awhile with this man who still knew how to make the heart sing. This lively, aged person who had a wonderful sense of humor. This gentle soul who understood that everyone delivering food to his home must worry about the same thing.

"I'm alive!" May I never forget to celebrate that fact and pass on that beatific angel's message.

NOTES

The compilers acknowledge with gratitude the publishers and individuals who granted permission to reprint the stories found within the pages of this book. In a few cases, it was not possible to trace the original authors. The compilers will be happy to rectify this if and when the authors contact them by writing to Zondervan, 5300 Patterson Ave. S.E., Grand Rapids, MI 49530. Each piece is noted in the order it appears in the book.

"Humbled by a Pine Tree" excerpt taken from *God Has Never Failed Me, But He's Sure Scared Me to Death a Few Times.* Copyright © 1998 by Stan Toler and Martha Bolton. Used by permission of RiverOak Publishing, Tulsa, OK. All rights reserved.

"The Almond Joy Incident" by Cathy Lee Phillips. This article first appeared in *Today's Christian Woman* magazine (November/December 1997), a publication of Christianity Today, Inc. Used by permission.

"Icebreaker SOS" excerpted from *Life Is Not a Dress Rehearsal* © 2000 by Sheri Rose Shepherd. Used by permission of Multnomah Publishers, Inc.

"A Complete Ensemble" is taken from *Living It Down by Laughing It Up,* © 2001 by Martha Bolton. Published by Servant Publications, Box 8617, Ann Arbor, Michigan 48107. Used with permission.

"Awkward Situations" is taken from *Worms in My Tea* by Becky Freeman with Ruthie Arnold. Copyright © 1994, Broadman & Holman Publishers. All rights reserved. Used by permission.

"Read My Lips" taken from *Welcome to the Funny Farm* by Karen Linamen, Fleming H. Revell, a division of Baker Book House Company, copyright © 2001. Used by permission.

"They Need Help!" by Thelma Wells, originally titled "What Would Jesus Do?" taken from *Boundless Love* by Patsy Clairmont, Barbara Johnson, Marilyn Meberg, Luci Swindoll, Sheila Walsh, and Thelma Wells. Copyright © 2001 by Women of Faith, Inc. Used by permission of Zondervan.

"Steaming in the Southwest" taken from *Mama Said There'd Be Days Like This* by Charlene Ann Baumbich. Copyright © 1995 by Charlene Ann Baumbich. All rights reserved. Used by permission.

Richard Lederer, "The Revised Nonstandard Bible," in *Fractured English* (Pocket Books, © 1996). Used by permission of the author.

"Just Kidding Around" pieces by Rhonda Mony, Kathy Plate, Karin C. Wooten, Nancy LaDuke, Elizabeth Sphar, Rhonda Reese, Mary Alderfer, Vesper Bauer, Judi Gaudio, Kathy Dinnison, and Carol Reasoner first appeared in the following issues of *Christian Reader,* a publication of Christianity Today, Inc.: (November/December 1996), (November/December 1996), (January/February 1997), (March/April 1997), (July/August 1997), (November/December 1997), (November/December 1997), (September/October 1998), (January/February 1999), (January/February 1999), (March/April 1999). Pieces by Gary Severson, Stephanie Gates, Marc C. Whitt, Sheri Lynn Essian, Tracy Potter, Sheila O'Connor, Martha Andersen, Rachel Swan, Vonda P., Sandy Y., Shawne B., Mary H., Shannon C., Rajendra P., Michele G., Wendy S., and Gina Doll first appeared in the following issues of *Christian Parenting Today,* a publication of Christianity Today, Inc.: (September/October 1998), (September/October 1998), (March/April 1999), (January/February 1999), (January/February 1999), (January/February 1999), (November/December 1998), (November/December 1997), (March/April 2000), (March/April 2000), (March/April 2000), (January/February 2000), (May/June 2000), (July/August 2000), (November/December 1999), (November/December 1999), (May/June 1998).

"I'll Catch a Later Bus" reprinted from *I'm Trying to Number My Days, But I Keep Losing Count!* Copyright © 1998 by Al Sanders. WaterBrook Press, Colorado Springs, CO. All rights reserved.

"If You Could Read My Mind" is taken from *The Lord Is My Shepherd and I'm About to Be Sheared,* copyright © 1998 by G. Ron Darbee. Used by permission.

"Celebrity Cover-Up" is taken from *Living It Down by Laughing It Up,* © 2001 by Martha Bolton. Published by Servant Publications, Box 8617, Ann Arbor, Michigan 48107. Used with permission.

"Two Cannibals in Love" taken from *Mama Said There'd Be Days Like This* by Charlene Ann Baumbich. Copyright © 1995 by Charlene Ann Baumbich. All rights reserved. Used by permission.

"For 25 Years I Hated My Mop" by Janice Crouse. This article first appeared in *Marriage Partnership* magazine (Summer 1989), a publication of Christianity Today, Inc. Used by permission.

"Wild Hares" taken from *Lighten Up!* by Ken Davis. Copyright © 2000 by Ken Davis. Used by permission of Zondervan.

"High Adventure in the Garage" taken from *Mama Said There'd Be Days Like This* by Charlene Ann Baumbich. Copyright © 1995 by Charlene Ann Baumbich. All rights reserved. Used by permission.

"Pulling Strings" is taken from *God Uses Cracked Pots* by Patsy Clairmont, a Focus on the Family book published by Tyndale House. Copyright © 1991 by Patsy Clairmont. All rights reserved. International copyright secured. Used by permission.

"Snore Warzzz" by Nancy Kennedy. This article first appeared in *Marriage Partnership* magazine (Winter 1997), a publication of Christianity Today, Inc. Used by permission.

"No Batteries Required" taken from *Welcome to the Funny Farm* by Karen Linamen, Fleming H. Revell, a division of Baker Book House Company, copyright © 2001. Used by permission.

"Beauty for the Beast" by Marti Attoun. Used by permission.

"Nightmare on Perfect Street" by Betty Smartt Carter. This article first appeared in *Marriage Partnership* magazine (Summer 2000), a publication of Christianity Today, Inc. Used by permission.

"I'm Surrounded by Teens with Uncommon Scents" by Marti Attoun. Used by permission.

"Like Death Warmed Over" is taken from *Worms in My Tea* by Becky Freeman with Ruthie Arnold. Copyright ©1994, Broadman & Holman Publishers. All rights reserved. Used by permission.

"*Yo Quiero* No Discount" used with permission from *Didn't My Skin Used to Fit?* by Martha Bolton. Copyright © 2000, Bethany House Publishers. All rights reserved.

"He's Baaaaaack" taken from *Lighten Up!* by Ken Davis. Copyright © 2000 by Ken Davis. Used by permission of Zondervan.

"When in Rome" by Shari MacDonald. Copyright © 2001. Used by permission.

"The Perfect Song" taken from *Duh-Votions* by Sue Buchanan. Copyright © 1999 by Sue Buchanan. Used by permission of Zondervan.

"Welcome to the Bat Cave" by Nate Adams. This article first appeared in *Marriage Partnership* magazine (Summer 1997), a publication of Christianity Today, Inc. Used by permission.

"I Yam What I Yam" is taken from *Living It Down by Laughing It Up*, © 2001 by Martha Bolton. Published by Servant Publications, Box 8617, Ann Arbor, Michigan 48107. Used with permission.

"Mommyrobics" by Nancy Kennedy. This article first appeared in *Christian Parenting Today* magazine (September/October 1996), a publication of Christianity Today, Inc. Used by permission.

"A Diet Prayer" by Victor Buono (1938–1982).

"Counting Fat Grams" taken from *Chonda Pierce On Her Soapbox* by Chonda Pierce. Copyright © 1999 by Chonda Pierce. Used by permission of Zondervan.

"Lamentations of the Father" is reproduced from *Lamentations of the Father*, Westminster John Knox Press. Copyright © 2000 by Ian Frazier. Used by permission of The Wylie Agency.

"Deck the Halls with Poison Ivy" is taken from *The Lord Is My Shepherd and I'm About to Be Sheared*, copyright © 1998 by G. Ron Darbee. Used by permission.

"Surprise, Surprise!" by Barbara Johnson taken from *We Brake for Joy!* by Patsy Clairmont, Barbara Johnson, Marilyn Meberg, Luci Swindoll, Sheila Walsh, and Thelma Wells. Copyright © 1998 by Women of Faith, Inc. Used by permission of Zondervan.

"Picky, Picky" by Nancy Kennedy. This article first appeared in *Christian Parenting Today* magazine (March/April 1999), a publication of Christianity Today, Inc. Used by permission.

"The Great Toaster Tart Conspiracy" by Randy Frame. This article first appeared in *Marriage Partnership* magazine (Fall 1996), a publication of Christianity Today, Inc. Used by permission.

"Dental Advice" is taken from *Out of Control*, Mark Lowry, copyright © 1996, Word Publishing, Nashville, Tennessee. All rights reserved.

"How to Have a Relationship with a Guy" is taken from *Dave Barry's Complete Guide to Guys* by Dave Barry, copyright © 1995 by Dave Barry. Used by permission of Random House, Inc.

"Airplane Babies" is taken from *Out of Control,* Mark Lowry, copyright © 1996, Word Publishing, Nashville, Tennessee. All rights reserved.

"Mr. Mom" by James R. Judge, M.D. This article first appeared in *Christian Parenting Today* magazine (May/June 2000), a publication of Christianity Today, Inc. Used by permission.

"Help! I've Got TMS!" originally titled "The Ravages of Tired Mother Syndrome" by Nancy Kennedy. This article first appeared in *Christian Parenting Today* magazine (March/April 1998), a publication of Christianity Today, Inc. Used by permission.

"Mama's On Hold" is taken from *Out of Control,* Mark Lowry, copyright © 1996, Word Publishing, Nashville, Tennessee. All rights reserved.

"Hello" is taken from *God Uses Cracked Pots* by Patsy Clairmont, a Focus on the Family book published by Tyndale House. Copyright © 1991 by Patsy Clairmont. All rights reserved. International copyright secured. Used by permission.

"And Her Husband Thought *He* Had a Stressful Job" excerpted from *Who Put the Skunk in the Trunk?* © 1999 by Phil Callaway. Used by permission of Multnomah Publishers, Inc.

"Free at Last?" by Pamela Shires Sneddon. This article first appeared in *Christian Parenting Today* magazine (September/October 2000), a publication of Christianity Today, Inc. Used by permission.

"I Dare You" by Luci Swindoll taken from *Joy Breaks* by Patsy Clairmont, Barbara Johnson, Marilyn Meberg, and Luci Swindoll. Copyright © 1997 by Patsy Clairmont, Barbara Johnson, Marilyn Meberg, and Luci Swindoll. Used by permission of Zondervan.

"Did I See That?" by Marilyn Meberg taken from *Joy Breaks* by Patsy Clairmont, Barbara Johnson, Marilyn Meberg, and Luci Swindoll. Copyright © 1997 by Patsy Clairmont, Barbara Johnson, Marilyn Meberg, and Luci Swindoll. Used by permission of Zondervan.

"Garth and Pat" taken from *Second Row, Piano Side* by Chonda Pierce. Copyright © 1996. Used by permission.

"You Drive Me Crazy," originally titled "We Aren't Real," is taken from *Choosing the Amusing,* Marilyn Meberg, copyright © 1999, Word Publishing, Nashville, Tennessee. All rights reserved.

"Playful People" by Marilyn Meberg taken from *We Brake for Joy!* by Barbara E. Johnson, Patsy Clairmont, Luci Swindoll, Sheila Walsh, Marilyn Meberg, Thelma Wells. Copyright © 1998 by Women of Faith, Inc. Used by permission of Zondervan.

"Hey, Good Lookin', Whatcha Got Burnin'?" taken from *Chocolate Chili Pepper Love*. Copyright © 2000 by Becky Freeman. Published by Harvest House Publishers, Eugene, OR 97402. Used by permission.

"Young Love Turns Daughter into Teen Cleaning Machine" by Marti Attoun. Used by permission.

"Household Skullduggery" by Renae Bottom. This article first appeared in *Marriage Partnership* magazine (Fall 1998), a publication of Christianity Today, Inc. Used by permission.

"Home Beautiful" by Marsha Crockett. This article first appeared in *Today's Christian Woman* magazine (September/October 1997), a publication of Christianity Today, Inc. Used by permission.

"The Fashion Plate on My Front Yard" by Marti Attoun. Used by permission.

"PMS: Psychotic Mood Swings" is taken from *Do Plastic Surgeons Take Visa?* by Kathy Peel, copyright © 1992, Word Publishing, Nashville, Tennessee. All rights reserved.

"A Fun Day Composting with Martha Stewart" taken from *Chonda Pierce On Her Soapbox* by Chonda Pierce. Copyright © 1999 by Chonda Pierce. Used by permission of Zondervan.

"Never Underestimate the Power of an Imperfect Woman" taken from *Welcome to the Funny Farm* by Karen Linamen, Fleming H. Revell, a division of Baker Book House Company, copyright © 2001. Used by permission.

"That Old Sew-and-Sew," originally titled "We Aren't Valued," is taken from *Choosing the Amusing,* Marilyn Meberg, copyright © 1999, Word Publishing, Nashville, Tennessee. All rights reserved.

"God's Timing" by Brennan Manning. Copyright © 2000 by Brennan Manning. Reprinted by permission of HarperCollins Publishers, Inc.

"I Could Lose Myself in Thought" taken from *Duh-Votions* by Sue Buchanan. Copyright © 1999 by Sue Buchanan. Used by permission of Zondervan.

"What's in a Name?" by Thelma Wells taken from *Boundless Love* by Patsy Clairmont, Barbara Johnson, Marilyn Meberg, Luci Swindoll, Sheila Walsh, and Thelma Wells. Copyright © 2001 by Women of Faith, Inc. Used by permission of Zondervan.

"And Edith with Them" by Barbara Johnson taken from *Boundless Love* by Patsy Clairmont, Barbara Johnson, Marilyn Meberg, Luci Swindoll, Sheila Walsh, and Thelma Wells. Copyright © 2001 by Women of Faith, Inc. Used by permission of Zondervan.

"Missing in Action" by Patsy Clairmont taken from *We Brake for Joy!* by Patsy Clairmont, Barbara Johnson, Marilyn Meberg, Luci Swindoll, Sheila Walsh, and Thelma Wells. Copyright © 1998 by Women of Faith, Inc. Used by permission of Zondervan.

"A Mirror Image" by Marilyn Meberg taken from *Joy Breaks* by Patsy Clairmont, Barbara Johnson, Marilyn Meberg, and Luci Swindoll. Copyright © 1997 by Patsy Clairmont, Barbara Johnson, Marilyn Meberg, and Luci Swindoll. Used by permission of Zondervan.

"Is It Love . . . or Is It the Flu?" by Sheila Walsh taken from *Boundless Love* by Patsy Clairmont, Barbara Johnson, Marilyn Meberg, Luci Swindoll, Sheila Walsh, and Thelma Wells. Copyright © 2001 by Women of Faith, Inc. Used by permission of Zondervan.

"I'm Alive!" taken from *Mama Said There'd Be Days Like This* by Charlene Ann Baumbich. Copyright © 1995 by Charlene Ann Baumbich. All rights reserved. Used by permission.

Look Who's Laughing!

BOOKS BY ANN SPANGLER

Daily Secrets of the Christian Life, Hannah Whitall Smith (compiled by Ann Spangler)
Don't Stop Laughing Now! compiled by Ann Spangler and Shari MacDonald
He's Been Faithful, Carol Cymbala with Ann Spangler
Look Who's Laughing! compiled by Ann Spangler and Shari MacDonald
Men of the Bible, coauthored with Robert Wolgemuth
She Who Laughs, Lasts! compiled by Ann Spangler
Women of the Bible, coauthored with Jean Syswerda
Women of the Bible: 52 Stories for Prayer and Reflection

BOOKS BY SHARI MACDONALD

A Match Made in Heaven
Don't Stop Laughing Now! compiled by Ann Spangler and Shari MacDonald
Humor for a Woman's Heart, compiled by Shari MacDonald
Humor for the Heart, compiled by Shari MacDonald
Look Who's Laughing! compiled by Ann Spangler and Shari MacDonald
Love on the Run
The Perfect Wife

Rib-Tickling Stories of Fun, Faith, Family, and Friendship

Look Who's Laughing!

Compiled by Ann Spangler & Shari MacDonald

Stories by: Barbara Johnson Patsy Clairmont John Ortberg
Chonda Pierce Becky Freeman Marilyn Meberg Luci Swindoll

ZONDERVAN™

GRAND RAPIDS, MICHIGAN 49530 USA

ZONDERVAN™

Look Who's Laughing!
Copyright © 2003 by Ann Spangler

Requests for information should be addressed to:
Zondervan, *Grand Rapids, Michigan 49530*

ISBN 0-7394-3807-7

All Scripture quotations, unless otherwise indicated, are taken from the *Holy Bible, New International Version®*. NIV®. Copyright © 1973, 1978, 1984 by International Bible Society. Used by permission of Zondervan. All rights reserved.

All rights reserved. No part of this publication may be reproduced, stored in a retrieval system, or transmitted in any form or by any means — electronic, mechanical, photocopy, recording, or any other — except for brief quotations in printed reviews, without the prior permission of the publisher.

Interior design by Tracey Moran

Printed in the United States of America

Contents

Preface

*W*illiam Makepeace Thackeray, a Victorian novelist, once wrote that "a good laugh is sunshine in a house." We hope that *Look Who's Laughing!* will not only add sunshine to your home but to your heart as well, easing your anxieties, giving much-needed perspective, and lightening whatever loads you might be carrying.

As we worked on the project over the past year, Shari and I have encountered our share of challenges in other aspects of our lives. But evening after evening as I set aside the pressures of the day and worked on the collection of material that eventually made its way into the pages of this book, I felt the pressure ease and slip away. Instead of ending the day worried or frustrated, I often slipped into bed with a smile on my face and a settled peace in my heart.

As you read through the stories, quips, and quotes in this book, we hope that you too will experience laughter's power to refresh and renew your soul, restoring a sense of balance regardless of life's difficulties.

We are grateful to the many people who have made this book possible, especially to the authors whose work it includes. Their ability to see the fun and funny side of life and their candidness about their own foibles and failings helps all of us to learn and relearn one of life's most important skills—the art of laughing at ourselves and our circumstances. Thanks also to the many publishers who kindly gave permission for use of the material in this book.

Particular thanks goes to Sandy VanderZicht, executive editor at Zondervan, who is also the editor of the two previous books in the series: *She Who Laughs, Lasts!* and *Don't Stop Laughing Now!* Sandy is a woman who laughs easily and heartily (even at my none-too-funny jokes) and who is quick to appreciate and enjoy the humorous side of life. Her guidance has been invaluable as we have worked on questions of content and structure, hoping thereby to tickle as many funny bones as possible.

We also want to acknowledge Dirk Buursma, our development editor, whose prayers and encouragement are greatly appreciated. Thanks also to Sue Brower, director of marketing for trade books. Sue and her creative team have energetically supported this book as well as its predecessors, making it their mission to spread the laughter as far and wide as possible.

To you, the reader, we hope for many days of lighthearted fun and ample joy as you read through the pages of *Look Who's Laughing!* You might even try, as I did, reading a few pages before bedtime and then tucking yourself in with a smile, experiencing the truth of the biblical saying that "a merry heart doeth good like a medicine."

—Ann Spangler

CHAPTER ONE

Men Are Funny, Women Are Hilarious . . . Together We're Hysterical

Man is the powder, woman the spark.
—Lope De Vega

Women like silent men.
They think they are listening.
—Marcel Achard

One Man's Treasure

G. Ron Darbee

I suppose I should have seen it coming, should have recognized the signs, picked up on the subtle hint. But after so many years of marriage, I really didn't want to believe it was true. Oh, she sent all the right signals, I guess. She even threatened a time or two. Maybe I loved her too much, trusted her too completely. When it finally happened—when all that trust shattered and her veil of secrecy lifted—there was no one left to blame but myself.

I went to bed early, consistent with my usual routine, but rather than falling directly to sleep, I waited. Because of my morning commute, it's not unusual for me to retire before Sue, anyway. I didn't think she knew of my suspicions, but later she claimed she did. In a way, I think she wanted to be caught, to get it out in the open and end the sneaking around.

About an hour later, Sue poked her head in the door, ensuring herself I was out for the night. I heard the fumbling of keys in her purse and the sound of the back door creaking before I rose and followed in pursuit. Stepping into the garage behind her, I caught her red-handed.

"Ah!" I said, in the manner of one who has just caught his spouse red-handed. "So what do you have to say for yourself?"

Sue spun around quickly, startled and caught off guard. Following her first impulse, she feigned surprise and pretended to gasp for breath, all the while attempting to hide something in the small of her back. I didn't fall for the clever ruse and demanded to see what she held behind her.

"It's nothing," Sue said. "Really . . . nothing." Her face displayed only guilt, and shame shone through the facade of shock.

"Nothing, is it?" I said. "We'll see about that. What have you got there? What are you hiding behind your back?"

"Don't make me show you," she pleaded. "Please, can we just go inside and forget about this? Pretend it never happened?"

"I don't think so, Sue. It's gone too far. I'll be seeing what you're hiding there now, if you please."

Slowly, cautiously, she pulled her hand around. I knew what to expect even before I saw it. "Those are my baseball cards, aren't they?" I said, my heart nearly pounding through my chest. "You've been cleaning out the garage again, haven't you?"

"Yes!" She said it defiantly, holding her head up high, ready to stand her ground. She had done it, yes, and she was glad.

"And you've been rummaging through my things?" I asked. "I suppose you've thrown away some of my stuff?"

"Yes," she answered, "and I'd do it again if I had the chance. It's all junk. Somebody had to clear it out of here."

So there it was, a turning point, a roadblock in our marriage. We could take the easy way, like so many other couples we knew, or we could try to work it out. Our life together was too important to both of us; we had made a commitment, a lifelong commitment.

"We can work this out, sweetheart," I said, in the spirit of reconciliation. "Let me see it all. We'll do this thing together."

That was one of the most difficult things I have ever done. Sue, like many women, doesn't know the first thing about memorabilia. She sees a box of baseball cards, an old ball glove—and immediately heads toward the trash pile. And the whole time our house is cluttered with real junk: photographs, old letters, and hand-me-downs disguised as family heirlooms.

"Show me what you've thrown away so far," I said, wanting to minimize the losses. She pointed toward a trash can nearly overflowing with my possessions. "Not my first ball glove!" I yelled as I extracted the crown of my earthly treasures. "You couldn't have meant to throw away my baseball mitt."

"It doesn't even fit you anymore," Sue said. "You couldn't possibly get your hand in there."

"But it has Ron Swoboda's signature on the thumb, Sue! How could you do this?"

"I don't see a signature on it," she said, squinting in the poor light of our garage.

"Well, it used to be on there," I said. "You can sort of make it out if you know what to look for." I continued rummaging through the pile. "Now wait just a minute. Do you know what this is?" I asked. "Do you know what you've thrown away?"

"Old baseball cards," Sue said. Accurate guess, but she obviously didn't get the whole picture.

"Not just old baseball cards, Sue. This is Mickey Mantle, 'Mick the Stick,' one of the greatest baseball players of all time. Do you know how much this is worth? I'll tell you. Several hundred dollars!"

"I apologize," Sue said. "I never would have thrown it away if I'd known how much it was worth. Can we sell it?"

"Sell it! This is my youth we're talking about, Sue. How much is my youth worth to you?"

"How much can we get?" she asked.

Determining that we were getting nowhere following that course, I switched gears slightly and attempted to gain the upper hand. "How much of *your* junk have you thrown away, sweetheart?" I asked.

"Over there by the shelves," she pointed in the direction of the washing machine. "A toilet brush that's seen better days, some slippers, and that cookbook your mother gave me."

I couldn't believe my ears. "The cookbook my mother wrote with her own two hands?" I asked. "You threw away Mom's Chronology of Darbee Cuisine? How could you?"

"It's not even a real cookbook, just a list of ingredients," Sue argued. "She didn't write down any amounts. What am I supposed to do—guess?"

"Okay, fine," I said. "Why are we saving this then?" I picked up an old encyclopedia volume and thrust it in Sue's direction. "Open the book, Sue, and you know what you'll find? Dead flowers. May I ask why we are saving dead flowers?"

"Those happen to be the first flowers you sent me," Sue said, as though that revelation was supposed to make a difference.

"They're still dead, Sue," I said. "And, quite frankly, I don't understand. Mickey you toss away without a second thought, and a dozen carnations get immortalized between the pages of World Book."

"Roses," she corrected. "They were roses, and I thought it was better to save them than expect new ones on occasion."

Immediately recognizing that this, too, was not a course I wanted to take, I changed directions one last time. "Sounds like we compromise," I said. "I'll tell you what, I don't mind if you keep the dried flowers. How's that?"

"Fine," she said, "and you can keep Sticky Mickey if it means that much to you."

"Mick the Stick, honey," I corrected. "Yes, it means that much to me. Why don't we try to get through the rest of this stuff tomorrow after we've both gotten some sleep. We'll get a fresh start."

"Okay, and I'm sorry I tossed your things without first considering your feelings."

We headed for the bedroom, hand in hand, the disagreement now behind us, when Sue asked another question. "By the way," she said, "what was the tooth you saved in the baby food jar?"

"Tell me you didn't throw away the tooth," I said. "That wasn't just any tooth, Sue. That tooth belonged to Dave Schultze, hatchet man for the Philadelphia Flyers back in the seventies. I picked it up off the ice after an Islanders game. At least I think it belonged to Schultze. Hockey players lose a lot of teeth, and it's not always easy keeping track *and* watching the puck, too."

"You took the man's tooth?" Sue asked in a voice that suggested disbelief. "Didn't you offer to give it back to him at least?"

"Nah," I said. "Those guys drop their teeth all the time. They're like souvenirs. If they really cared about their dental work, they wouldn't be playing ice hockey, now would they?"

"I guess not, but I still think you should have at least offered," she said. "And, by the way, the tooth goes."

"Let's talk about it in the morning, sweetheart."

"The tooth goes."

"Goodnight, Sue," I said.

"Goodnight."

As we drifted off to sleep, I thought about how some people can't seem to appreciate the finer, more sentimental things in life. And for all this time I had lived under the impression that women were the more emotional partners. It's just lucky she didn't find my collection of athletic footwear. I'm sure she would have burned them.

Light His Fire

Becky Freeman

I am not, by any stretch of the imagination, what you would call a naturally wild and wanton woman. But I'd been married fifteen years, and I felt our marriage needed a little—spice.

It all began with a romantic suggestion I gleaned from a book titled *Light His Fire*. The author, Ellen Kriedman, suggests that wives use their ingenuity to come up with imaginative ways to have fun seducing their mate. The book assured me that, done properly, this technique should fire up the "I feel a chill in the air" times most couples experience at some point in their relationship.

Nothing new here, really. Ever since the days when perky Mrs. Marabel Morgan first suggested we Christian women greet our husbands at the door dressed in plastic wrap and/or an apron, we wives have spent a couple of decades trying to outdo the Total Woman. Personally, I have come to the conclusion that such efforts leave me feeling more like a Totaled Woman. Not that I hadn't given wild and creative tactics my best shot, mind you.

One night as I stepped out of the shower wrapped in a towel, I spied the lights of Scott's pickup in the driveway of our home. Our closest neighbors were raccoons and possums, so I didn't worry about the undraped window overlooking the drive. Suddenly I could almost hear Dr. Kriedman whispering in my ear. *Why not? After all, you're married to the guy. Be playful! Be sexy! Have some fun with your man!*

So I dropped the towel and stood there in front of the window wearing nothing but my best seductive smile. As it happened, Scott was not alone. This night he had with him our good friend Gary, husband of my dear friend Mary. As the two men walked casually toward the house (I learned later), Scott glanced toward the window, returned for a second to his conversation with Gary, and then jerked his head back toward the window, his eyes wide, his mouth agape. He then alternated between trying to divert Gary's eyes from our bedroom window and gesturing frantically for me to run for cover.

Lamentably, although it is easy to see *into* a lighted home from the dark, it is quite difficult for the one standing inside the house to see *out* into the dark. Because of this phenomenon, I imagined Scott must surely be whooping it up out there in the night air. I even thought I heard him egging me on with playful wolf whistles. Later I would discover the "whistles" were actually high-pitched sounds made by Scott's vocal chords desperately searching for the natural range of his voice. In any case, I simply responded to what I had assumed was my husband's enthusiastic reaction.

Finally, having safely escorted Gary into the kitchen, Scott breathed a sigh of relief and began to relax. Observing that nothing could undo the damage that had already been done, my husband nonchalantly poked his head into the bedroom.

"Hi, hon," he said casually. "Gary's with me."

My screams, I'm sure, awakened every possum and raccoon in the surrounding square mile. I thought I would die. My thoughts were frenzied. *I've* just flashed my best friend's husband! It doesn't get any worse than this. Of all the stupid antics—this absolutely tops the list! I vowed to avoid Gary for the rest of my life. I couldn't possibly face him again without dissolving into a puddle of shame and embarrassment.

The next morning, Mary—Gary's wife—called bright and early. "Becky," she said brightly, "Gary asked me to deliver a message to you." Switching to a deep French accent, she went on. "He says to tell you, 'Becky, jou look mahvalhlous.'"

When the laughter finally began to subside on her end of the line, Mary added, "And, hey, I just want you to know, since I've been feeling a bit under the weather lately, this probably *made* his week."

Because they both had a great sense of humor, we all recovered fairly quickly. With time and understanding, I am now able to hold a normal conversation with Gary without benefit of a paper bag over my head.

The Window Story has already made its way through our small town—down grocery store aisles, across neighborhood fences, into most of our fellow parishioners' ears between services—and is probably being translated into several foreign languages. My best friends, and even my husband, love to tell it at appropriate gatherings when conversation hits a lull.

After that little escapade, one would assume I would have laid to rest any impulse to do something wild and crazy and romantic—for at least a while. One would assume.

Then one evening, feeling rather amorous, I stepped out of the bathtub and noticed a large, yellow, transparent bag hanging over the towel rack—a bag that had been used to cover Scott's dry-cleaned shirts. Viewing all that plastic, I thought I heard voices again. This time it was the Total Woman speaking. *If at first you don't succeed, try, try again.*

Inspired, I draped the mustard-colored wrap around my torso, ingeniously holding it together with a couple of bobby pins I had found in the sink. Slinking toward the bedroom where my husband was reclining with a good book, I opened the door with a flourish. He continued to read, so I loudly cleared my throat. He finally glanced up, shook his head as if to clear it, frowned in bewilderment, and scratched his chin. Not quite the reaction I had anticipated. It got worse.

"What have you done to yourself now?" Scott asked sincerely. "You've made your entire body look like one of those supermarket meat trays of pickled pigs' feet!"

I wasn't as crushed as you might expect from that verbal blow to my ego. I had to admit, a last-minute glance in the bathroom mirror had filled me with a few serious doubts. I had gone into this mission knowing its outcome was chancy at best. But I was no longer in a wild and crazy romantic state of mind either. As to my pork-minded husband's chances for an evening of love, I have just one thing to say—"That little piggy had none."

Egg Money

Anonymous

The elderly pastor was searching his closet for his collar before church one Sunday morning. In the back of the closet, he found a small box containing three eggs and one hundred $1 bills. He called his wife into the closet to ask her about the box and its contents.

Embarrassed, she admitted having hidden the box there for their entire forty-five years of marriage. Disappointed and hurt, the pastor asked her, "Why!?" The wife replied that she hadn't wanted to hurt his feelings.

He asked her how the box could possibly have hurt his feelings. She said that every time he had delivered a poor sermon, she had placed an egg in the box.

The pastor felt that three poor sermons in forty-five years was certainly nothing to feel bad about, so he asked her what the $100 was for.

She replied, "Each time I got a dozen eggs, I sold them to the neighbors for a dollar."

Pearly Gates

John Ortberg

A man appears before the pearly gates.

"Have you ever done anything of particular merit?" Saint Peter asks.

"Well, I can think of one thing," the man offers. "Once I came upon a gang of high-testosterone bikers who were threatening a young woman. I directed them to leave her alone, but they wouldn't listen. So I approached the largest and most heavily tattooed biker. I smacked him on the head, kicked his bike over, ripped out his nose ring and threw it on the ground, and told him, 'Leave her alone now, or you'll answer to me.'"

Saint Peter was impressed. "When did this happen?"

"A couple of minutes ago."

Pause for Concern

Dave Meurer

Solve the Mystery: An ill-fated family of four is stranded in a car on a country road in South Dakota during the worst blizzard of the century. One person has numb toes, one person's teeth are chattering, one person is shivering, and one person is fanning herself and saying, "Gracious, it is so *hot* in here."

> **QUESTION:** Which one is experiencing menopause?
> **HINT:** If you answer correctly, you may get whacked with a spatula.

I had never even heard the word *menopause* when it decided to pay my mom a nice little visit (in the sense that a forest fire pays Yellowstone a nice little visit). I came home from school one day and walked in the door and said, "Hi, Mom," and she erupted in a geyser of tears, collapsed on the sofa, and sobbed, "Go ahead, just rub it in!"

I turned quizzically to my dad, who was wildly making the universal gesture for "Meet Me in Ohio!"

Dad drove me across four county lines before he cleared his throat and announced, "Your mother is going through 'The Change.'"

"The change of what?" I asked.

Dad bit his lip.

"Son, there comes a time in every woman's life when her body decides that her childbearing days are over. Her hormones are in a state of upheaval, and it is exhibited in moodiness, hot flashes, tears, and the ability to rip the doors off a Brinks armored truck if chocolate is inside. Just try to be understanding."

That directive turned out to be easier said than done.

The term "try to be understanding" implies that there is something that can, in fact, be understood—like algebra or mathematical word problems, which at least involve logic. Menopause is more complex than quantum physics, and no rules of logic apply . . .

Although it will still be several years before The Change descends on our house, the Meurer household is already in training for this momentous event. We hold monthly drills called PMS, which is sort of like training for a National Guard exercise except that it's more dangerous and we don't even get free uniforms.

Women believe it is tremendously unfair that they have to endure PMS, childbirth, *and* menopause, because they think men pretty much get off scot-free. But they are mistaken. While it is true that women have to do the labor thing and the childbirth thing, and endure the cramps, aches, pains, water retention, bloating, hot flashes, sudden fits of weeping, hormone-driven maniacal mood swings, and embarrassing OB/GYN exams, they need to bear in mind that guys have to *live in the same house with them* while all this is happening. So we males are certainly shouldering our share of the suffering. Hey, I think you could even argue that guys are doing *most* of the heavy lifting, because sometimes we even have to go to the store late at night to buy Midol for our women folk.

WHACK, WHACK, WHACK!!! OW, OW, OW!!!

You may recall that in the biblical account wherein God told Abraham that the pitter-patter of little feet would soon be heard around the tent, Sarah, who was nearly one hundred years old, laughed. While the text tells us it was a laugh of unbelief, we can conjecture that one component of this unbelief may have taken the form of Sarah thinking to herself, "Surely, *the Lord would not make me go through menopause TWICE?!? I can't* believe *it!*"

Be that as it may, the happy couple did get a baby out of the ordeal—it's just that half of the happy couple was a bit happier than the other and had less stretch marks.

But it is all a package deal. The entire PMS/pregnancy/menopause thing is a wondrously orchestrated system God has created so that we can bring children into the world to nurture and teach and then release into adulthood to start the amazing process all over again—with menopause serving as an "off switch" so that women finally get a break and do not have kids at the age of one hundred unless God is really trying to make a major point.

Although we don't understand why much of this has to be kind of an unpleasant experience for women, we need to trust that, in the grace and goodness of God, there is, in fact, a reason for it. At minimum, we can be thankful that, except for those late-night Midol runs, men pretty much get to skate. Works for me!

WHACK, WHACK, WHACK!!! OW, OW, OW!!!

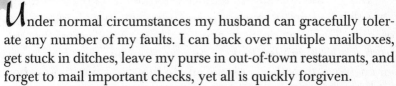

Showdown at the Hoedown

Becky Freeman

$\mathcal{U}$nder normal circumstances my husband can gracefully tolerate any number of my faults. I can back over multiple mailboxes, get stuck in ditches, leave my purse in out-of-town restaurants, and forget to mail important checks, yet all is quickly forgiven.

But in our earlier married life there was one thing my husband had never been able to tolerate, not even for a second, and that was for me to be in a negative mood. His attitude was, *Get over it and get over it yesterday.* Here was an area in our marriage where I had come to feel I wasn't being given any slack in the ol' fishing line—no leeway to express even one moment of plain old everyday grumpiness. Once every month we added my drop in hormones to Scott's lack of tolerance, and we had an explosion just waiting to happen. Unfortunately, one time happened to coincide with my birthday.

Scott and I were driving to Dallas, Texas, to meet my parents at a country-western family steak house—The Trail Dust—to celebrate. The Trail Dust had long been a family favorite; it had a wonderful band and was one of the few wholesome places where we could go to two-step, waltz, or dance the Cotton-Eyed Joe. Mother and Daddy were getting to be quite the fancy country-western dancers, and we had always enjoyed each other's company, so we were looking forward to the evening out with them.

As we were driving I mulled over the variety of special occasions we'd celebrated at this steak house over the years—Scott's graduation from college, numerous birthdays, and a couple of anniversaries. Then, however, I recalled a couple of special

25

celebrations that had been a little hard on my ego. On my thirtieth birthday, for example, the bandleader had coerced me into coming up to the front, donning a white cowboy hat, and galloping around the dance floor on a stick horse while the packed-out restaurant sang "Happy Birthday to You." Now isn't that special? I was stuck in one of those classic unavoidable dilemmas. If I declined to trot around the floor like an overgrown child on a stick horse, I would have looked like a spoilsport. If I accepted the invitation, I would look like an idiot. Better to be an Idiot than a Party Pooper, so I pranced proudly with my head held high and my dignity still somewhat intact.

But I remembered yet another celebration dinner at the Trail Dust that had pretty much stripped me of any remaining vestiges of pride. That evening, Scott and I had been seated across the table from some rather dignified young men from our church—one was an engineer, the other a physician. To this day I don't know how it happened, because I had certainly not been drinking anything stronger than root beer, but as I was debating a serious point, I became airborne and somehow fell straight back in my chair and onto the floor. There I sat in my ladder-back chair, staring at the *ceiling* instead of across the table at the two young men.

Of course I was wearing a dress. Of course I landed with my boots sticking straight up in the air. As nonchalantly as he might have reached for a fallen set of keys, Scott scooped me up and, without a word, set me back in the upright position. Didn't lose a beat. Just propped me up like a rag doll and went right on with his meal and conversation. The two gentlemen, as I recall, sat poised with forks in midair, blinking as if to be sure of what they had just seen.

As we drove toward my birthday celebration, I recalled these past events and felt suddenly uneasy about another Trail Dust celebration. As Scott and I neared the halfway point on the highway to the familiar steak house, my general uneasiness turned to strong irritation, coupled with a sudden high-dosage bolt of low self-esteem, and things went downhill from there.

"So why don't you like my dress, Scott?" I began.

"I didn't say I didn't like your dress!"

"Well, you didn't say you *did,* either. And you didn't say I looked pretty tonight. You always tell me I look ravishing when we go out. What is it? Do I look heavy? Are you embarrassed to have me as your partner?"

"I'm not going to have this conversation, Becky."

"You are talking to me, so you *are* having this conversation."

Silence followed for the next thirty minutes. I guessed maybe we *weren't* having this conversation after all. When we pulled into the restaurant parking lot, I could stand it no longer.

"I can't believe you ruined my birthday dinner by refusing to tell me I look ravishing!"

Then I flounced out of the truck, slammed the door hard enough to loosen every tooth in his head, and marched into the steak house. I was pretty sure Scott would follow me, even though my behavior surely wasn't all that ravishing. After all, it was my birthday, and we were meeting my parents, for goodness sake. But did I mention that my husband has a wee stubborn streak?

I walked into the restaurant and glanced back over my shoulder, expecting to see a properly penitent husband trailing just behind. There was a huge empty space instead. So I made up a plausible excuse to tell my parents. I told them that Scott had probably gone to get some gas and would be right back, all the while inwardly hoping that what I said would turn out to be the truth. I kept a sharp eye peeled for him—even praying that he would walk through those swinging doors any minute and bring the standoff to an end. But no sign of my tall husband graced the entry. After about twenty minutes I ran out of excuses. We were into a standoff to rival the one at the O.K. Corral. But no longer up to a shootout, I began to cry into my iced tea.

Not knowing what else to do, Daddy asked me if I would like to dance, and I managed to nod. So I "Waltzed Across Texas" in my father's arms while the tears poured down my cheeks over the fact that my birthday dinner had been ruined, that my husband was behaving like a stubborn mule sitting out in the parking lot, and, most of all, that I was not ravishing tonight.

Finally, I told my parents that Scott and I had had a little tiff on the way to the restaurant. They both managed to feign surprise and registered the appropriate sympathy for me. Then I told them that if they would excuse me I had to go out to the parking lot to apologize to my hardheaded, insensitive husband.

I found Scott sitting in the truck, his hard head resting against the steering wheel. As soon as I opened the door, Scott took a good look at my tearstained face. "Becky," he said grimly, "what time of the month is it?"

How *like* a man—so totally irrational!

"It's my birthday. That's what time of the month it is! Did you know that it is my *birthday?* How can you stand me up on my *birthday?* And in front of my *parents!*"

"Becky, I'm sorry," he said, shaking his head as if to clear it. "I just don't know what to *do* with you. You're like a different person when you hit a certain time of the month. You hate yourself. And you try your best to pick a fight with me. And it works every time! You've got to do something!"

I felt tremendous relief that he wasn't going to leave me stranded there and began to hope that the evening could be salvaged. I even toyed with the remote possibility he might be a tiny bit right.

"Well," I said, sniffing and trying to smile, "I'll make you a deal. I'll see a doctor soon if you'll come inside and do the Cotton-Eyed Joe with me."

When we walked inside the restaurant to our table arm in arm, Mother shook her head and grinned.

"You know, you two are a lot of trouble—but you're never more trouble than you're worth. Let's eat!"

We made it through the evening—and even managed to have a good time. Once as I waltzed in my husband's arms, he stopped and whispered in my ear something that I desperately needed to hear.

"Miss Becky, you look ravishing tonight."

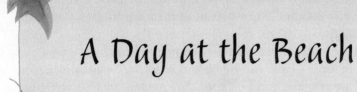

A Day at the Beach

Chonda Pierce

There's nothing like a late-night telephone call from the local police department to shake up your day.

My best friend, Alison, owns a place near Charleston, South Carolina, just off the coast. For the last several years I've gone there for at least a week to do nothing but eat, sleep, shop, and shop. For me, it's a place to park my brain and to replace all the city air in my lungs with ocean air.

But this particular year, late at night, while Alison and I were in a heated battle of Rummikub (only the greatest board game ever invented), the phone rang. Alison's son, Justin, answered. After a short moment all the blood drained from his face, and we heard him say, "You'd better talk to my momma." Alison took the phone and held it so we could both hear.

"Sorry to bother you so late tonight, ma'am," the nasal voice said. "My name is Sergeant Lipton, and I'm just making a few routine calls to residents of the community to say we believe we're close to an arrest of Crazy Eddie."

"Crazy Eddie?"

"Yes, ma'am. If you've been listening to the news, you're probably aware of his escape earlier in the day. We've been all over this island with dogs and cops and soldiers and swamp buggies. And now–"

"So he's still loose?" Alison interrupted. Her husband was working two hundred miles away, and my husband, David, wasn't supposed to fly in until the next day. So there we were in a tiny beach house, Alison and me, with three children and a crazy man who had just escaped from prison and had somehow outrun a swamp buggy.

"Well, he's sort of loose," said Sergeant Lipton.

"Sort of loose? How can he be sort of loose?" said Alison.

"Because it's late, and he's probably exhausted after wrestling the gators and—"

"What are you talking about?"

"Well, we had him cornered in a swamp on the island's southeast side, and a gator jumped him and—"

"And what?"

"And he killed the gator and got away."

"He what?"

"But like I said, we're really close to an arrest."

"How can you be so sure?" I hollered into the receiver.

"Because we've cornered him at the Seaside Mall," Sergeant Lipton continued and then paused, as Alison and I wondered what that had to do with anything. "And if I've done my homework right, ma'am," he added, "one good mall—no matter what part of the country it's in—can literally suck the life out of any man, no matter how strong or how crazy he might be."

Something clicked inside my head, and I took the receiver from Alison, who had also turned very pale by now. "David, is that you?" I asked.

Sergeant Lipton—Crazy Eddie . . . David began to cackle on the other end.

"That's *not* funny," I told him. "It's David," I said to Alison, and the blood began to return to her face, faster than was probably healthy.

"I'm going to kill him," she said, not caring how many witnesses overheard.

"Just settle down, Alison," I told her after I'd finished "speaking" with David and hung up the phone. "Besides, he won't be here until tomorrow."

David came in late the next day and couldn't wait to go down to the beach. Alison and I had cooled down a bit, but we still made David carry the cooler, the towels, and all the beach toys for the two-block walk.

"I can't believe you guys fell for that," said David, as he tottered barefoot down the drive, arms full of beach stuff. Alison and I didn't say a word, trying not to encourage him. "I mean, Sergeant Lipton! I made up the name from a tea box right there on the spot."

Hahahahahahahahaha!

Just before we reached the end of the drive I heard Alison say, "You know, you might want to wear some sandals. It's been very hot, and the road might be—"

"Ouch! Ouch!" David whooped as he danced around in a tiny circle. The cooler lid flopped open and closed, all the beach towels slid to the ground, plastic shovels and buckets flew off to the right and left. "Hot! Hot! Hot!" he yelled. On his tiptoes, trying to find a way off the hot pavement, he made a beeline for the skinny grassy island in the median.

Again I heard Alison say, just before he got there, "Watch out for the sandspurs!"

But David had already hopped onto the sandy, grassy patch and, for just a second, seemed to find relief. His peaceful expression didn't last long though, before his face twisted into the most painful expression I'd ever seen. He raised one foot and lowered it and then raised the other, as though he were climbing invisible stairs. Whenever he would lift up a foot, we could see all sorts of sticks and grass and prickly things stuck to the bottom—stuff he couldn't shake off.

Sandspurs!

I'm not sure who started to laugh first. It may have been me, or Alison, or perhaps even the children. All I know is that we were laughing so hard we could barely stand up. I couldn't catch my breath. Tears began to flow down Alison's face. The children were hopping around like David—cackling and laughing. Alison managed to pull her video camera from its bag and start to shoot, but the video is so bouncy it's hard to watch.

David lay on his back on the hot pavement and stuck both feet straight up in the air. The bottoms of them were covered with the prickly, green sandspurs.

Alison finally came to the rescue and made him roll over onto one of the big beach towels. (This is where the video begins to steady somewhat, and we can get a better look at all the sandspurs in the bottoms of his feet.)

That day convinced me that God is still working on me (and Alison), because—after a bit—both of us began to pick off the little prickly things from the bottoms of David's feet and toss the stickers to the side. David just lay there in the middle of the drive, legs raised high and feet swaying back and forth in the breeze that blew in from the ocean (we never made it there that day), repeating, "Ouch, that hurts. Ouch, that hurts."

"Okay, Sergeant Lipton," Alison said. "This will probably hurt a little—but not as much as wrestling gators."

Pluck. Pluck. Pluck.

After several long minutes, we helped David hobble back to the house. We split up the towels and toys between the kids, and Alison and I carried the cooler back home.

Weeks later I finally sorted out what happened. (Before that, every time I'd get close, I'd start to laugh, and that's as far as I could get.) Eventually I could see God's mercy playing out that day. I realized that, no matter how much we'd like to see someone get what's coming to him, there's always a place for compassion—for mercy. No matter how much David had frightened us the night before, it was right for us to help him when he needed us.

Now, I think Alison may still have some sorting out to do. When I asked her what she learned from the experience, she simply said, "That God can use even lowly sandspurs to dole out justice on his people when they stray."

Give it time. I believe she's still a bit upset with Sergeant Lipton.

The Offering

Anonymous

One Sunday a pastor told his congregation that the church needed some extra money and asked the people to prayerfully consider putting a little extra in the offering plate. He said that whoever gave the most would be able to pick out three hymns.

After the offering plates were passed, the pastor glanced down and noticed that someone had placed a $1,000 bill in the offering. He was so excited that he immediately shared his joy with his congregation and said he'd like to personally thank the person who placed the money in the plate.

Rosie, from all the way in the back, shyly raised her hand. The pastor asked her to come to the front. Slowly she made her way to the pastor. He told her how wonderful it was that she gave so much, and in thanksgiving he asked her to pick out three hymns.

Her eyes brightened as she looked over the congregation, pointed to the three most handsome men in the building, and said, "I'll take him and him and him."

Slapstick

Becky Freeman

Just when I think my life is growing dull and I'm running out of material, something seems to fall in my lap from out of nowhere.

It's a laid-back Sunday evening. Or at least it was. The family seemed content, and all of them looked happily occupied. Some were sprawled on the living room couch watching a movie, one was soaking in the bathtub, another was reading a book. So I thought I'd sneak off for a few minutes to work on this manuscript.

Suddenly the body of a large man fell against the door, knocking it open as he collapsed at my feet. I recognized him as my husband. He had contracted into a fetal position, holding both legs against his chest. As I helped him to the couch, he winced—and through his clenched teeth I understood him to say, "You'll never believe what I did."

"Oh? What makes you think I wouldn't believe it, baby?"

I cautiously untied his shoes and helped him out of his jeans. At this point he began to see the humor in the situation. He was laughing and moaning at the same time. I could see a large scratch across one thigh—and whatever it was that had given him the scratch had also torn through his jeans in the process. On the other leg, a large goose egg was already beginning to swell on his right kneecap. It hurt to look at it. I ran into the kitchen for ice and asked Zeke to help me move his dad into the living room, where I gave him a couple of pills for his pain.

Once we were able to assess my husband's wounds and determine that nothing was broken, I asked for details. "So would you like to talk about it now?"

"Well, it's really embarrassing," he said.

I thought of all the dangerous situations my husband had put himself in as he worked on our house every weekend—wiring high-voltage electrical circuits, lifting heavy beams, operating circular saws from lofty perches, and, of course, hanging from the rafters by one hand with a caulk gun in the other. I thought to myself, *Nothing my husband did to injure himself would surprise me.*

I was wrong.

"Come on, Scott," I probed. "I promise I won't yell at you. What did you do this time? Were you trying to move that table saw without asking for help? Did you fall between the beams? Did the truck trailer collapse on you? What?"

He grinned sheepishly. "Remember that metal workbench I moved from the neighbor's house to our backyard today? Let's just say that while I was running around in the dark, I found it."

"Should I ask why you were running outside in the dark?"

"Maybe that wouldn't be such a good idea."

"Come on, I can't stand the suspense. Tell me."

"Well, you know how our septic system has been overloaded with all the rain we've been having? So I thought I'd be frugal and go outside behind a tree in the dark, and—well, you know. I'd just finished two large glasses of iced tea, so I guess I was in a hurry to get to the woods. That's when I ran into the workbench and turned a flip into the night air."

So collapsed was I with laughter that I laid my head on Scott's shoulder and wiped the tears away. He was in the same condition, though every time he laughed it also brought on a moan.

"So, Scott," I gasped, "what you're trying to tell me is that you nearly broke both legs trying to ... "

"Yes. Are you satisfied now?"

"Yes, I am. I really am. Scott?"

"What?"

"Can I use this?"

"What do you mean?"

"Can I write about it?"

"Becky, you're like a vulture circling weakened prey. Every time anybody does anything stupid, there you are, like Lois Lane with her pad and pencil. Am I nothing but *material* to you?" But even as he said it he was laughing, so I felt pretty sure I was close to getting the go-ahead.

"Oh, Scott, you know I love you with all my heart, and I am so sorry you are in pain. But how could you question my motives? Didn't I just give you my very own pain medication a few minutes ago?"

"What pain medication? I thought you gave me some Tylenol."

"Well, we're out of Tylenol. So I gave you some of my Midol PMS multi-symptom relief tablets."

"What??? You gave me girl pills!?"

"See how cranky you are? You needed those pills. You'll feel much better in a few minutes."

"What do those things do?"

"Well, they keep you from fussing at those who love you."

"Is that so? And how?"

"They make you go to sleep and render you incapable of communication."

"Hmmm—well, I *am* feeling kind of drowsy." His eyelids began to droop.

I waited a few more minutes before I spoke again.

"So it's okay with you, honey, after you drift off to sleep and everything, if I go back out to my office and write about this?"

"Um ... what? ... I'm so tired ... whatev ... "

"I'll take that as a yes," I said, and dashed for the computer.

It's now the morning after the "accident." I rolled over in bed about 6:30 A.M. and woke my husband from his peaceful slumber by seductively wrapping my leg around his swollen knee. Honestly—I forgot! Once he stopped shrieking, he managed to get dressed for work. As he hobbled around in his pitiful condition, I asked him, "So, Scott, what are you going to tell the gals at work this morning about how you got your limp?"

"I'll say it was a skiing accident. Or maybe I got sideswiped by a truck. Which story do you think sounds more manly?"

"Well, don't worry," I answered, batting my eyelashes. "Your little secret is safe with me."

"Suuure it is. I'll proofread the chapter tonight."

It is now the *day after* "The Day after the Accident." A few hours ago, as I was putting my makeup on in the bathroom, the body of a large man fell against the bathroom door, knocking it open as he fell to the floor. Guess who? Same song, second verse. He was once again holding his knee and curled up in the fetal position.

"Oh, Scott," I said as I helped him sit up, "what have you done now?"

"Well, it's embarrassing," he moaned, gingerly examining his wound.

"It's broad daylight. Please tell me you weren't looking for a tree—"

"No, no, no. It wasn't that bad. This time I just whacked my leg with a two-by-four."

"Hold on a second. Don't say another word. You hop in the tub and soak your knee while I run to get a pad and pencil."

I was back in a flash.

"OK, Scott. Now tell me again what happened, and don't leave out any details."

"Well, there's not much to tell, really. I was trying to get the porch post aligned, so I picked up a two-by-four and gave the post a few hard whacks—only on one of the backswings I whacked my sore leg."

My husband seems to be stuck in a painful slapstick comedy routine. And here he was, *literally,* slapping himself with a stick. I am truly sorry he's in pain, but you have to admit, he's been entertaining.

Some days it's really a lot of fun to be married.

CHAPTER TWO

Just for Laughs

*No man [or woman] who has once heartily
and wholly laughed can be
altogether irreclaimably bad.*
–Thomas Carlyle

*Laughter is a tranquilizer
with no side effects.*
–Arnold Glasgow

Insurance Claims

Anonymous

The following are actual statements found on insurance forms, where drivers attempted to summarize the details of an accident in the fewest words possible:

- I thought my window was down but found it was up when I put my head through it.
- The other car collided with mine without warning of its intention.
- The guy was all over the road. I had to swerve a number of times before I hit him.
- I pulled away from the side of the road, glanced at my mother-in-law, and headed over the embankment.
- In my attempt to kill a fly, I drove into a telephone pole.
- I had been driving for forty years when I fell asleep at the wheel and had an accident.
- I was on my way to the doctor with rear-end trouble when my universal joint gave way, causing me to have an accident.
- The pedestrian had no idea which direction to run, so I ran over him.
- The indirect cause of the accident was a little guy in a small car with a big mouth.

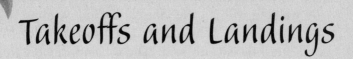

Takeoffs and Landings

Anonymous

*O*ccasionally, airline attendants endeavor to make the "in-flight safety lecture" a bit more entertaining. Here are some real examples that have been heard or reported:

- "There may be fifty ways to leave your lover, but there are only four ways out of this airplane."
- "Your seat cushions can be used for flotation, and in the event of an emergency water landing, please take them with our compliments."
- "Smoking in the lavatories is prohibited. Any person caught smoking in the lavatories will be asked to leave the plane immediately."
- This is an actual joke heard on Southwest Airlines just after a very hard landing in Salt Lake City, Utah—one of the most bone jarring ever experienced. The flight attendant came on the intercom and said, "That was quite a bump, and I know what y'all are thinking. I'm here to tell you it wasn't the airline's fault, it wasn't the pilot's fault, it wasn't the flight attendant's fault—it was the asphalt!"
- An airline pilot wrote that on this particular flight he had hammered his ship into the runway really hard. The airline had a policy that required the first officer to stand at the door as the passengers exited and to give a smile and a "thanks for flying XYZ Airline." He said that, in light of his bad landing, he had a hard time looking the passengers in

the eye, thinking that someone would have a smart comment. Finally everyone had gotten off except for a little old lady walking with a cane. She said, "Sonny, mind if I ask you a question?" "Why, no, ma'am," said the pilot. "What is it?" The little old lady said, "Did we land, or were we shot down?"

Courtroom Follies

Anonymous

The following were recorded on transcripts from actual courtrooms:

Q: What is your date of birth?
A: July fifteenth.
Q: What year?
A: Every year.

Q: What gear were you in at the moment of the impact?
A: Gucci sweats and Reeboks.

Q: All your responses must be oral, OK? What school did you go to?
A: Oral.

Q: How old is your son—the one living with you?
A: Thirty-eight or thirty-five, I can't remember which.
Q: How long has he lived with you?
A: Forty-five years.
Q: What was the first thing your husband said to you when he woke that morning?
A: He said, "Where am I, Cathy?"
Q: And why did that upset you?
A: My name is Susan.

Q: Sir, what is your IQ?
A: Well, I can see pretty well, I think.

Q: Did you blow your horn or anything?
A: After the accident?
Q: Before the accident.
A: Sure, I played horn for ten years. I even went to school for it.

Q: Do you know if your daughter has ever been involved in the voodoo occult?
A: We both do.
Q: Voodoo?
A: We do.
Q: You do?
A: Yes, voodoo.

Q: Now, Doctor, isn't it true that when a person dies in his sleep, he doesn't know about it until the next morning?

Q: The youngest son, the twenty-year-old, how old is he?

Q: Were you present when your picture was taken?

Q: Was it you or your younger brother who was killed in the war?

Q: Did he kill you?

Q: How far apart were the vehicles at the time of the collision?

Q: You were there until the time you left, is that true?

Q: How many times have you committed suicide?

Q: So the date of conception [of the baby] was August 8th?
A: Yes.
Q: And what were you doing at that time?

Q: She had three children, right?
A: Yes.
Q: How many were boys?
A: None.
Q: Were there any girls?

Q: You say the stairs went down to the basement?
A: Yes.
Q: And these stairs—do they go up also?

Q: Mr. Slatery, you went on a rather elaborate honeymoon, didn't you?
A: I went to Europe, sir.
Q: And you took your new wife?

Q: How was your first marriage terminated?
A: By death.
Q: And by whose death was it terminated?

Q: Can you describe the individual?
A: He was about medium height and had a beard.
Q: Was this a male or a female?

Q: Is your appearance here this morning pursuant to a deposition notice which I sent to your attorney?
A: No, this is how I dress when I go to work.

Q: Doctor, how many autopsies have you performed on dead people?
A: All my autopsies are performed on dead people.
Q: Do you recall the time you examined the body?
A: The autopsy started around 8:30 P.M.
Q: And Mr. Demmington was dead at the time?
A: No, he was sitting on the table wondering why I was doing an autopsy.

They Said It in the Church Bulletin

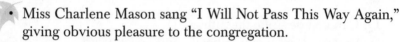

Anonymous

- Miss Charlene Mason sang "I Will Not Pass This Way Again," giving obvious pleasure to the congregation.
- Bertha Belch, a missionary from Africa, will be speaking tonight at Calvary Memorial Church in Racine. Come tonight and hear Bertha Belch all the way from Africa.
- Members of the outreach committee will make calls on people who are not afflicted with any church.
- Evening massage–6:00 P.M.
- The audience is asked to remain seated until the end of the recession.
- Low Self-Esteem Support Group will meet Thursday from 7:00 to 8:30 P.M. Please use the back door.
- FASTING CONFERENCE. The cost for attending the Fasting and Prayer conference includes meals.
- Our youth basketball team is back in action–Wednesday at 8:00 P.M. in the recreation hall. Come out and watch us kill Christ the King.
- Ladies, don't forget the rummage sale. It's a chance to get rid of those things not worth keeping around the house. Don't forget your husbands.
- The peacemaking meeting scheduled for today has been canceled due to a conflict.
- Barbara remains in the hospital and needs blood donors for more transfusions. She is also having trouble sleeping and requests tapes of Pastor Jack's sermons.

- A songfest was hell at the Methodist church Wednesday.
- Thursday night Potluck Supper. Prayer and medication to follow.
- The rosebud on the altar this morning is to announce the birth of David, the sin of Rev. and Mrs. Adams.
- Weight Watchers will meet at 7:00 P.M. at First Presbyterian Church. Please use large double door at the side entrance.
- Don't let worry kill you, let the church help.
- For those of you who have children and don't know it, we have a nursery downstairs.
- This being Easter Sunday, we will ask Mrs. Lewis to come forward and lay an egg on the altar.

Strictly Classified

Anonymous

The following entries come from classified ads in newspapers:

- Free Yorkshire Terrier. 8 years old. Hateful little dog.
- Free puppies: 1/2 Cocker Spaniel, 1/2 sneaky neighbor's dog.
- Found: Dirty white dog. Looks like a rat ... been out awhile ... better be reward.
- Snow blower for sale ... only used on snowy days.
- Tickle Me Elmo, still in box, comes with its own 1988 Mustang, 5L, auto excellent condition $6800.
- Full-sized mattress. 20 Yr. warranty. Like new. Slight urine smell.
- Nordic Track $300, hardly used, call Chubby.
- Bill's Septic Cleaning ... "We haul American-made products."
- Georgia peaches, California grown–89 cents lb.
- Nice parachute: Never opened–used once.
- Tired of working for only $9.75 per hour? We offer profit sharing and flexible hours. Starting pay: $7–$9 per hour.
- Exercise equipment: Queen size mattress and box springs–$175.
- Our sofa will seat the whole mob. 100% Italian leather.
- Joining nudist colony! Selling washer & dryer $300.
- Open house. Body shapers toning salon. Free coffee and donuts.
- For sale by owner: Complete set of Encyclopedia Britannica. 45 volumes. Excellent condition. $1,000 negotiable. No longer needed. Recently married; wife knows everything.

CHAPTER THREE

Born to Laugh:
Of Humor
and Kids

When I grow up, I want to be a little boy.
—Joseph Heller

*When I was a kid
my parents moved a lot,
but I always found them.*
—Rodney Dangerfield

Kids:
The Original Workout

Chonda Pierce

People go to a lot of trouble to work out. Some will ride a bike for thirty minutes, climb steps for fifteen minutes, and run for another twenty. These are the people who can burn off enough calories to offset a dozen donuts, a lemon-filled éclair, and *three* bites of Death by Chocolate (using a tablespoon). These are people with no life.

And it doesn't matter how terrible they look, either. When they walk out of the gym all sweaty, sticky, messy, and oftentimes smelly, people will actually stop them to say, "Oh, you look wonderful!"—just because they know they've been working out.

My girlfriend Angela and I got a good workout just the other day. She called me at 7:00 A.M. and asked, "Are you dressed?"

"Blue spandex with a fuchsia oversized sweatshirt," I answered.

"Oh, that color has always looked so good on you," she said.

"Thanks. How about you?"

"Well, I just bought one of those jogging outfits, the kind made from that slick parachute material."

"What color? Purple, I hope."

"Purple."

I squealed. "I bet you look *soooo* cute."

"So, you're ready?" I asked.

"Yeah, come on over."

My kids were already at school, so I hopped in my van and headed over to Angela's.

When I arrived, I found she had started without me. She was lugging a car seat about the size of a small recliner out the front door. "I've got this, if you want to help Brittany," she called with a grunt. Brittany is her six-year-old daughter. (Angela's purple outfit did look great, and I told her so.)

Brittany still had her "sleepy" hair, so I grabbed a brush and pushed and pulled the bristles through the tangles. Then I twisted a rubber band around bunches of hair to make pigtails. "Looks good," I announced. "Now go brush your teeth."

Just then her three-year-old brother, Austin, dashed past me in his stocking feet. Angela was close behind, wagging one shoe at him as she ran. I found the other shoe in the living room, picked it up, and fell in behind Angela, who was behind Austin, who was heading up the stairs. Angela took two steps at a time until she reached the very top, where she crawled the last few. I paced myself, feeling the stretch and strain of each hamstring. I caught up with her at the top, where we both collapsed to catch our breath.

"Did you see which way he went?" she asked.

I looked down the hall in both directions and shook my head. "You go that way, I'll go this way. If he makes a move for the steps, yell and I'll head him off."

"Good plan."

We headed off in separate directions, both crawling for stealth—and because neither of us was ready to stand up just yet. I felt my lower abdominal muscles tighten with every baby crawl I took. Angela caught up with Austin at the foot of his Winnie the Pooh bed. Together we wrestled his shoes on him. Once we tied the laces, I stood and massaged my upper arms. That was tough.

"Okay," Angela announced, brushing her hair out of her face and fixing it back into the purple tie that matched her warm-up suit. "Is everyone ready to get in the van?" Austin took off like a shot, and we gave chase again. Down the stairs we went, my calves screaming out with every step.

Angela did five laps around the kitchen island before I took the baton and did four more. Then Austin swerved into the living room, and Angela swooped him up—just like we had planned. "Gotcha!" she said.

"I'll get the door," I panted.

"Meet you at the van," she said to me, holding Austin around his chest, his two feet squirming in all directions. Angela was holding on tight, biting her lip, reaching back for a little extra something I'm sure she never knew she even possessed, her face turning a shade that came close to matching that of her suit.

She plopped Austin into his car seat, and together we tugged and pulled and cinched harnesses, braces, and straps. Brittany was so much easier—just pull and click the grown-up seat belt. But her backpack weighed almost as much as Austin. I carried it from her upstairs bedroom and passed it off to Angela, who lugged it down the back steps and rolled it into the van with a giant "Umph!"

We both stood there for a few moments, catching our breath and studying our handiwork. With the sleeve of my new shirt, I dabbed at the beads of perspiration on my forehead while Angela adjusted her hair. "Ready to roll?" she asked me.

"Ready," I said. "You drive."

The drive through the neighborhood wasn't too bad, a few turns here and there, a few stop signs. But once we entered the main highway, the story was different. Still, Angela handled the traffic like the seasoned mom she is. She worked the turn signal, pumped the brakes, and mashed the gas pedal. I noticed that whenever she gripped the wheel, like during a lane change, her knuckles would turn white. Then, at a stop sign or traffic light, they would flush back red as she loosened her grip.

We went to Brittany's school first. I hopped out, yanked open the van's side door, and unfastened Brittany, who skipped along the sidewalk and into the building. I squat-lifted her backpack and waddled in behind her.

When I got back to the van, Angela already had swapped seats with me. She was flexing both hands to rub away the tingles and bring back the circulation. "Your turn," she said to me with a smile.

I started out slow and easy, but then the right turn signal went out. "Got a burnout on the right!" I called over to Angela. She nodded and rolled down her window. I did the same. When we reached Austin's day care, which happened to be on the right, I stuck out my left arm and pointed back over the van. And—just in case whoever was behind me didn't understand what I was doing—I began to pump my arm up and down, like one of those lighted signs where the arrow seems to be moving across the side of a building. I looked over and saw Angela hanging out the passenger window, stabbing a finger into the air in the direction of Austin's school. I'm sure we appeared very effective to those behind us—fuchsia and purple arms flashing out from each side.

We made the turn safely and unbound Austin, taking turns carrying him to his classroom because he didn't want to walk. When we left the day care, Angela drove us to the mall. We walked past the fitness center, where a lot of people were dressed just like us. We found a place in the food court that sold chocolate donuts and coffee and snacked until the stores opened.

Later we went shopping for more workout clothes. I bought a chartreuse top with black piping and some spandex pants to match. (Angela said I looked like a frog, but I was also thinking about the burned-out turn signal in her van and how important it can be to be visible.) Angela bought this adorable bright-yellow fleece sweatshirt for 60 percent off. She looked like a canary, but it would help with the turning also. On our way out, we passed someone we recognized from church.

"Hello," our friend said. She was dressed in an Ann Taylor business suit and really could have tucked her shirttail in. (She looked a bit slouchy.)

"Hi," we both said, clutching our new purchases. My collar was still damp with sweat, and my muscles still ached from Brittany's backpack, so I walked with a slight hitch. Angela's hair had come out of the purple tie, and she was trying to push it out of her face.

Our friend looked at us, then glanced up at the fitness center sign behind us. As if she had it all figured out, she smiled and said, "You girls are looking just wonderful!" I wished I could have said the same about her. But it goes to show, you can get away with a lot of disasters if you wear a sweat suit.

Pearls of Wisdom

Assorted Kids

Never trust a dog to watch your food."

Patrick, age 10

"When your mom is mad at your dad, don't let her brush your hair."

Taylia, age 11

"A puppy always has bad breath—even after eating a Tic-Tac."

Andrew, age 9

"Never hold a dustbuster and a cat at the same time."

Kyoyo, age 11

"If you want a kitten, start out by asking for a horse."

Naomi, age 15

"Felt-tip markers are not good to use as lipstick."

Lauren, age 9

"When you get a bad grade in school, show it to your mom when she's on the phone."

Alyesha, age 13

"When you want something expensive, ask your grandparents."

Matthew, age 12

"Never smart off to a teacher whose eyes and ears are twitching."

Andrew, age 9

"Wear a hat when feeding seagulls."

Rocky, age 9

"Never flush the john when your dad's in the shower."

Lamar, age 10

"Forget the cake, go for the icing."

Cynthia, age 8

Masterpiece

Anonymous

A kindergarten teacher was observing her classroom of children as they drew. She would occasionally walk around to see each child's artwork.

As she got to one little girl who was working diligently, she asked what the drawing was.

The girl replied, "I'm drawing God."

The teacher paused and said, "But no one knows what God looks like."

Without missing a beat or looking up from her drawing, the girl replied, "They will in a minute."

God Is Watching

Anonymous

Up at the head table in the cafeteria, one of the nuns had placed a big bowl of bright-red, fresh, juicy apples. Beside the bowl she placed a note that read, "Take only one. Remember, God is watching."

At the other end of the table was a bowl full of freshly baked chocolate chip cookies, still warm from the oven. Beside the bowl there was a little note, scrawled in a child's handwriting, which read, "Take all you want. God's watching the apples."

Ultimate Sacrifice

Anonymous

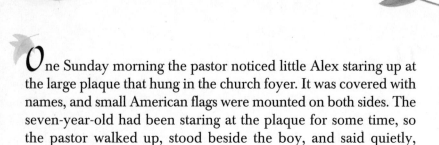

One Sunday morning the pastor noticed little Alex staring up at the large plaque that hung in the church foyer. It was covered with names, and small American flags were mounted on both sides. The seven-year-old had been staring at the plaque for some time, so the pastor walked up, stood beside the boy, and said quietly, "Good morning, Alex."

"Good morning, Pastor," replied the young man, still focused on the plaque. "Pastor McGhee, what is this?" Alex asked.

"Well, son, it's a memorial to all the men and women who have died in the service." Soberly, Alex and the pastor stood together, staring at the large plaque.

Little Alex's voice was barely audible as he turned to the pastor and asked, "Which one—the 9:00 or the 10:30 service?"

Dear God

Assorted Kids

Dear God,

Maybe Cain and Abel would not kill each other so much if they had their own rooms. It works with my brother.

Larry

Dear God,

I read the Bible. What does "begat" mean? Nobody will tell me.

Love, Allison

Dear God,

Did you mean for the giraffe to look like that, or was it an accident?

Love, Norma

Dear God,

Who draws the lines around the countries?

Nan

Dear God,

Instead of letting people die and having to make new ones, why don't you just keep the ones you have?

Timmy

Dear God,

Thank you for the baby brother, but what I prayed for was a puppy.

Love, Joyce

Dear God,
     If we come back as something, please don't let me be Jennifer Horton, because I hate her.
                                                    Denise

Dear God,
     We read Thomas Edison made light. But in Sunday school they said you did it. So I bet he stole your idea.
                                                    Sincerely, Donna

Dear God,
     I didn't think orange went with purple until I saw the sunset you made on Tuesday. That was cool.
                                                    Love, Sam

"Bet I Can!"

Marilyn Meberg

Sometimes I think about the "least likely" humans I have known, those who seemed incapable of letting a smile, giggle, or laugh escape from their frozen lips.

Eighty-year-old Mrs. Davidson falls into the frozen-lip category. Yet, as a child I found her fascinating. A good part of my fascination was undoubtedly that she would occasionally shout out disagreements during my father's preaching. I, on the other hand, wasn't even allowed to interrupt during second-grade reading group, much less during Dad's sermons. I was tremendously envious of all she got away with.

Since she lived within walking distance of our parsonage, I loved dropping in on her. She never seemed particularly glad to see me; instead she appeared indifferent to my visits.

One night at supper my parents quizzed me about why I liked visiting Mrs. Davidson. I think they were concerned that she might find me a nuisance or that she might hurt my feelings. I told my parents I liked her animals and loved the smell of her few bales of alfalfa, but more than that, I wanted to make her laugh. Both parents put down their forks and looked kindly at me.

"Honey," my father said, "I've never even seen Mrs. Davidson smile, much less laugh."

One of the things we did as a small family of three was make various bets. Dad always was betting my mother about some academic subject he was sure he was right about, only to find out he was totally wrong. That never seemed to squelch his enthusiasm, however, and the bets continued as long as they lived.

Thinking I might get in on the betting game, I said to my parents, "I'll bet I can get Mrs. Davidson to laugh before I'm in the third grade!" Rising to the challenge, they agreed and said they hoped I would win the bet. Mom asked what kind of payoff I wanted.

"French toast for breakfast every Saturday morning for six weeks," I said without hesitation.

For at least a month I tried every conceivable thing I could think of to make Mrs. Davidson laugh. I told her jokes; I told her all the bad things Lester Courtney did in school; I even did acrobatics for her. No response.

Then one day, as I was heading up the path toward her messy property, I was attempting to perfect my imitation of how Mr. Brownell walked. Mr. Brownell had caught his leg in a threshing machine at some point in his life, and the accident resulted in the most memorable walk I'd ever seen. Whenever his weight landed on his bad leg, his whole body would veer dangerously out of balance. But somehow the flapping of his arms caused him to catapult in the opposite direction until everything appeared to be back in order. His head moved in perfect rhythm to all this disjointedness. It was quite a feat.

I had been working on this imitation for some time—purely for my own sense of accomplishment. My efforts were interrupted by the sound of what could only be likened to a donkey's braying. It grew louder and louder until finally I located where the noise was coming from. Mrs. Davidson was leaning against the side of her chicken house—laughing. She laughed so long, so loud, and so hard it made me a little nervous. It seemed to me that making that much noise could kill a person.

"Well, Mr. Brownell," she finally gasped, "how nice of you to visit me," and then she went into another braying episode.

When I triumphantly announced to my parents that I had won the bet, they were concerned that the laughter had come at the expense of another's misfortune. I explained that I had been working on the walk for weeks but never intended it to be used for Mrs. Davidson. In fact, I further explained, I had no idea she was watching me until I heard her laugh. Apparently convinced that my heart was not cruel, I was rewarded with French toast every Saturday for six weeks.

"Yes, Ma'am!"

Sheila Walsh

My son, Christian, and I often revisit a familiar discussion on manners. He does well for a four-year-old boy, but he seems to have the Walsh trait of brain leakage, and occasionally all my reminders slip out.

We were flying to Dallas, Texas, and the flight attendant asked Christian if he would like to have wings to pin on his ball cap.

"Yes, I would!" he replied enthusiastically.

"Yes, ma'am," I reminded him.

"Yes, ma'am," he mimicked, looking at me as though I might be ruining his chances of having a meaningful relationship with this darling blond flight attendant.

Later that night he sat on my lap while we sang our favorite nighttime songs. When we were finished, I asked him if he remembered our discussion on the plane.

"Yes, ma'am," he replied with a grin.

"I know you think I make a fuss about things like that, Christian, but it's important to show respect for your elders."

He looked at me and laughed. He waited for me to join in. I didn't.

"Mommy, that was funny," he said, a little confused.

"Why was that funny?" I asked sternly.

"How can I show respect for my elbows?"

How often do we do that with the Lord? He says, "Trust"; we hear, "Try." He says, "Rest"; we hear, "Strive." He says, "I love you just the way you are"; we hear, "I love you, but I'd love you a bit more if you'd change a few of your bad habits."

Thank you, Father, that you're willing to keep talking to me, even when I don't get it! Amen.

Dig deep into the Word of God. All the right words are in there!

Kids Say the Craziest Things

Assorted Kids and Adults

I had been teaching my three-year-old daughter, Caitlin, the Lord's Prayer. For several evenings at bedtime, she would repeat after me the lines of the prayer. Finally, she decided to go solo. I listened with pride as she carefully enunciated each word, right up to the end of the prayer: "Lead us not into temptation," she prayed, "but deliver us some e-mail. Amen."

And one particular four-year-old prayed, "And forgive us our trash baskets as we forgive those who put trash in our baskets."

A little boy was overheard praying: "Lord, if you can't make me a better boy, don't worry about it. I'm having a real good time like I am."

A Sunday school teacher asked her little children, as they were on the way to the church service, "And why is it necessary to be quiet in church?" One bright little girl replied, "Because people are sleeping."

The preacher was wired for sound with a lapel mike, and as he preached, he moved briskly about the platform, jerking the mike cord as he went. Then he moved to one side, getting wound up in the cord and nearly tripping before jerking it again. After several circles and jerks, a little girl in the third pew leaned toward her mother and whispered, "If he gets loose, will he hurt us?"

A woman invited some people to dinner. At the table, she turned to her six-year-old daughter and said, "Would you like to say the blessing?" "I wouldn't know what to say," the girl replied. "Just say

65

what you hear Mommy say," the wife answered. The daughter bowed her head and said, "Lord, why on earth did I invite all these people to dinner?"

My four-year-old son, Kyle, was unsuccessfully trying to open a bottle of children's vitamins. After watching several vain attempts, I explained, "It's made so only mommies and daddies can open it." After tiring of his struggle, Kyle relinquished the bottle. As I easily opened it for him, Kyle stared in amazement and asked in a breathless voice, "How does it know you're a mommy?"

Angela Mitchell, Kansas

My eight-year-old daughter, Candace, loves to spend time at her grandma's house. But I wondered if she spent too much time there when recently she sat down and started fanning herself, saying, "Whew! I'm having a hot flash. I hate hot flashes!"

Rebecca Stuhlmiller, Washington

When her dog and a pet goat died, my five-year-old stepniece, Whitney, was told that the animals were now in heaven. All was well for a few weeks—until Whitney and her mother, Ella, went for a walk. Ella explained that God made the flowers, the trees, and the bugs. "Where's God?" Whitney asked. "In heaven," her mother replied. Whitney moaned sympathetically. "What happened to him?"

Robin Martinez, New Mexico

I was at the beach with my four-year-old son, Pauly, when we discovered a dead seagull lying in the sand. "Mommy, what happened to him?" Pauly asked. "He died and went to heaven," I told him. Pauly thought for a moment, then said, "Did God throw him back down?"

Mary L. Shaw, Florida

My son, Zachary—age four—came screaming out of the bathroom to tell me he'd dropped his toothbrush in the toilet. So I fished it out and threw it in the garbage. Zachary stood there thinking for a moment and then ran to my bathroom and came out with my toothbrush. He held it up and said with a charming little smile, "We better throw this one out, too, 'cause it fell in the toilet a few days ago."

Jacqueline Bay, British Columbia

66

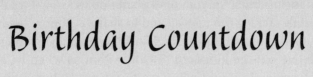

Birthday Countdown

Barbara Johnson

Andy was miffed when he didn't get the part he wanted in the Christmas pageant. He had hoped for the role of Joseph but got stuck being the innkeeper. So Andy decided to pull a fast one and get even with Joseph when he came with Mary, looking for a place to stay.

"Come right in, folks," innkeeper Andy told them. "I've got plenty of room."

Perplexed, Mary looked at the startled Joseph, who quickly rose to the occasion.

"Hey, this place is a real dump," he said, poking his head inside. "I'd rather go out and sleep in the stable."

Whatever happened to the wit and wisdom that served us so well as kids? Why can't we employ them when middle age baffles us? Experts say innate creativity begins to disappear at about the age of eleven because we stop using it. We become progressively less curious and spontaneous.

Youth is not a time of life but a state of mind. It boldly takes risks, seeks adventure, hopes for the best, and displays courage. You are as young as your faith is strong.

The actor Jimmy Stewart stayed young until the day he died at the age of eighty-nine. Although extraordinarily talented, he remained genuinely touched by the fact that he was a celebrity.

One time a stranger put his hand out and said, "Mr. Stewart, I don't guess it means much to you, but I want you to know I think you're wonderful." Taking the man's hand to shake it, Jimmy held on to it tightly, looked him in the eye, and said, "It means everything to me."

We live out the kingdom of God within us when we treasure each other like that and when we find ways to turn unfortunate things around. Laughter is one of those ways. Laughter stirs the blood, expands the chest, electrifies the nerves, and clears the cobwebs from the brain. If you laugh a lot, when you are older all your wrinkles will be in the right places!

If you live to be one hundred, your heart will beat 3,681,619,200 times, pumping 27,323,260 gallons of blood weighing over one hundred tons. (If you end up tired, you've earned it!) Think about making every heartbeat a happy one.

Actually, I think living to be one hundred would be great, but living to fifty twice would be so much better. The way to do it is to get one year younger each year after your fiftieth birthday. So on your fifty-first birthday you turn forty-nine, at sixty you are forty, and so on. I'm not saying lie about your age; actually grow younger every year!

The first rule for this (you'll start looking younger, too) is to scatter joy to everyone you meet. There is no more effective beauty secret. The second rule is to exercise regularly—and the best heart workout is reaching down and lifting someone else up. The third and last rule is to guard your enthusiasm—in fact, let every experience in life multiply it.

You can't turn back the clock, of course, but you can wind it up again. As a recycled teenager, insanity may be your best means of relaxation. The secret to growing younger is counting blessings, not birthdays. Don't grow up; grow down. You'll know you're getting the idea when you begin buying cereal for the toy, not for the fiber.

If you keep it up long enough, sooner or later you'll grow down from teenager to toddler. Uh-oh, there is one thing about being a two-year-old that could take all the fun out of getting younger. Beware the toddlers' creed: *If I want it, it's mine. If it looks like mine, it is mine. If I take it away from you, it's mine. If I had it a little while ago, it's mine. If I give it to you and change my mind, it's mine.* No wisdom there; this breaks every rule of growing down. Skip this stuff, then hop and jump to infancy—that blissful time when you have no more responsibility than to eat and sleep and bask in the love of your family. No one will blame you for an occasional wakeful night or fussy afternoon. Dependent on others, enjoy the minutes as they fall through the hours—on your way to eternity.

CHAPTER FOUR

For Wives and Moms Only

When you get to the end of your rope,
tie a knot and hang on.
—Franklin Delano Roosevelt

Out of all the things I've lost in life,
I think I miss my mind the most.
—Anonymous

You'll Never Have to Dust Again

Chonda Pierce

I don't know why I said yes to the fellow—maybe because never having to dust again sounded so . . . romantic!

"You mean, not even a little?" I asked him on the telephone.

"If you get this thing set up right," he answered, "use it frequently—like every day—then you can take all your old dust rags and throw them away. And then there are the health benefits for your children."

"For the children?"

"Yes, ma'am. Helps them to breathe easier."

"Really?" Anything to help my children breathe easier must be a good thing.

"Oh, yeah."

"Well, then," I said, "I guess we need to talk."

"How about tomorrow night?" he asked. "I'll have someone in your neighborhood who will be glad to demonstrate our machine for you."

That sounded perfect, and so the next night I warned David—before he had a chance to take off his work boots and walk around in his stained socks, or loosen his belt or something like that—that we had company coming.

Soon a man showed up at the front door, carrying a big black notebook under one arm and dragging R2-D2 at his side.

"Come right in," I said.

"My name's Chuck." He let go of the little robot to shake our hands. We led him into the living room, and he wheeled his contraption right along with him. "So you hate to dust?"

"It's no big deal, really," David said.

"Hate it with a passion," I interjected.

"Then you're going to love this." Chuck took a seat on our sofa and plopped the big notebook down on the coffee table in front of him. "Oh, would it be possible to get a drink of water?"

I left and returned with a glass of water to find Chuck and David bent over the robot, examining and punching buttons.

"It's a vacuum cleaner!" David said, looking up and smiling. "Chuck says this thing will pick up a bowling ball!"

"Why would you want to pick up a bowling ball?" I asked.

"If it can pick up a bowling ball," explained Chuck, "imagine what it can do with a speck of dust."

David whistled at that overwhelming notion.

"Here's your water," I said, handing over the glass. "Now tell me about the no-dusting part again."

Chuck took the glass and turned it upside down so that water and ice plopped right on the carpet in the middle of the living room floor. "Oops," he said, but he didn't seem too upset about his mess. "Good thing I've got the model 500 series A with me." He plugged his contraption into the wall, pulled out a coiled hose, telescoped out a silver wand, flipped on a toggle switch, and with a whine and a blare, the squatty little machine came to life. Chuck aimed the nozzle at the puddle on the carpet. The ice rattled as it got sucked up the silver wand, and in two seconds the spot was clean and nearly dry.

"Wow!" David said, as the whine of the machine died down.

"Kind of loud, isn't it?" I said.

"I'll bet you can pick up nuts and bolts with that thing," said David.

Chuck nodded.

"And wood chips!"

Chuck nodded again.

"And—"

"What about the dust?" I interrupted before we wound up back at the bowling ball. "And the easier breathing for the children?"

Chuck's face brightened. "Ah, yes, the dust and the breathing. Let me explain that, but first, let me show you some pictures." He turned the black notebook so David and I could see it easily and then began to flip through some laminated pages. He turned until he came to a big color photo of a space alien with giant, toothy chompers and long, hairy legs, and an antlike body with big, bulging eyeballs. I pulled back in disgust.

"Scary, isn't it?"

My hand was over my mouth, and I was afraid I wouldn't be able to speak, so I just nodded.

"Caught a big bass once with something that looked like that." David leaned in to get a good look at the picture.

"This," began Chuck, tapping the alien in his notebook, "is a dust mite. The picture's been blown up about a hundred times because the real mite is only the size of a dust speck." Chuck paused to allow us to soak in the dust-sized alien.

"Ma'am, how many children do you have?" he asked me.

I found my voice and eked out a weak, "Two."

Chuck dropped his head, rubbed the back of his neck, moved his hand up to his forehead, rubbed his eyes, and finally landed at his chin before saying in a most somber voice, "Then you need to hear this."

"Hear what?" David said.

"That these dust mites," he thumped the big, glossy photo on the table, "could be everywhere in this house. Even in the beds where your children sleep—heaven forbid."

"How can we get rid of them?" I asked.

"How can we zap 'em?" David slapped a fist into an open palm.

Chuck walked over to his machine and unfastened the hose. "Just leave this off, pour water into this opening until it's full, and press the start button." He pressed the button again, and the thing whirred to life for the second time that evening. For a couple of minutes, a thunderous roar filled the room. He finally punched it off. "If you do that on a regular basis, no more dust, no more dust mites. And your children can breathe easier and rest peacefully."

"Not while it's running." David massaged his eardrums.

"And how long should I let this thing run?" I asked.

"About an hour," he said.

"An hour!? And how often?"

"Every day."

"Just don't leave any bowling balls out, right?" David said, but Chuck ignored him.

"And how much does something like this cost?" David asked.

Chuck pointed at the picture of the dust mite on my coffee table and said, "To rid your home and your children's beds of these ... these ungodly creatures—sixteen hundred dollars."

David's eyes grew as large as the dust mite's enlarged one hundred times. "We didn't pay that much for our car."

Chuck broke all the numbers down for us. He even told us how many dust mites could fit on the head of a pin and explained that, with one push of a button, we could wipe out thousands, maybe even millions, of the little buggers. When it became clear to David how we actually were paying less than a penny per mite, the deal wasn't such a bad one after all.

And me? Well, I wheeled that little robot man all over the house and sucked up pillows and curtains and Legos and little green army men—and got real close to the cat once. For a while, I would turn on the machine every day and leave it in the middle of the room to roar and whine for at least an hour, sucking up the evil dust mites.

Twelve years later, we still have that old machine—and it's paid for now. I don't know how many dust mites were conquered with it over the years. Probably not many, because the thing was too stinking loud to live with. Sometimes David would hop about on the carpet and then announce to me that he had squashed enough for today, just so I wouldn't turn on the machine. Other times he and the children would hop around and have big dust mite–squashing parties. I would always make refreshments.

Sometimes our good intentions can drown out what's really important to a family. David and I wanted so badly to wage war against all the dust mites of the world. But what God reminded me of—and in the roar of a vacuum cleaner, no less—was that there are more important things we can do for our children, such as teach them the truths of God. And that's hard to do with something as loud as a 747 roaring in the living room every day.

Our battle against dust mites goes on. Today, when we sit down on a sofa for family time, we like to think we squashed a few for the cause. But what we have to pass on to our children doesn't have anything to do with a vacuum cleaner.

So if you're interested in a vacuum that can pick up bowling balls, it'll be at our next yard sale—financing available.

What Part of "Ten Items or Less" Don't You Understand?

Chonda Pierce

The young woman's hand seemed to move in slow motion. All I could do was stand—frozen—and watch as she reached higher and higher, until her fingers twisted around a cotton string that was attached to a beaded chain that was attached to a light switch. With a quick yank on the string, the plastic number three began to blink. Then, still in slow motion, she lifted a black phone from its cradle and spoke into its mouthpiece. Her tired voice rang throughout the store: "Price check on aisle three, please. Price check on aisle three." It looked like another long day at Stal-Mart.

And I was next in line, too! I thought I had picked a good line. The woman in front of me had only two items—but one of those turned out to be a turtleneck sweater with no price tag. After the cashier made her announcement, she stepped away from the register, folded her arms, and leaned against the wall of her little cubicle, getting comfortable. Now, this was not the first price check I'd lived through—housewares, electronics, kids' wear, I'd had lots of experience. But women's wear was big trouble.

I know women who will pick up a blouse and fall in love with it. But as the day goes on, usually somewhere in the automotive section, the love affair ends, and the blouse is left hanging from a spark-plug display. "It's okay," the woman says. "It gives the workers something to do." And I'm convinced that part of the workers' job is to remove the price tag before they find its real home.

By the time that blouse can be matched up with similar blouses that do have a price tag, I was thinking, *my ice cream will be melted, my cab-*

bage wilted. Yes, I should have known that a turtleneck sweater was trouble.

I gritted my teeth, gripped the buggy handle, and pulled back from aisle three. For a moment I just hovered in the No-Buy Zone—you know, that big area in front of the registers where you don't shop, but you cruise back and forth in search of the perfect checkout line. I noticed the light for aisle seven was on, so I set out. My wheels squawking, I yanked the cart a hard right rather than try to roll the long way around the popcorn display. (Someone always puts up the oddest displays in the No-Buy Zone. Cheaper than speed bumps, I guess.)

Aisle seven would take you even if your cart was crammed full and overflowing—or even pulling a second cart in tow, like the train that cut me off. The train's driver saw me coming, I know she did, and if it hadn't been for the box of Cap'n Crunch that came flying out of the second cart, I'd have beat her to the belt. But I had to brake hard to avoid the cereal box, which allowed her carts to zip in just before mine. The mother ushered and tugged her buggies into the channel. With a hard look, I studied the toddler in the second cart as it passed by me. He was grinning, mouth smeared with something sweet. He waved at me and pointed at the Cap'n Crunch. I smelled a conspiracy.

No time to lament. I spun the cart 360 degrees (barely missing the display for Titanic bath soap).

Number three was still flashing, the cashier still resting. But now light one was on—and the lane was empty! I pushed the cart hard and felt my cargo shift. On the way past three, I noticed the woman who wanted the turtleneck was pulling and tugging at the sweater, searching inside the neck, under the arms, everywhere, for that elusive price tag.

I slowed and cruised into aisle one at a safe speed. There to greet me was a young girl with lavender eye shadow, green lipstick, and black fingernail polish. (I am not making this up.) In between the chomping sounds she made on her wad of bubble gum (bigger than my fist), she was talking to the cashier at the register next to her about Billy Earl and something about a fistfight with Ernestine and how "Mama's done kilt 'em both." (I'll interpret for you later.) In the middle of her sentence, she glanced my way for a split second, long enough to say, "Sorry, ma'am, but this is the express lane. Five items or less." I kept waiting for her to say, "Just kidding" or, "Come on in. I'll take you anyway," but she didn't.

Rather than move, I studied my load. I didn't have too much. "I think I'm close on the count here," I told her, ashamed at how pleading my voice sounded.

Just about the time Billy Earl had done went down to Tucson and bought a double-wide, she put one hand on her hip and finally looked at me. "Maybe you are close," she said. "But sometimes we have customers who have small emergencies, like sick children at home, or they've run out of diapers, or they need batteries for their flashlights because the power has been knocked out. Things like that. That's what this aisle here is for, so people with real emergencies don't have to wait so long."

I looked back. There was no one behind me. "There are no emergencies right now!"

She chose not to hear this and instead said, "Perhaps you should try ..." she paused as she scanned across the aisles, "... aisle three. It looks like she can take you over there." And she went back to planning her outfit for whenever Billy Earl got back from Tucson.

I looked over to aisle three and saw that the light was on and not flashing. "You're serious?" I asked. I studied the hostess of aisle one, but all she did was shrug her pretty little shoulders and say, "Store policy."

I jerked the buggy backwards, the wheels grinding and bouncing and leaving a dotted black skid mark on the tile floor that someone would later probably have to use a giant buffer to remove.

The cashier at aisle three saw me coming; I know she did. And I saw her leaning back against her little cubicle, arms folded, yawning. I clipped a tin of popcorn on the way past and sent it wobbling into the path of an oncoming buggy. I thought about the little toddler in buggy number two, tossing out boxes of Cap'n Crunch that worked like mortar shells to keep incoming buggies away, and felt rather proud of this tactic. But before I arrived at the conveyor belt, before I could grab up that little baton and slap it down on the black surface to keep someone else's groceries from getting mixed up with mine, the yawning cashier picked up a cone-shaped object that advertised cigarettes and set it down on the belt. Below the advertisement was the note, "This Register Closed."

"You mean *after* me, right?" I said.

"Sorry, but it's my break time." She yawned, slipped out of her cubicle, and walked away.

"Aisle seventeen is open with no waiting," blared a voice over the PA system. Again I reversed out of the aisle and turned my buggy in the direction of aisle seventeen, which was so far away I doubted my own strength and stamina to make it that far, just past the flea and tick display. Frozen in place, I couldn't move. In moments, my heart slowly sank as I watched a tiny buggy (at least it looked tiny from that far away) slip into the spot marked aisle seventeen. I could only lean forward on my buggy, parked motionless beside a cardboard cutout of the Titanic, and watch my hope slip away. But I wasn't going to cry.

I knew then that I had no other option. I began to throw items overboard—Pringles, plastic coat hangers, shoe polish, some fuzzy socks with rubber grips on the bottoms, and at least a half-dozen other odds and ends—until I was down to five items. (The socks dangled dangerously from the bow of the Titanic, but that would give the workers something to do.) Then, with renewed determination, I turned my buggy about and aimed again for aisle number one—the express lane.

"Hi, remember me? Just waiting to hear if Billy Earl got the double-wide back to Tennessee." (Okay, I'll admit I said it with a bit of sarcasm. She was not amused.) Before she could say anything, I told her, "I have five items, and I'm in a hurry—this is an *emergency.*"

She smiled because that was what she was supposed to do. "Did you find everything you needed today?" she asked, as she began to scan my items.

I had kept a pair of big, fuzzy house shoes, and she picked them up and studied them as though they were a puppy. "How cute!" she squealed. She turned them over once, twice, without finding what she was looking for. When she reached for the cotton string that dangled just above her head—the string that was attached to the chain that was attached to the flashing light—I grabbed the shoes from her and laid them on the chewing-gum rack beside the register.

"I'll get those some other time," I said.

She looked confused. "But they're *so* cute!"

I took my four items and left, wadding up my shopping list and stuffing it into my pocket as I walked. Before I could get to the door, I heard a voice on the PA. I recognized it as the sleepy voice of the cashier on aisle three. She was asking for a price check from women's wear on a pair of fuzzy socks with rubber grips on the bottoms.

Later that evening, my husband called to tell me he was on his way home. "Can I pick up anything for you on my way?"

I pulled the crumpled shopping list out of my pocket and flattened it out on the counter. "As a matter of fact," I said, "while you're out ..."

Gourmet Napping

Becky Freeman

I used to think I didn't have time for such luxuries. A nap? Are you kidding? In the middle of my hectic day? Puh-lease. Or I might take one but wake up feeling frazzled and guilty. There was always this fast-forward tape going on in my head, taunting me with a singsong, "You're getting behind-er, you're getting behind-er." I thought if I just kept doing and doing, staying focused on my to-do list, no matter what—or who—interrupted my day, I could actually, eventually, catch up.

Then one bright morning, I had this incredible moment of enlightenment and realized The Truth. There is no such place as "All Caught Up." It only exists out there in our imaginations along with Oz and Santa's Workshop and Never-Never Land.

Why didn't the grown-ups tell us this when we were kids? I don't know, I simply don't know. Perhaps they, too, are still struggling under the illusion that it exists somewhere out there. You may have to grieve a little over the loss of this fairy-tale catch-up land. You'll find it a healthy, cleansing experience, though. Because in the long run, I guarantee you'll be thankful I told you the hard truth right now—before you waste any more time chasing a dream. When you give up on the existence of "All Caught Up," you are free to do all those wonderful things you were waiting to do until you arrived there. Like, for example, taking a guilt-free nap.

I have learned, the hard way, that taking a short nap is the best thing I can do when I'm plagued with hurry-upitis. I used to cram, pray, recite, and practice before a speech. Now I look for a good

81

place to snooze for twenty minutes instead. I'm convinced that God goes inside our brains and cleans house in there when we resign control of the universe long enough to let go and drift into a short sleep.

I've actually elevated napping to a gourmet experience. Let's say it's a springtime afternoon loaded with deadlines, housework, phone calls, and a hundred obligations, and I begin to feel the pressure building inside. (I love the title of Julie Barnhill's new book *She's Gonna Blow!* Any woman who's been there knows what built-up tension feels like and how everyone around you can pick it up.)

Like a movie producer who yells, "Cut!" I've learned to stop, walk away from the middle of the action, and melt like a boneless chicken into my quilt-laden hammock.

I soak up the warmth of sunshine on my skin and watch the play of light on the leaves in the trees overhead. Then I imagine my brain is a lot like the world before God fixed it up: dark, formless, and void. Very void. And I pray, "Father, hover over me the way you hovered over the formless deep, and create order out of the chaos that is now my mind."

As I imagine myself cocooned in his Spirit, I almost always fall into a deep, peaceful sleep. Then I wake up in a few minutes, refreshed, without a trace of guilt.

CAN YOU BELIEVE IT? Trust me, this sort of experience has been a long time in coming. Now there are books on Power Napping, and a number of corporations are even beginning to create Napping Rooms—realizing that the long-lasting effects of fifteen minutes of rest are more effective than caffeine infusions from the coffee station.

"How can I stop for a nap when I have so much I should be doing?" you may ask. Here is the answer. You get three times as much accomplished in one well-rested hour as you do in three hours of plodding along half awake. Take an hour to sleep and an hour to work, and you gain a whole extra hour to play with. Okay, I'll admit I just made that up. But you're just going to have to trust me on this one.

For you more scientific types, I do have some objective research proving that one nap a day will increase the number of your highly creative periods. It has to do with hypnopomping and hypnagogging. Really. I'm not making this up.

Hypnopomping actually refers to that period of time just before we are completely awake, when our mental pictures are a mixture of dreams and our own created images. It is considered one of the most productively creative periods. Hypnagogging, on the other hand, is that time just before we are asleep. Again, it is when images are a mixture of dreams and thoughts under our control—another highly creative state of mind.

Thomas Edison had an unusual technique for putting that hypnagogic state to work. He would doze off in a chair with his arms and hands draped over the armrest. In each hand he held a ball bearing, and below each hand on the floor were two pie plates. When he drifted into the state between waking and sleeping, his hands would naturally relax and the ball bearings would drop on the plates. Awakened by the noise, Edison would immediately make notes on any ideas that had come to him.

I wish someone would explain why, if we are such a brilliantly advanced nation, American forefathers let the concept of a Nationwide Nap slip through the cracks of the Constitution? I appreciate that Ronald Reagan took naps while he was president. I, for one, miss having him in the Oval Office—relaxed enough to take a little snooze now and then. His mere napping presence was soothing. (After all, if *the president* could nod off, what was there for the rest of us to worry about?)

In Latin America, they deal with midafternoon slumps by embracing The Siesta. The English have a countrywide sleepy-time breather they disguise as a tea party. Again, it takes place in the late afternoon, and because the English are the way they are, they call it High Tea. One of England's most celebrated citizens, William Shakespeare, penned the poignant words, "O, sleep, O gentle sleep [beloved nap time!], Nature's soft nurse."

Indeed, a short sleep is a healing balm.

Now, if you'll excuse me, the birds are tweeting outside my office window, the quilt-covered hammock is calling—and so off to hypnagog I go.

Chatting with Martha Stewart about My To-Do List

Chonda Pierce

Last night I had another dream about Martha Stewart. She showed up at my house early in the morning, just after the kids had gone to school. We sat in my huge sunroom (which I don't have in real life—that's how I knew it was a dream) and talked like old girlfriends while a small jazz ensemble played in a far corner by the fountain that had real koi fish swimming about and several thousand dollars in change underwater where people had stopped to make a wish. Martha and I were sipping our coffee. (Just some cheap decaffeinated stuff I had bought at Kroger's.)

"So your kids are in school?" she asked.

"Oh, yes. Long ago," I answer.

"Children are so cute," she said, sipping her coffee. "I would love to have watched them make their own breakfasts and prepare their own lunches to take."

"Me, too."

"You mean you didn't watch them?"

"I mean they didn't make their own breakfasts, let alone their own lunches."

She set down her coffee cup slowly and said, "You mean you prepared for both of them?"

"*And* myself *and* my husband."

"Oh, my." Her forehead wrinkled.

"Oh, Martha, enough about that. I've been dying to ask you something. On that show you did last Christmas, did you really make your own salt and pepper?"

Martha cut a glance about the room to make sure we were alone (with the exception of the jazz ensemble and the fish, of course). Then she confided, "I have to be honest."

I leaned in closer.

"Someone else quarried the salt."

"No!"

She nodded. "Of course, I grew and harvested the pepper and ground it myself. *And* I filled the shakers." She smiled and seemed pleased with herself. She nodded her approval to the jazz ensemble and then looked around the room. "This is such a lovely room. Did you make it?"

"Oh, heavens no. Are you kidding? I just dreamed this thing up. I have so much laundry to do, when would I find time to make glass and glue it together like you would?"

"Laundry? What do you mean by laundry?"

"You know, separating the darks from the whites, the towels from the delicates."

"Then what?"

"Then I put them in the washer, add soap—"

"I can make soap."

"Make sure all the socks are turned right-side-out—"

"All of them?"

I nodded. "And then dry—"

"Dry?"

"And fold—"

"Fold?"

"And put away."

"Where?"

"Why, into the proper chest of drawers or closet. Or at least in neat little stacks in the corner of the room."

"I hadn't thought about that. So how long does a job like that last?" she wanted to know.

I paused for a long moment—for effect, I admit, and to give her an opportunity to swallow her last drink of coffee—before saying deliberately, *"Forever."*

She put a hand to her mouth, and I feared maybe I hadn't paused long enough. "I hadn't thought about that," she said.

"Oh, please," I said, "enough about laundry. Do tell me about that crumpet party I saw on your show once."

"Crumpets are boring," she said.

"Then tell me about how you made your own paper for the invitations."

She dismissed this with a wave and said, "Just like any other paper—wood pulp, et cetera." Then, lowering her cup from a fresh swallow, she asked, "Have you ever vacuumed your carpet?"

I nodded.

"I mean, like a *whole* room?"

"Try a whole house," I said, trying not to sound as though I were bragging.

She gasped.

"And then I usually dust," I added.

"Dust what?"

"The furniture."

"I can build furniture," she said.

"I know, Martha, and you're quite good."

Just then the phone rang, and I answered, "Oh, yes, I'm expecting you. I'll be here with Martha Stewart ... Okay, I'll ask." I covered the phone and asked Martha, "The plumber wants to know why the hot water valve is always on the left and cold on the right."

"Tell him," Martha said, "to watch this Sunday's program."

"Watch her this Sunday," I said into the phone. "Besides, this is *my* dream, and I'm having my *own* chat." I hung up and said, "That was the plumber. He'll be here in a bit."

"Plumber? For what?"

"Toilet's stopped up."

She set down her coffee and pushed it away. "How do you do it?"

"Do what?"

"Take care of your children and your husband, do the laundry, vacuum, dust the furniture, take out the trash—you do take out your own trash?"

"Only when it's full."

"And *then* cook?"

I nodded, but I had never thought of my day as quite so overwhelming, so daunting a task, until I heard Martha Stewart lay it out so plainly.

I shrugged and said, "Practice, I guess."

The plumber showed up, gave Martha a big hug, and told her how great her spinach quiche recipe was. He dragged out a big coiled cable with a giant electric motor that uncoiled the cable across the room and into my toilet. After a few moments, the plumber spun it backwards and pulled out Bongo, my son's favorite Beanie Baby.

"So *that's* where that went!" I said, spraying it down with some Shout and dropping it into the washer, which was set for the very next load. Zach would be excited when he got back from school.

The plumber asked for Martha's autograph (on an old nasty plunger of all things), picked up his auger, and left.

I retrieved a mop from the garage and wiped up some size-thirteen prints from the vinyl floor.

"*Why* do you do this?" Martha asked, the exasperation evident in her voice.

"Do what?"

"All this," and she waved an arm about my big sunroom, but she meant my whole house. "The laundry, the dusting, the vacuuming, the mopping–"

"Don't forget the windows."

"You do windows? *Why?* Couldn't you just hire someone to take care of menial tasks like these so you would have more time for other things, like weaving napkins with an interlaced monogram or crafting reproductions of Early American Shaker furniture?"

Now that the plumbing seemed to be taken care of, I filled Martha's cup with more coffee. The dark liquid warmed the cup; sunshine poured through the glass overhead and warmed everything else. I noticed the streaks and the dust, so I added "Clean the sunroom" to my to-do list. I'd take care of it as soon as Martha left.

I carried the pot of coffee back to the kitchen and dragged the mop behind me, thinking about Martha's question. The jazz ensemble was playing something perky now as I answered her. "Perhaps in *your* dreams things like that can happen, Martha, but not in mine."

Glancing at my watch, my heart thumped. Any minute my kids would be barreling in the door looking for an after-school snack. I pulled a box of Little Debbie snack cakes out of the cupboard and laid them on a plastic plate. No, I didn't make them myself, but the kids won't care. They'll be too busy ripping open the wrappers, and I'll be too busy hearing about their day. I'm pretty comfortable with that. Suddenly I felt a little sad for Martha.

On the way past the fountain, I flipped in a quarter and made a wish.

CHAPTER FIVE

Lookin' So Good!

*The LORD seeth not as man seeth;
for man looketh on the outward appearance,
but the LORD looketh on the heart.*
—The Bible, 1 Samuel 16:7 KING JAMES VERSION

*My idea of strenuous exercise
is to fill the bathtub and lie back,
then pull the plug and fight the current.*
—Barbara Johnson

The Bra of My Dreams

Cathy Lee Phillips

The Madras School girl's rest room was packed with fourth graders washing up after morning recess. I was elbowing my way through the crowd when Betsy Fowler's shrill voice rang out above the chatter.

"Well, look at this. My bra strap just won't stay in place."

An uneasy silence enveloped the Madras School girl's rest room. Betsy shoved a very obvious white strap underneath the shoulder of her sleeveless pink and white polka-dot shirtwaist dress and smiled smugly.

I hated her at that moment.

It didn't matter that, being the largest girl in the class, she would naturally be the first to need a bra. It didn't matter that, as an only child, Betsy was constantly showered with gifts from adoring parents. All that mattered was that Betsy Fowler was the first girl in the Madras School fourth grade to wear a bra, and she had succeeded in making the rest of us aware of the fact. Though it was not discussed openly, I firmly believe that, right then, every girl in that rest room silently vowed to secure a bra before sundown. Me included.

Needless to say, I concentrated little on science and arithmetic the rest of that Monday afternoon. I wanted a bra in the worst way, and by the time the final bell rang it was an obsession. I rode the bus home in silence, daydreaming of the scene that would surely unfold when I arrived home. I would walk up to Mama and calmly announce, "Mother, it is time. I must have a bra."

She would take me in her arms and shower me with kisses while shedding a bucket of maternal tears over how quickly I had grown up. Together we would drive to town, where, with great ceremony, we would choose the perfect bra. It would be pure white, decorated with lace and a tiny pink flower adorning the front. In my fantasy, this would be a special day my mother and I would recall fondly for the rest of our lives.

As the bus stopped, I jumped off and raced up the driveway. Mama stood at the kitchen sink, and—my fantasy abruptly abandoned—I blurted, "Betsy Fowler has a bra, and I've just got to get one!"

Mama slowly dried her hands. She took one step back and looked at me squarely for several agonizing seconds before muttering five horrible little words: "You don't need a bra!"

Need? Who said anything about need? It never dawned on me that I *needed* a bra. The situation was simple: Betsy Fowler had a bra, and therefore I wanted one.

I didn't care about the job a bra performed. I was not suffering from "cleavage envy," nor did I want anything to put into the bra. I simply wanted a bra. Immediately! I wanted to stand in the Madras School girl's rest room and push a lacy white bra strap underneath the shoulder of a sleeveless dress.

The look on Mama's face, though, told me that she simply did not understand my situation. Furthermore, she had no intention of showering me with kisses, shedding maternal tears, or driving me to town for a precious white bra decorated with lace and a pink flower.

My fantasy died right there in the kitchen on Posey Road.

Life was brutal. By suppertime I was convinced that the next morning I would be the only fourth-grade girl attending Madras School braless. Horrified, I did what any other normal fourth-grade child would do—I nagged, I pestered, I whined. I accused my mother of not loving me, of not caring about either my reputation or my general well-being. I compared her unfavorably to mothers of my classmates. I brooded and sulked, while murmuring Betsy Fowler's name under my breath. I was obnoxious and bratty. But I was persistent, and when I climbed into bed on Thursday night, my godly and beleaguered mother surrendered.

"I will pick you up after school tomorrow, and we will go to town and buy you a trainer."

A TRAINER!?

I began to worry. A trainer? What was a trainer? Was it a bra? If so, was it lacy and white? Did it have a pink flower on the front? And furthermore, was I ready for a trainer? I didn't know training was involved in this particular growth process. Didn't the contents of a bra just grow naturally? What was I supposed to train them to do? And what if I trained them wrong? After all, I was only nine years old; without realizing it, I could disfigure myself for life. Training? This was a lot of responsibility to place on a fourth grader.

I hardly slept at all.

True to her word, Mama was waiting for me when the final school bell rang. My stomach hurt, and I was afraid I would throw up long before we walked into Kessler's on the Court Square in Newnan.

Inside, we met a tall lady with gray hair and tiny glasses perched on the end of her nose.

"We've come to purchase a bra," Mama announced. Over the top of her glasses the gray-haired lady looked at me with the same expression my mother had given me earlier in the week. She didn't say those five little words, but I knew she was thinking them.

"I think we need a trainer," she said. My stomach began to hurt again.

Taking a second look at me, she walked toward a rack holding small pastel boxes. She opened a blue box and held up a trainer. My stomach relaxed, and I began breathing normally. It was a bra— and it was perfect! It was a brilliant white. Lace decorated the bottom, and to my delight, a petite pink flower sat front and center. Trainer or not, it was the bra of my dreams. Surely Betsy Fowler had no finer bra.

"We'll take it," Mama announced. I left the store without saying a word, but as I walked toward the door, I was sure everyone was staring at me, fully aware that a bra rested inside my brown shopping bag.

Later, I placed the bra safely inside my top drawer, where it would remain until I dressed for school Monday morning. I slept peacefully that Friday night, quite happy with myself for getting exactly what I wanted.

Monday morning came. I awoke before the alarm sounded. My dress had been carefully chosen—pale yellow tulips on a blue background. It was sleeveless, of course, thus allowing my bra strap to make an appearance at a strategic moment during the school day. The garment felt quite strange, but I was confident it would feel more natural the longer I wore it. Climbing aboard the school bus, I felt like a true woman of the world. With one meager appearance of a simple bra strap, I planned to personally wipe that smug look off the face of Miss Betsy Fowler.

Arithmetic—definitely not my favorite subject—was my first class that day. To my surprise, I knew the answer to the first question the teacher asked. Raising my hand enthusiastically, I discovered, to my horror, that my bra went with it!

Instead of staying in its intended location, the garment slithered up my chest and crept rapidly toward my neck. I instantly lowered my hand and turned crimson with embarrassment. Were bras supposed to do this? Hoping no one was watching, I hunched over my desk, discreetly tugging and yanking, trying desperately to return the bra to its proper position.

As I made my final adjustments, the teacher called my name.

"Cathy, could you come to the board and show us how to work this problem."

I walked slowly to the front of the room, selected a piece of chalk, and lifted my arm to write the numbers on the blackboard. As I did, the bra lurched upward. It climbed toward my throat, twisting and pinching as it moved. Had some demon, intent on ruining my life, gained control of this innocent garment? The bra kept crawling higher and higher until it seemed ready to shoot through the neck of my dress. I was sure everyone in the class could see an abnormal wrinkle crisscrossing my chest. Holding me in its tight grip, the wicked combination of elastic and lace threatened my dignity and bound my upper chest until I could barely breathe.

Excusing myself quickly, I ran to the bathroom. I was no longer interested in showing my strap to Betsy Fowler and the other girls in my fourth-grade class. I was interested in pure, basic survival.

My mind raced as I jerked the bra back into place. What could I do with this cursed object? I had no purse. I couldn't just stuff it into one of my books. Surely one of the boys in class would find it, and I would die from the resulting ridicule. I couldn't throw the bra away—Mama would never let me hear the end of it. I couldn't call home sick and listen to my mama's "I told you so" the rest of the day.

There was no alternative. I had to wear the horrible contraption until the end of the day. I could do it, I told myself, as long as I didn't move my arms. Thus I spent the rest of the day walking like a short robot programmed to keep my arms glued tightly to my side.

I stepped off the bus that afternoon completely humiliated. Walking silently to my room, I removed that cursed garment and stuffed it in the back corner of my dresser drawer. I prayed I would never see it again.

Mama never mentioned the bra again. Neither did I. But when the time was right and I *needed* one, we returned to Kessler's and bought a suitable bra for me. Because I then possessed the necessary anatomical components, the bra stayed easily in place.

I have worn many bras since that horrible day at Madras School so long ago. I have worn underwires and cross-your-hearts. I have worn two-hookers, four-hookers, back-hookers, and front-hookers. I have worn T-backs, U-backs, posture bras, and sports bras. I have worn strapless bras, bras with comfort straps, and bras with frayed straps held together with a few strategically placed safety pins. I've worn white bras, black bras, ivory bras, and once, on a dare, a leopard-skin bra. Occasionally, I still wear a bra with a tiny pink flower on the front.

Ironically, there are now many times I don't *want* to wear a bra at all, but nowadays I really *need* one.

I can still recall clearly that awful day in the fourth grade. Would I have been more patient had I known just how many bras were in my future? Probably not. I was controlled completely by my wants. My needs were not an issue. And though quite a few years have passed since I was in the fourth grade, I still struggle with this same problem.

It is a hard thing to realize that I do not always know what is best for me. Mama knew best in the fourth grade. God knows best today and every day.

Grant me the wisdom I need, O Lord, to praise you for meeting my needs—and to trust your wisdom when it comes to controlling my wants.

Step Right Up

Patsy Clairmont

I can identify with Zacchaeus in that I have a difficult time finding a place high enough to let me see a parade. Visibility is limited when you're five feet tall. I've spent a lifetime on my tiptoes, calling up to others, "What's going on?"

I know I'm supposed to take comfort in the saying "dynamite comes in small packages." But I don't want to blow up; I want to grow up.

Sitting tall is also a challenge because invariably, a seven-foot-two-inch fellow will plant himself in front of me at church. I then have the joy of staring for the next hour at the seams in his shirt and his nappy neck. It's like trying to watch a ball game through a billboard.

Hugging is often a strain as we shorties have to reach past our stretching points to squeeze a neck. It's such a rumpling experience and requires readjusting everything from hat to hose.

As a speaker, I frequently find myself peeking over lecterns in my attempts to spot the audience. It's difficult to retain the interest of people when their view consists of your forehead and eyebrows. I have stood on many creative booster stools so I could see and be seen.

At one retreat, the kitchen workers brought me a box of canned juice to stand on. It worked fine until my high heel poked between two cans and I jerked sharply backward. I grabbed the lectern, catching myself just before doing a topsy-turvy somersault. My disheveled appearance resulting from my stage aerobics made me look juiced.

I have perched on many piano benches to speak. Because they're pieces of furniture, I always remove my shoes before stepping up. Smooth nylons on shiny-finished wood equals slick chick in action. It's like trying to speak on ice skates—possible but risky.

To elevate me enough to be seen at one church meeting, the staff quickly piled up two stacks of hymnals, five deep. As I turned to look at my audience from one side of the auditorium to the other, the books would swivel. At one point the right-foot stack headed east while the left-foot stack headed west. Those shifting stilts kept me divided in my concentration, as I was concerned I would leave with a split personality.

I've stood on milk crates, suitcases, tables, and kiddie stools. Once I was precariously placed on a wooden box whose weight limit I obviously exceeded. It creaked threateningly throughout my presentation as I closed in prayer, a soloist began to sing, and I cautiously stepped down. Relieved that I hadn't burst the boards, I walked down the platform steps to take a seat. At the last step, my heel caught in the microphone cords, and I crash-landed in the front row as the singer was belting out "Amazing Grace." I obviously was not Grace, although in a discussion later, we thought it was amazing I could survive my teeter-totter platform and then splat when I arrived on solid ground.

It's difficult to be taken seriously when you're sixty inches short. People have a habit of referring to shorties as "cute." "Cute" is what you call a toddler, a house without a future, or the runt of the litter.

I tried to increase the presentation of my stature by wearing tall clothes. But more than once, while walking up the front steps in sanctuaries, my heel slid into the hem of my long skirt, toppling me across the altar, where I looked like some sort of short sacrifice.

I shortened my skirts and added shoulder pads to my jackets in an effort to give an illusion of tallness without tripping myself.

Then one time I was in Washington, and when I was introduced, I grabbed my suit jacket and slid into it as I headed for the stage. I had been speaking for about fifteen minutes when I turned my head to one side and noticed that my left shoulder was four inches higher than my right. Evidently the pad, rather than conforming to the shape of my shoulder, perched on it. Up to that point, I was the only one in the auditorium who hadn't noticed. I was speaking on being dysfunctional and suggested that this perched pad was proof of my expertise in the subject. When I finished speaking, the mistress of ceremonies approached the steps with the back of her dress tucked into her panty hose. That took a lot of pressure off me.

Another time, I was sharing the stage with a statuesque and elegant friend who, as I was speaking, noticed that my mega shoulder pad had slid off my shoulder and into my blouse. She reached in through my neckline and fished down my back in her attempt to retrieve it. I was stunned but continued to speak as though I didn't notice she was shoulder-deep into my clothing. Well, I lost the audience as everyone became hysterical watching her catch my illusive inches and pat them securely back into place.

I wish my height were my only struggle with smallness. Unfortunately, I'm also shortsighted in my faith. I'm one of those "if I can see it, then I can believe it" people.

Zacchaeus was a small man who shinnied up a sycamore tree to give himself a boost. To that extent, I can identify. But his next move made the difference for him in a way lengthened robes or mountainous shoulder pads under his togas never could. He inched out on a limb to glimpse the Savior. He risked the shaky-limb experience of faith and responded to the Lord's invitation, not only to come down, but also to grow up.

That day he stepped down from his own efforts to see and be seen and stepped up to the call of the Lord. Zacchaeus still lacked inches, but he gained insight and walked away a giant of a man.

Faith is a believe-it-first proposition, with no promise that I'll get to "see it" regardless of how many boxes I climb. That's scary—like going out on a limb, huh, Zac?

Face-lift

Barbara Johnson

A stranger called me one day and asked if I would like to have a face-lift.

"Who is this again?" I asked, dumbfounded that such a call came from out of the blue. As I spoke, I leaned around the corner so I could peek at my face in the hallway mirror. I puckered my mouth just a little, trying to find my cheekbones.

The woman laughed and said she worked for a plastic surgeon who had just performed a face-lift on a friend of mine. She explained that when the doctor did a face-lift, he offered a big discount to any patient who gave him the names of four friends who might also be interested.

"She ... she thought I needed a face-lift?" I stuttered, lifting my chin indignantly to smooth out the creases in my neck. "She said I would be interested?"

"Well, uh, I guess she did," the woman said, a little embarrassed when she realized that my friend (*former friend,* I was thinking) hadn't prepared me for her call. "But it sounds like you're not interested, huh?"

"You got *that* right!" I answered. I hung up the phone, trying to decide whether to feel hurt, angry—or old. When I glanced into the hall mirror again, my face had contorted into a disgusted frown. For one brief moment I saw the droopy eyelids, the neck creases, the wrinkles everywhere. Then, just as quickly, I decided to laugh about the whole thing. And what do you know? My face lifted all by itself!

To Bean or Not to Bean

Marilyn Meberg

*W*hen Beth and Steve decided to get married in Italy, I realized I would need a coat! This southern California damsel did not even own a winter coat because she rarely needed one. But, I reasoned, if we were all going to traipse to Europe in the dead of winter, do the tourist thing by going to Paris first, and then do the wedding thing, I needed to ward off the potential of freezing to death.

L. L. Bean is a mail-order house in Freeport, Maine, whose catalogs I pore over regularly. I love that place! Almost all of my wool-cashmere blazers have come from there, and my turtlenecks and sweaters as well. There's something irresistibly fun about simply picking up the phone, calling the toll-free number, and chatting with one of their amiable salespersons as I give my order. I always find out how cold it is there and then of course point out that we in southern California are basking in seventy-degree sunshine. (That's an unattractive side of me I'm not proud of, but I seem to continue to express it in spite of my avowed disapproval.)

When my bright-blue quilted goose-down coat with optional zippered hood arrived, I felt ready for any temperature. It claimed to be lightweight for easy packing as well as for wearing, and indeed it was. In fact, it proved so efficiently to retain my body heat, I never once felt cold in spite of freezing temperatures in Paris. I basically just cooed and smiled from the depths of my goose-down cocoon the entire three days we "did" Paris prior to going on to Italy.

Since then, this coat has cuddled and cocooned me many times—sitting on cold bleachers waiting for the Rose Bowl Parade to start, traveling to other cities whose temperatures nearly rival those of wintertime Paris, and then again just last week when we all went to New York for Thanksgiving. (I'd have died without her encompassing warmth while standing rinkside at Rockefeller Center.)

Perhaps now that I have so drawn you into my inordinate affection, as well as appreciation, for "Bean," perhaps you'll understand how startled I was to suddenly realize one morning as we all walked down West 75th Street to Amsterdam Avenue that no one in New York was wearing a bright-blue quilted goose-down coat except me. Everyone was wearing a long black, brown, or tan wool coat. On the heels of this realization came a delayed flashback. I thought, *I don't remember anyone in Paris wearing a bright-blue Bean either.*

I caught my reflection in a window as we hunched our way down Amsterdam Avenue to Sarabeth's for breakfast. *You know, Marilyn, you really look like a walking sleeping bag. I hate to tell you that, but you stick out in a crowd. There* are *no other walking sleeping bags in all of New York!* I was crushed.

After we'd given our breakfast order I turned to my son and said, "Jeff, I want your absolutely honest response. Do you like my coat?"

Jeff stared at me for a minute and then eyeballed the crush of not only my coat but the coats of Pat and Carla on the seat beside me. He said, "You mean the Bean?"

"Yeah, the Bean."

"Well, Mom, because of your happy attachment to her in Paris, I really care only that you continue to be pleased with her."

I looked closely at him to be sure he wasn't doing that Ken Meberg thing. "Jeff, what do you think of my Bean?"

"Mom, uh—she's great for certain places and occasions."

"Jeff, is she good for New York?"

"Probably not, Mom."

"Jeff, was she good for Paris?"

"She kept you warm—but otherwise, no, Mom, she belongs somewhere else."

I looked at my gorgeous, fashion-plate daughter-in-law and said nothing. She too had the grace to say nothing.

My dear friend Pat, whose fidelity to truth-telling is often a challenge to me, offered, "I can tell you the exact place where Bean is appropriate."

Perking up, I asked, "Where?"

"She would be appropriate for you to wear for duck hunting. You know, those places where people lie low and then rise up from the marshes with guns pointed and shoot at ducks who suddenly fly out of nowhere."

I stared at her in total disbelief. "Pat, that's a terrible image. I can't imagine ever lying low to shoot a duck."

"Well, if you change your mind, you've got the coat for it!"

Fortunately, our food arrived, and I settled into my Florentine omelette with extra-crispy bacon on the side. The subject of my Bean didn't come up again.

I must admit there was a slight decrease in my usual ebullience as we went about our activities following breakfast. I was busy settling the Bean issue. So what if I were the only walking bright-blue quilted person in New York, or Paris, or Amboy, California, for that matter! Why do I have to mirror everyone else's subdued earth-tone wool look? I don't! I love my Bean! I'm cozy and warm in my Bean—and as Jeff pointed out, "We can always find you in a crowd!"

What more could one ask from a coat! That settled it: there would be no severing of my relationship with Bean. She stays, and so do I. Nestled beneath several layers of lightweight goose down, I continued our New York activities, secure in the knowledge that I was the only genuinely warm person in the entire city!

Isn't it remarkable how uncomfortable we can become if we don't blend in to our environment? But without God-given uniqueness, everything would look the same, taste the same, and feel the same. What a bore! And what a loss.

Snaggletooth

Luci Swindoll

One of my favorite television commercials has no words. A young woman walks into a shop and admires a bathing suit on a mannequin. With a look of self-satisfaction, she picks up the exact same suit, disappears into a dressing room, and throws her own clothes over the door; after a couple seconds, she lets out a blood-curdling scream. It's a powerhouse endorsement of the diet the commercial recommends. I laugh every time I see it as I munch away on my Snickers bar.

How many times do we look in the mirror and find no words to express what we see? The mirror talks. We scream. Thelma Wells has a good idea. She says, "I'm fully clothed when I look in the mirror 'cause I don't want nuttin' talkin' back to me." Well put.

Recently I had a little screaming fit in front of my bathroom mirror. The dentist had attached a temporary cap on one of my permanent front teeth, which he had earlier filed away to a tiny squared-off yellow stub. That night when I was brushing, the cap fell off into the sink and disappeared down the drain.

At first, with the movement of the toothbrush and a mouthful of toothpaste, I couldn't tell it was gone. I just had a virtual sense of vacancy. Then, running my tongue across my front teeth, I felt nothing more than that stub. The cap was gone. For good. Forever. Forsooth! (Actually, I thought something else, but you don't want to know.)

I smiled into the mirror, then screamed. In short, I panicked. And I rarely panic. Generally I'm very calm, and little makes me lose my cool. But losing my tooth! Well, I lost my cool. I moaned, groaned, whimpered, and wailed. (It's hard to do all that at the same time, but I managed.) I looked in the mirror, hoping a second glance might bring back the tooth, but saw only that awful, gaping hole.

While pacing the hallway, I asked the Lord to take my life. I prayed for the return of Christ. This gaping hole in my mouth was a serious problem. I was leaving at dawn the next morning for Cincinnati, Ohio.

With an unsteady hand I eventually dialed my dentist at home and told him that I had to speak to 15,000 women at a conference that next day and I had no front tooth. I just knew he'd say, "Oh, honey, I understand. You come to the office right now, and I'll fix everything." But he didn't. He promised to meet me the next morning before my flight.

The *next morning?* He might as well have said in my next life-time! Needless to say, I had a restless night envisioning the most embarrassing moment of my life surrounded by a sea of laughing women.

The next day Dr. Baumann and I both showed up early, and the replacement took place. A very caring, kind man, he looked at me and said (with both fists and several tons of metal in my mouth), "Luci, what if you had to speak with that stub showing? You're still the same person inside, aren't you?"

That'th eathy for you to thay, pal. But you know what? It's true. No matter how different I look on the outside, I'm still me behind the snaggletooth. And I'll be me when I'm completely toothless one day! God, have mercy.

Sometimes the hardest thing in life is being ourselves. We so want to be somebody else. For years I sang with the Dallas Opera chorus, playing the part of other people. It was great. I wore wigs, corsets, fake eyelashes, heavy makeup, and costumes in order to become a waitress or a factory worker, a nun, courtesan, school-teacher, soldier, witch, dancer, or lady-in-waiting. Whatever was called for, I became that. Interestingly, even my friends in the cho-rus used to say, "My favorite thing about all this is that I don't have to be me."

The next time you stand in front of a mirror and want to scream, try to remember that *God* made that face. That smile. Those big eyes, crooked teeth, and chubby cheeks. You are his creation, called to reflect him. Spiritual transformation doesn't come from a diet program, a bottle, a makeover, or a mask. It comes from an intimate relationship with the Savior. Because of his gracious nature, he looks beyond our snaggletoothed grin and appreciates us for who we really are. So we can, too.

Look Good, Smell Good!

Chonda Pierce

The other day I read a story about a new suit for men—a scented suit, as a matter of fact. I'm not kidding. They make them in South Korea, and these suits sell for about $400. (Do you know how many pine-tree air fresheners you can buy for that?)

The secret to the suit, I read, are these microscopic capsules implanted in the fabric. These capsules pop open when rubbed or shook to release the scent of lavender, peppermint, or pine. Okay, stop laughing; this is a true story!

I can see where something like this could come in handy. Every time David and I get lost and I make David go into one of those convenience stores to ask for directions, he comes back smelling like Marlboro country. But if he had one of those lavender-scented suits, he could do a little two-step in the parking lot and come wafting back into the car smelling like a butterfly bush. That's when one of those suits would be nice.

But I can think of a few instances in which smelling like a pine tree could be the worst thing—take bears, for instance. That could be dangerous to your health, especially if you're walking through the Smokies one afternoon on your way home from church.

And I don't think I would want to wear one of the lavender-smelling ensembles, either. Not during the heavy periods of cross-pollination (such as the months of April and May)—because of the bee problem.

But what if not only scented *suits* caught on in a big way but also scented clothing of all kinds? Why stop with peppermint, lavender, and pine? Why not take the scented thing as far as it will go? It only makes sense to me.

If you ask people what two things they like the most, many would probably say food and clothes. So why hasn't someone thought of this before? This is a great idea! Children's clothing could be the fun smells of jelly beans, bubble gum, and ice cream. Adults could wear grown-up smells such as fried chicken, okra, and squash (or just meat and potatoes for people like my husband).

Food-scented clothing could help boost sales for some small businesses. For instance, if you sell pizzas and you want to drum up a little extra business, just jump into your pizza-scented coveralls, grab some business cards, and head out to the mall. Waiters could actually wear the soup of the day so, when you ask them, they don't just stand there going, "Ahh ... ahh ... I'm not sure, but I'll find out." They could just sniff their shirtsleeves, and they would know.

Food-scented clothing could help one's self-esteem. I love the smell of popcorn, but I hate the way my feet smell after being hot and sweaty in my sneakers all day. But what if I had popcorn-scented socks? Then, at the end of the day, my feet would smell just like a bowl of Orville Redenbacher's extra-buttery. (Everyone would love me!) And what could be more relaxing than, after wearing my roast-beef-with-gravy pantsuit all day, to come home and slip into my chocolate brownie pajamas?

Dressing for the seasons would be more fun than simply "flannel in the winter and rayon in the summer." On the coldest days, I'd love to wear my chili con carne sweatshirt with my saltine mittens. And on really hot days, I'd wear something fruity, like watermelon or kiwi.

And think of the time food-scented clothing would save, too. Instead of standing in front of the closet every morning and wasting all that time trying to match up colors, I could simply match smells (and plan for supper at the same time).

I know there would be some problems. "You can't wear fish with pasta," someone would say. But look at not only all the different choices that would be available to you but also the combinations. Of course, my husband would be happy to knock around in the ground beef sweatshirt and pants, with cheese socks, pickle

T-shirt, and a ketchup ball cap—smelling like a cheeseburger all day. Me? I'd love to take a gourmet clothing lesson or two and be a different casserole every day—perhaps even a quiche every now and then.

I don't doubt that clothes would still be a marker of status. It would be obvious (without labels) who was wearing the filet mignon skirt and jacket and who was wearing the cheap sirloin skirt and jacket. There would be those who would insist on wearing a caviar camisole or perhaps an escargot dinner jacket, just because they thought they should.

I don't doubt, either, that some fake stuff would be going on, causing us to be more aware of the scams and to watch for imitation crabmeat sweaters, powdered milk blouses, ground turkey slacks—things like that. We would have to be on guard constantly and schooled regularly to distinguish the genuine from the pretend. (Imagine your embarrassment at attending a formal function wearing what you thought was a genuine lamb chop sequined gown only to discover it was some soybean by-product.)

Meeting people would be more than just shaking hands and asking about their jobs. "Oh, I just love the smell of that outfit! What is it? Egg roll? Without MSG, right?" But the downside of this is that complete strangers would stop you to sniff your clothes. "Sorry. I thought I detected the aroma of cabbage stew." (The lesson here is not to borrow someone else's jacket and then embarrass yourself because you don't know the difference between a trout and a salmon.)

And I can imagine the conversations I would have. "Chonda," my friend would call to say, "what are you wearing tonight?"

"Since we're just going out to the mall, I figured I'd wear my black olive slacks and that pimento blouse I showed you the other day."

"Oh, shoot, I was going to wear my pimento top, too, but don't you think that will be too much pimento?"

"Not at all. David's wearing this nifty egg salad sweater that I got him for Christmas, so we should be okay. We'll just make sure he stands between us. What about your husband?"

"Well, he has this pickle thing he could wear."

"Any mayonnaise or cream cheese?"

"Just in dress slacks, but I think he wanted to go a bit more casual. How about mustard boxers?"

"Perfect."

Food-scented clothing may be the best idea since the Y2K-scare books. (I wish I had invented those.) It will encourage us to love our neighbor more. (I've stood in line next to people I could have loved a whole lot more if they had just smelled like a Salisbury steak.) And I believe food-scented clothing will also help people to lose weight. I mean, if you walk around all day smelling like meat loaf, the last thing you're going to dig into is a fatty meat loaf recipe that night. (If your weakness is bratwurst, the same thing holds true.)

Going to the mall would be like going to Luby's Cafeteria. Going to Luby's Cafeteria would be like going to Sak's Fifth Avenue. Food and clothes, clothes and food—together at last. Life would be good!

But I was just wondering: Will I need more closet space, or a bigger refrigerator?

Big Hair Day

Cathy Lee Phillips

It was a big hair day. I made that decision on a whim, little knowing the events it would set into motion. This was a few years ago, when "big" hair was in style and I had just received a new perm in my auburn (absolutely no gray, of course!) locks. Because my curls were shoulder length, I occasionally used a variety of accessories to corral my hair into a sleek ponytail or other various styles. However, on this particular day I opted for the tousled, carefree, "big hair" look—a decision I would live to regret. I finished the style with half a bottle of Mega Spritz, a gluelike spray that provided my big hair the power to withstand a hurricane.

My husband and I were in a hurry that morning. Jerry was flying to Colorado Springs, Colorado, for a convention of the United Methodist Association of Church Business Administrators. I would fight the Atlanta traffic going toward the airport, drop Jerry off in time to catch his flight, and then fight more traffic to reach my office on the other side of Atlanta.

My schedule that day was quite full—it included a lunch appointment and several afternoon meetings. Leaving my office that afternoon, I fought more traffic, ran a gazillion errands, met friends for dinner, and returned home well after 11:00 that dark night.

Though I was completely exhausted, I was proud that my big hair sill looked fresh, thanks to its three-inch glaze of Mega Spritz.

Crawling into bed that night, I was almost asleep when I realized I had forgotten one very important task. Rhett and Ashley were two beautiful cocker spaniels—one black and one blonde—who did not want to suffer hunger pangs all night long. Feeding them was normally Jerry's job, but he had safely arrived in Colorado and had no intention of flying home to feed two cocker spaniels, no matter how special they were.

"Those two dogs will surely live until morning," I rationalized, "and they could actually stand to lose a pound or two." I snuggled deeper under the covers and punched the pillow into a comfortable position.

I tried to sleep, but the faces of those two lovable old dogs appeared each time I closed my eyes. I was warm and comfortable and did not want to crawl out of bed. But there was a bigger issue at stake.

I, Cathy Lee Phillips, am afraid of the dark. I grew up where there was talk of boogers and monsters and haints and such—a virtual smorgasbord of creatures just waiting to grab and torment me in the night. *(A word of explanation may be necessary for the Yankees or the very young among us:* Haint *is an old Southern word meaning anything scary, frightening, or just generally creepy.)* Though talk of these creatures took place during my childhood, I remained convinced that boogers and monsters and haints still awaited me in the dark.

So, while I was warm and comfortable in bed that night, I basically did not want to face the terrors of the dark. But my love for these old dogs prevailed, and I reluctantly climbed out of bed, pulled a purple chenille robe over my still perfect big hair, and slipped my feet inside my Nikes.

What a picture I was that midnight—a weirdly dressed, scared-of-the-dark, big-haired preacher's wife facing boogers and monsters and haints to undertake a mission of mercy for two beloved cocker spaniels.

Rhett and Ashley lived in a "doggie condo" behind our parsonage. Inside their fence was a shed that housed them, a riding mower, assorted junk, and an ample supply of Wal-Mart Old Roy dog food. It also housed an abundance of flies, quite possibly attracted to the halo of Mega Spritz encircling our house.

What I did not know—and what Jerry failed to tell me before he boarded his flight that morning—was that the shed also housed something else that dark night. You see, my dear husband decided to tackle the problem of those pesky flies with an age-old remedy—yes, flypaper. About two inches wide, the flypaper came in little canisters that hooked to the roof of the building and hung approximately three feet from the ceiling. The desired effect, of course, was that flies and mosquitoes would innocently crash into this sticky substance where they would remain until their bodies became lifeless.

Jerry, I must say, was *very* efficient when it came to dealing with annoying flying creatures and was not content to simply suspend one or two strips of flypaper. No! He virtually covered the ceiling of that little shed with a truckload of sticky strips hanging down several feet.

As I bent down to open the plastic container of Wal-Mart Old Roy dog food, I luckily avoided the flypaper. But as I stood up straight (all five feet zero inches of me), my big hair felt a tug. My head was pulled backwards, and I was suddenly encased in something unknown and very sinister. In the eerie darkness I did not realize that it was me, not the mosquitoes, that the flypaper had captured so skillfully.

Sections of flypaper seized my big hair, while others slapped at my face. The harder I fought, the harder my unknown enemy fought back. The flypaper seized my hair and the fuzzy material of my chenille robe. It stuck to me as I flailed my arms and bravely battled the boogers and monsters and haints I vividly envisioned. My heart pounded as I shrieked, and with great effort I finally broke free from the invisible enemy tormenting me. I raced toward the safety of the parsonage, where I slammed and bolted the door and tried to breathe normally again. Running to the bathroom, I faced my reflection in the large mirror. It was *not* a pretty sight. Staring back at me was a terrorized preacher's wife complete with Tammy Faye mascara running from my panic-stricken eyes, while my big hair looked as though it had been brushed in a blender and dipped in Mega Spritz and flypaper.

It was well past 3:00 A.M. before my heart stopped pounding and the final remnants of flypaper were pulled from my big hair.

While I have never looked a roll of flypaper in the face again, I still have days when terror and darkness grip my heart. There is much to fear in our imperfect world. My advice for handling those fearful moments? Boldly face those days with your hair small and your faith big, and walk confidently with a loving God who understands your anxiety and gently whispers, "Fear not!"

CHAPTER SIX

Nothing to Do but Laugh: Life's Most Embarrassing Moments

Man is the only animal that blushes.
Or needs to.
—Mark Twain

The problem with people
is that they're only human.
—Calvin and Hobbes

Slippery Slope

Betty Malz

I had driven three hours with my friend Gloria Hutchens to speak at Sauk Center, Minnesota, for a Saturday night church rally. It was November 6—my birthday. We arrived there only ten minutes before I was to be introduced. While Gloria went to tell the pastor that we had made it, I went downstairs to the rest room. As usual, the ladies' room was full—and about twenty women were waiting in the hallway. The men's room was empty. I figured I'd temporarily claim the territory, so I slipped in. No one had seen me, and no one would ever know.

Well, they had recently remodeled the rest room and had covered the cement steps that led up to the "white throne" with a very slick gray porcelain-finish paint. Although I stepped carefully, I whacked my head on the overhead plumbing. I winced and felt a painful knot on my head, but I knew it would be all right. But when I started up the steps, my high wooden heels slipped. My feet went out from under me, and I cracked the back of my head on that cement. When I woke up, I was at the bottom of the steps. My back now hurt more than my head, and my belt was broken. I could hear the congregation singing upstairs. I could not see my feet, and soon I realized that the heels of my shoes had run right through a plasterboard wall and were protruding into the hallway in the dust of white, chalky powder.

I heard two men talking in the hall. One said, "What is this?" The other opened the door and answered, "I believe it's our speaker." "Not anymore," the first one remarked. "She'll never make it. She may be a writer, but she can't read." Then he called out, "Do you know you're in the men's room?"

"Yes," I muttered, although I didn't see what difference that made at this point in the game.

Then came the second dumb question. "Are you hurt?"

I couldn't help but reply, "No, I'm not hurt. I always exit the rest room this way."

I was determined I was going to speak. I assured them I would be okay, put my broken belt in my purse, and struggled to the platform. Somehow I got through the evening, but the pastor could tell that something was wrong. After the rally, when I told him my story, he wouldn't believe me until he'd gone to check it out for himself. You should have heard the roar!

All the way home that night I moaned. I couldn't sleep, and the next day the doctor told me I'd broken my tailbone—snapped off the last three tiny bones at the end of my spine. I didn't even try to explain the accident to the doctor.

Weeks later I got a letter from the pastor's secretary telling me that they didn't repair the hole but posted a sign that read, "Betty Malz was here."

Looking back now, the whole story is hilariously funny, and I can laugh about it. But, as the psalmist said, I had to endure the night of weeping before I was able to experience the joy that comes in the morning.

A River Runs Down It

Charlene Ann Baumbich

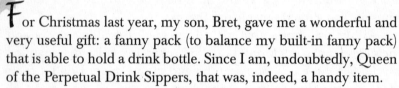

For Christmas last year, my son, Bret, gave me a wonderful and very useful gift: a fanny pack (to balance my built-in fanny pack) that is able to hold a drink bottle. Since I am, undoubtedly, Queen of the Perpetual Drink Sippers, that was, indeed, a handy item.

Before my husband, George, and I left on our annual trek to the local county fair, I filled 'er up and strapped 'er on. After walking around for about an hour and finishing my second tankful, so to speak, it was time to hit the john. Right now!

Since it was a very hot, sticky day and since a strapped-on fanny pack makes loosening clothing so much more difficult, I unsnapped it from around my waist and hung it around my neck so I could negotiate the necessities without impairment.

In the nick of time, I was free to do my duty. Whew! But by midstream, a horrible sensation struck me. In the heat and desperateness of disencumbering myself from the tacky clothes, I must not have gotten something pulled down right. To make it worse, it was beyond my capabilities to shut off the tap, so to speak. I was stunned, humiliated, and wet.

Then the light dawned. I hadn't secured the pop-up top on the drink bottle dangling from my neck. Although my shorts were a mess, I was relieved to find out that the situation wasn't what I had first believed it to be.

But relief was brief, because suddenly I saw them—the dancing feet of the lady in the stall next to me. The stream of water that had run down my leg had quickly flowed in her direction. Of course, she didn't know that the stream had originated from my water bottle, so I quickly hollered, "It's not what you think! It's my water bottle."

My reassurance did nothing to stop those dancing feet that were trying to hover, one at a dancing time, above the floor and out of the stream.

I exited the stall before her and dutifully waited to show her exactly what had happened. I had become nearly hysterical with laughter by this point.

When the lady exited her stall, I tried, accompanied by my own peals of laughter, to give her a quick demo as to what had happened. She didn't laugh, she didn't smile, she didn't wash her hands. She simply left me standing there alone, wearing wet pants and babbling and laughing.

The next lady who entered the bathroom took a swift up-and-down look at me, and she didn't laugh, either.

Dear Lord, thanks for helping me to laugh at myself. Especially when I'm the only one who thinks I'm funny. Okay, so the joke's on me, but at least I get it!

Gourmet Goodies

Patsy Clairmont

My friend Lana learned some lessons about exactitude when her son's girlfriend invited her for a birthday dinner. It turns out this gal was a gourmet cook, and Lana said it was one of the best meals she had ever eaten. Everything had been prepared exactly as it should have been.

Lana's only disappointment was that some of her good friends didn't get to sample this excellent fare.

So Lana was elated when a second invitation arrived to attend an open house and to bring guests of her choice—exactly what Lana had hoped for, gourmet goodies and all. Lana regaled her friends about this dream-come-true cook.

When they arrived, Lana and her enthusiastic friends gathered in the living room and selected cozy seats around a tray of lovely appetizers. Eager to sample them, Lana's guest Beverly selected an item and dipped it into the candle-heated sauce. She took a bite, chewed, and swallowed—and then began to spit. She tried to dispose of the rest of her gourmet treat into her napkin while shaking her head in disgust.

Lana was aghast. "What's wrong?" she whispered to her friend.

"It's terrible," Beverly choked out quietly.

"Don't be silly," Lana replied, beginning to feel defensive. Then to prove her friend wrong, Lana picked up the identical item, dipped it into the sauce, and popped it into her mouth. Her eyes began to grow larger, and she looked for a place to get rid of the disgusting stuff lodged in her burning mouth. Her now-experienced friend handed her some napkins. Lana was confused, embarrassed, and nauseated.

She decided the offending culprit was something in the raspberry sauce. When one of the kitchen helpers walked through the room, Lana meekly asked about the sauce's contents.

"Sauce?" said the woman. "Why, that's liquid potpourri!"

Later Lana had to admit the evening hadn't exactly gone as she thought it would. The good news? Lana and Beverly had the sweetest breath for weeks afterward!

Putting on the Ritz

Cathy Lee Phillips

The Ritz Carlton? Well, maybe I can adjust my schedule."

The rat! For several weeks I had been begging Jennifer to go to the beach with me, but a variety of scheduling conflicts had kept her close to home. So, being an independent woman of the world, I decided to go by myself. *I've been to college and I hold a steady job,* I thought. *I certainly can go to the beach by myself.*

I called my travel agent with my criteria: I wanted to practically roll out of the bed and onto the beach. And I wanted something relatively close to my hometown. I didn't want to spend my entire vacation driving to and from my destination.

Within the hour my travel agent called back. "Have I got a deal for you," she practically shouted with excitement. "In fact, if you don't take this, I will."

The Ritz Carlton, Amelia Island, Florida. They were offering a special rate of $159 per night for a suite that normally rented for $650 per night. The Ritz Carlton! I had never visited a Ritz before, but I knew of their reputation for being the ultimate in pampering and luxury.

"Book it!" I told my travel agent.

Next, I called Jennifer to gloat. She was my best friend, a fellow PW (Preacher's Wife), with a temperament so like mine it was frightening. Most people thought we were sisters because of our similar looks and personality. Of course, because I had no gray hair, people naturally thought I was the younger sister.

Our husbands pastored neighboring United Methodist churches in Cherokee County, Georgia. Therefore, we saw each other often at community and church events. We quickly became close friends. Jennifer was a teacher, with a long summer vacation, so it seemed sensible that she could accompany me to the beach. But her summer calendar filled quickly that year. It seemed that she had no time for pitiful little me—until I mentioned the Ritz Carlton. Like me, she only knew of the Ritz by reputation and couldn't pass up the chance to spend a few days in this luxury resort.

In short, Jennifer somehow changed her plans, and on a hot July afternoon, these two preacher's wives from Cherokee County turned toward the beach. Over the six-hour drive we talked and laughed like two teenagers at a slumber party. We sang along with the radio and even played word games to pass the time.

As we neared the island, however, we began to think seriously about something important to both of us—snacks! We were on vacation; everyone knows that calories do not count while you are on vacation. We had no idea what edibles the hotel would offer, so we made a quick stop at a convenience store for the basics:

√ Two cases of caffeine-free Diet Coke
√ DoubleStuf Oreos
√ Cheese and crackers
√ Cherry Pop Tarts for breakfast
√ One bag of Almond Joy candy bars
√ An oversize bag of bright-orange cheese puffs
√ One disposable razor, because Jennifer had forgotten to shave her legs

In our old shorts and tank tops we made quite a scene as we raided the convenience store. We paid in cash so no one would know our names.

We arrived at Amelia Island about twenty minutes later and looked for signs to the Ritz Carlton. Distracted by our chatter, we missed the turn. Realizing we were lost, we decided to head toward the water—since the hotel was on the beachfront. We would find it eventually. In the distance we spotted a large hotel with a beautiful blue roof and turned toward it.

"I'd like to stay at a place like that just once before I die," Jennifer remarked. Hoping we might find the Ritz in the general area of that beautiful building, we drove toward it. As we approached, we finally saw the signs that would direct us to the Ritz Carlton. Making one last turn, we suddenly discovered that the large hotel with the blue roof *was* actually the Ritz Carlton!

I stopped the car just short of the entrance.

"I feel completely outclassed," I whispered, looking at my old shorts and tank top. And Jennifer still had not shaved her legs. Not knowing what else to do, I shifted the car into drive and slowly approached the hotel.

An army of uniformed attendants descended upon the car. "Welcome to the Ritz Carlton. May we get your bags? Please let me valet-park your car while you check in. Did you have a pleasant trip?"

Walking inside, Jennifer and I surveyed the tall ceilings, the ornate furnishings, the fresh flowers, and the strict attention to detail. Just then a nicely dressed bellman brought our luggage cart into the lobby. Glancing over, I realized that the oversized bag of cheese puffs had pushed through the top of our brown bag of snacks. The bag rustled loudly as the cart moved.

I wanted to register under an alias!

Jennifer, meanwhile, used the "I think I'll stand off to the side and pretend I don't know her" approach. After all, the room was reserved in my name, and no one even knew that Jennifer Huycke existed.

Laugh on, Jennifer, I thought to myself. *At least my legs are freshly shaven!*

The bellman led us to our accommodations on the sixth floor. The foyer opened into a suite that was easily larger than my first apartment. The sitting room was beautifully decorated in tones of green, with an overstuffed sofa and chairs and a large color television. A separate bedroom was equally posh, with two queen beds, desks, and a tall armoire holding another large television. An immense hallway held two large closets, complete with thick terry cloth Ritz Carlton robes. There was also a safe for our valuables (maybe the cheese puffs?). A large private balcony overlooked the beach and a perfectly manicured courtyard. Three separate marble bathrooms completed the ensemble.

"Are your accommodations suitable, Mrs. Phillips?" the bellman asked.

"Perfectly," I replied.

When he left the room, Jennifer and I squealed with delight. The place was gorgeous—and it was ours for the next three days!

"Where is the phone!" Jennifer shrieked. "I have to call Dick and tell him about this place!"

We looked around the suite and found a variety of phones—six in all. Choosing one on a table next to the sofa, Jennifer remarked, "Wow, look at all the buttons on this phone. I wonder what they all do."

"Just don't call Alaska or do anything to embarrass me," I instructed, remembering that the registration was in my name only.

Lifting the receiver, Jennifer punched in a series of numbers that connected her with the parsonage in Cherokee County. Dick was not home, but in our excitement we proceeded to leave a very long and very silly message describing our arrival at the Ritz Carlton. With great animation we related everything—from the uniformed attendants meeting our car to the orange bag of cheese puffs gliding through the lobby on our luggage cart. Jennifer described the room in detail—from the posh furnishings to the magnificent view.

While she talked, I explored the suite and found, to my amazement, that each bathroom was equipped with a telephone. It hung on the wall next to the toilet. So as Jennifer continued to babble, I picked up the extension from the bathroom in the foyer and said, "Hey, Dick, I am using the phone in the bathroom. Just think, I can go to the bathroom and talk to you at the same time. This phone is in bathroom number one. You don't believe me? Well, I'll prove it."

And I held the receiver at an angle that would pick up the sound of the toilet as I flushed it. Continuing with this theme, I walked into the next bathroom.

"Hello, Dick. I am in bathroom number two. It has a gray marbled floor, a large tub, and a mirror that covers the whole wall. And guess what? There is a phone next to this toilet, too! Just listen."

And I flushed toilet number two.

"Dick, this is me in bathroom number three. We have another marble floor and a shower with a glass door. There are tons of towels and Ritz Carlton toiletries. And, of course, there is a phone. Listen to this!"

And I flushed toilet number three.

Jennifer and I were red-faced by the time we completed our bizarre message. We were having a great time!

"Now, I've just got to call Mom," and Jennifer again began pushing buttons on the large phone. Before the connection was made, however, she stopped, turned pale as a ghost, and placed the receiver on the base.

"What?" I demanded. "What's wrong?"

For a few brief seconds she was completely quiet, still pale. Then she spoke in a subdued voice.

"Someone from the hotel office spoke to me when I began dialing," she relayed. "I could hear giggling in the background as they gave me some phone instructions."

"What instructions?" I practically shouted.

Still pale and obviously horrified, Jennifer said, "They told me that I should depress the conference-call button before I made my next call. And they called me *Mrs. Phillips*."

This could mean only one thing: the staff in the hotel office had heard our entire ridiculous, absurd, laughable conversation. I turned pale myself. Jennifer was obviously telling the truth. I knew she was—she would *never* have used the word "depress." She would have used "push" or "press," instead. She's a kindergarten teacher, after all!

For me, the most awful part of this nightmare was that the operator had called her *Mrs. Phillips*. The Ritz Carlton did not know Jennifer at all; they only knew that the room was registered to *Mrs. Phillips*. They even knew my home address and my credit card number.

"I'm never leaving this room," I said, completely humiliated.

Jennifer confessed, "I think I want to go home."

Silence filled the room—at least for a few minutes—until Jennifer began a soft giggle that quickly matured into a loud belly laugh. It took me a few minutes longer to see the humor in the situation, because I was, after all, *Mrs. Phillips*—the registered guest.

We laughed until our sides hurt. We laughed until we rolled off the sofa and onto the dark green carpets. We laughed until tears rolled down our faces. We laughed until we each had to use one of the three bathrooms in the suite.

The Trouble with Peanuts

Barbara Johnson

Recently someone sent me a silly story about a preacher who visited an elderly woman from his congregation. As they talked, he nibbled from a bowl of peanuts on the coffee table. They visited for nearly an hour, and by the time the preacher was ready to leave, he had eaten the whole bowl of peanuts. A little embarrassed, he told the woman, "I have to apologize. I really just meant to nibble a few peanuts."

"Oh, that's okay," the old lady reassured him. "Ever since I lost my teeth all I can do is suck the chocolate off them anyway."

CHAPTER SEVEN

Raising Laughs:
Humor and Parenting

Parents are the last people on earth
who ought to have children.
—Samuel Butler

Oh, what a tangled web do parents weave
when they think that their children are naive.
—Ogden Nash

Bare Witness

Phil Callaway

It's BATH NIGHT. Around the world hurried and harried parents seize precious moments to rest and recharge while their children set uncontested Olympic records in the dunking and "I got more water on the walls and ceiling than you did" events.

At our peculiar house on this particular night, a four-year-old and his younger brother are all wet. The older is constructing a bubble bath beard on the younger. I can't help overhearing their conversation:

"Did you know that you've done bad things?"

"Yeah." It is one of three words one-year-old Jeffrey knows. The other two are "yep" and "uh-huh."

"You have done sins," continues the four-year-old kindly.

"Yep."

"And you shall go to hell."

"Yep."

"Hell is hot."

The one-year-old is making a hole in the soap bar.

"But you can go to heaven. Do you want to go to heaven?"

Jeffrey sips some bathwater before responding: "Uh-huh."

"Then ask Jesus into your heart."

"Yeah."

"I'll pray for you, okay?"

"Yep."

Moments later an excited four-year-old stands before his parents–dripping wet, wearing a smile. "Daddy! Mommy! Guess what?"

128

"What, Stephen?"

"Jeffrey asked Jesus into his heart."

Jeffrey is one. You might say that he's a baby Christian.

"Rachael!" A few days have passed since Stephen claimed his first trophy. He is on a roll, and he isn't about to stop now. Especially at mealtimes. "Did you know that you've done bad things?"

"No." It is two-year-old Rachael's most common response.

"You have done sins," the four-year-old continues, undaunted.

"Haven't." Rachael is trying to stab a pea with a fork.

"Yes, you have."

"No. Haven't ... "

"YES!"

"NO!"

"YEEEEEESS YOU HAVE!" The witnesser throws part of a sesame seed bun at the witnessee. The bun misses. There are sesame seeds everywhere.

"All right, Stephen. Come with me."

Down the hall we go, hand in hand. He is unsure of the consequences. I can't think of a thing to say. Kneeling down, I hold him tight. Ah, my son. The bare witness. "Don't throw things at your sister."

"Okay," he says, and he wiggles free. "One more thing," I say, as he disappears around the corner. "You will sweep up those sesame seeds."

Evening has come. The children are tucked in. Mom is out with my VISA card, and I am in bed reading. A little pajama-clad figure with bare feet slowly pokes his head around the corner. "Hi," he says.

"Stephen, you should be asleep." My tone is unconvincing. He knows his father is a softy when it comes to bedtime.

"What are you eating?"

"Grapes."

"Are they good?"

"Come here and see." I pull down the covers, and he crawls in. Grapes are better shared.

"What are you reading?" he asks, looking at the book I'm holding—a best-seller I don't read enough.

"It's the Bible. Do you want me to read to you?"

"Yep."

"I'm reading from a book called Matthew. Remember the song you like, 'I don't wanna be a Pharisee, 'cause they're not fair you see'? Well, one of the Pharisees asked Jesus what he wanted him to do most of all. Do you know what Jesus said?"

"What?"

"He told him to love God with everything he had—and do you know what else?"

"What?"

"He told him to love others like he loved himself. Don't you think it's more important to love others than to tell them about Jesus? You've been telling Rachael and Jeffrey about Jesus, and that makes me glad. But they need to see how kind you are to them before they'll believe what you say about Jesus. Love them, Stephen. Grown-up Christians like to talk about *contacts* and *souls*. Sometimes we sort of throw buns, too, but we don't talk very often about loving those who don't know Jesus. We need to love people so they begin to ask us why."

My son has been silent. Undoubtedly, he's impressed with my verbose rhetoric. I mean, let's face it. This has been pretty good stuff. I look over at him. His mouth is wide-open, but not with awe. He is sound asleep. Perhaps all this advice was really meant for me.

Good Grief!

Karen Scalf Linamen

When Kaitlyn turned eleven, she wanted one thing and one thing only for her birthday. Pet rats. I didn't ask my husband, Larry, what he thought about the idea. After all, there are just some things for which it's easier to obtain forgiveness than permission. Instead, I peeled open the Yellow Pages and looked under pets— and before you could say, "Mouse droppings," Cecelia and Megan had come to live with us.

They were adorable, all white and inquisitive and good-natured. The little ladies had been a part of our family for about a week when I looked into their glass cage and noticed something tiny and pink wiggling next to Cecelia. I blinked. Stared. Blinked again. It was a baby rat. I called the pet store. The woman on the other end of the line sounded puzzled. "She must have been pregnant when she left here, although I didn't think either of those rats were nearly old enough. And I'm amazed there's only one baby. I've never heard of a rat giving birth to a litter of just one. Oh well. Think of it as a two-for-one special. Or maybe three-for-two. However you count 'em, congratulations and good luck."

Kacie, then two and a half, bonded immediately with the baby. Forget watching *Rugrats*—Kacie watched our own rats and daily monitored the progress of our tiny guest.

Everything was going great until one morning I looked into the nest and discovered that the baby rat had died during the night.

My biggest concern was how to tell Kacie. Larry and I discussed it at length. I voted for the straightforward approach, but

Larry wondered if Kacie was too young to understand the idea of death—and in the end I agreed.

You know that old saying "what a tangled web we weave"? Well, I started weaving the very afternoon the baby rat died. After disposing of the tiny body, I pulled Kacie onto my lap and gently explained that the baby rat had simply "gone away." This was my first mistake. "Gone where? Who took it out of the cage? Does Cecelia know it's gone? Did it walk, or go in a car? Where did it go? When is it coming back? Who's going to feed it while it's gone? Is it visiting its family? Is Cecelia sad the baby's gone? Can we go find the baby?"

I tried to answer all her questions. But in my attempt to protect her, I tried to answer her questions without actually giving her any accurate information. This, of course, led to more questions, and one thing led to another until . . . Two hours later, I called my mom in a panic. "I don't think I handled this very well," I explained. "I started off nice and vague, but Kacie bombarded me with so many questions that I guess I got a little carried away, and now, well, now she thinks the baby took a train to rat heaven. She's roaming the house, yelling, 'Baby rat, where are you?' trying to convince it to catch the 6:15 back home. This has gotten entirely out of hand."

When my mother responded, I could hear the smile in her voice. "Karen, it's simple. Here's what you need to do and say . . . " I followed her instructions to the letter. My conversation with Kacie went without a hitch. I pulled the tiny body from the trash and let Kacie see and even touch the lifeless form (thank God for antibacterial soap!). I chose my words carefully when explaining how the baby rat had died. I didn't want to say the little rat had fallen asleep and would never wake up—what if Kacie became afraid to fall asleep herself? I didn't want to say the mother forgot to feed it— what if Kacie missed a meal and began to fear for her life? No, I had to pick a cause of death that had no easily identifiable counterpart in Kacie's world.

I told her the mother rat sat on the baby. I rarely, if ever, sit on my children, so this was probably a pretty safe choice.

I suggested we bury the baby in the backyard, but Kacie wasn't ready for that quite yet. It took three days of talking and looking and touching before she was ready to say good-bye. Then we took the baby rat into the backyard and buried it under a cedar tree. This was Kacie's first encounter with death.

Awhile later Larry's grandmother died. When we heard the news, we packed up our van and drove from Texas to Arizona to be with other family members as we grieved the loss, remembered the legacy, and celebrated the life of Eyla Linamen.

Of course, this also meant that I found myself with yet another opportunity to talk to Kacie about loss. Thankfully, Kacie was nearly four years old by now and had matured a little since our tiny pet took the train to rat heaven.

I thought about calling my mom again for advice. But Kacie wasn't the only one who had developed since the untimely passing of Baby Rat. I had learned a thing or two myself, and I was ready to handle this one on my own.

For just a heartbeat I wondered whether Kacie would be traumatized or comforted by viewing her great-grandmother's body. Then, remembering Cecelia's dear departed baby, Larry and I agreed that a straightforward, concrete approach was the best path.

We let Kacie view the body, which she found intriguing. Then I sat down with her on a sofa in the foyer of the funeral home and tried to explain what she had just observed. This is what I said:

"Kacie, yesterday you played all day, didn't you? You ran and played and got all dirty and messy. And at the end of the day, you needed to take a bath, so you went into your room, took off all your clothes, and ran naked into the bathroom. When that happened, you were in one room and your clothes were in another. Could your clothes run and play anymore? Could they move all by themselves? Of course not. They lay crumbled on the floor, worn and discarded, unable to stir or shift or move by themselves. But you weren't crumpled on the floor, were you? You were in the other room, naked, laughing, and playing in the water.

"That's what happened to Great-Grandma. That's what will happen to all of us one day. Our bodies are like clothes. We wear them for a while. We run and play, and after a while our bodies get wrinkled and worn. And when they're pretty much worn-out, Jesus helps us to climb out of them. He lets us leave them crumpled on the floor, and we run on into heaven. That's where Great-Grandma is. Her body is here, but she's in heaven."

Kacie thought for a moment. I knew I was in trouble when she said, matter-of-factly, "So Great-Grandma is naked in heaven?"

"Yes, well," I hedged, "I don't think she's still naked. I think God gave her another body to wear. You know, kind of like when you put on pajamas after your bath."

Kacie looked at her body and tugged at the skin on her arm. Then she looked at me. "How did Great-Grandma take off her body? I don't know how to take off my body. Can I climb out of my body, too?"

"Um, not exactly. We can't do it ourselves. Jesus has to help us. Only he knows when our bodies are worn enough and it's time for a new one."

"But how?"

"How?"

"How does Jesus do it?"

"Do what?" I was stalling for time.

"Get our bodies off us?" I had no choice; I had to tell her.

That afternoon, Kacie ran to Larry's dad, climbed into his lap, and asked loudly, "Grandpa, did you know that God unzipped Great-Grandma's body? Great-Grandma's body has an invisible zipper."

Dad blinked. "A zipper?"

"Yep. Everybody's does. We don't know where it is, so we can't unzip it ourselves. Only God knows about the zipper."

"I didn't know that."

"Yep. And do you know what happened then?"

"I can't say that I do."

Kacie's eyes widened with excitement as she leaned in close and blurted, "Great-Grandma ran naked into heaven!"

Perhaps I should have called my mother for advice after all.

Bite My Tongue!

Sue Buchanan

From the time Dana was born, we prayed that she would marry the right person someday and that it would be God's choice, not ours. It took Dana a long time to show even the slightest interest in boys. She was a late bloomer. By the time she was in eleventh grade, we'd pretty much pegged her as antisocial and slightly boring. Yes, I know she is my very own daughter and that's a cruel thing to say, but sometimes a mother has to face facts.

Then, in her senior year, she discovered the harp, and suddenly she was known. She was in demand to play at every event—talent shows and musicals, and she even became a member of the Nashville Youth Symphony. One night when she returned from a rehearsal—we always waited up to help her unload, lamenting the fact she hadn't chosen to play a piccolo—she had with her the cutest, tallest, most muscular, blond-haired boy you ever laid eyes on. Balanced on one of his shoulders was the harp. Heretofore, it had taken the three of us to manipulate it out of the station wagon, into the house, and up the stairs. *Whoosh,* went the wind out of Wayne's sails, when he realized that he might never be needed again. If for no other reason than that, we knew this boy couldn't possibly be the one.

After the blond Adonis came a total opposite: a dark, fun-loving Jewish boy, and we all fell in love, especially Wayne after he discovered David couldn't move the harp by himself. My guess is, knowing David, that even if he could have, he was smart enough to play the game.

It wasn't unusual for Dana and David to come home late after a date and barge right into our room, ready to entertain us with their evening's adventures. It was fun while it lasted. We knew deep down that David wasn't the one; his background was very Jewish, and Dana's was very Christian. Each recognized that their heritage was part of who they were, and neither intended to change.

In college Dana met Barry, and it didn't take long for us to figure out that this was the one! Watching the two of them together was like watching six-year-olds who simply took delight in each other's presence. Barry's parents, Bonnie and Miles, whom we'd met and fallen in love with, were having the same thoughts we had: these two were meant for each other. In our minds, Bonnie and I were planning a wedding. We chose the colors for our dresses, for heaven's sake!

The problem was that Dana and Barry didn't cooperate! Dana assured us that they could *never* date; they were best friends. "Almost like brother and sister," she said. They graduated from college with no wedding in sight.

Every year, Dana and Barry and their other best friends, Deba and Cary (also not a couple), took a vacation together. Throughout the year, they would visit each other: Barry would come to Nashville, or she would go to Middletown, Ohio. They dated other people, and if he broke up with someone, she was by his side to comfort him. If she broke up with someone, Barry was there, hugging, patting, consoling.

Looked like love to me, but what do I know? I'm just the mother.

Once when I was planning a business trip to Columbus, Ohio, Dana insisted that, instead of flying, I should drive so she could go with me. The plan would be to drop her off in Middletown on the way and pick her up on the way back. Things went according to plan. I dropped her off, continued on to Columbus for a couple of days, did my work, and returned to the designated meeting place in Middletown—the Bob Evans restaurant. They were there, and I pulled in next to them. And I waited. I waited and waited and waited!

When I glanced their way, I could see they were in heavy conversation. I waited!

Even though I tried to keep my glances at a minimum, I couldn't help but notice after a while that Dana was becoming more and more animated. Not in a good way. I knew my daughter well, and I recognized "not in a good way" when I saw it. I waited!

For forty-five minutes I waited, and at last Dana jumped out, slammed the door, threw her duffel bag in the backseat of my car, slammed the door, jumped in the front seat, and slammed that door.

"Go!" she ordered. "Go!" She didn't look back. She didn't wave. And there was certainly no sisterly kiss blown through the breeze—the kind you would expect to see when best friends part.

The look on her face was the look you save for someone who just killed your pet parakeet. She was steaming! Smoke was coming out of her nostrils.

I bit my tongue!

"The nerve of him," she said. "You'll never believe it! You will *never in a million years* believe it!"

I bit my tongue.

"Mother, I am so mad!" she said. "He loves me." It was like she'd just been proposed to by the Ayatollah! She slapped the dashboard for punctuation.

I bit my tongue.

"He's loved me for years. Can you believe it?"

I bit my tongue.

"Know what he said? He said he wants to get married, but he can't wait for me forever." She slapped the dashboard.

"He says he'll have to find someone else if I won't marry him. Can you believe that?" Another slap on the dashboard.

I bit my tongue.

"'Of course, find someone!' I told him. 'Of course, get married! We're just best friends. Always were, always will be.'"

There was a moment of silence, followed by another slap on the dashboard. I noticed that her poor hand was bright-red from the trauma.

As for me, I was thinking I could taste blood running down my throat as a result of my tongue biting! I wondered if the emergency room in the next town was equipped to handle severe carpal tunnel syndrome and tongue biting trauma.

"I'll tell you one thing, though," she said, eyes flashing. The dashboard punctuation was now coming with every word she expelled. "*Whoever* he marries better understand our relationship!"

I could contain myself no longer. I burst out laughing. I'd just taken a mouthful of iced tea, and I spewed it all over me, the dashboard, and the windshield.

"*What!*" she screeched like a banshee, her face now between me and the road, presenting another problem that might end in the trauma center.

"I can promise you," I said, "whoever he marries *won't* understand the relationship."

It was quiet the rest of the way home.

The friendship somehow continued—unchanged as far as I could tell. In the fall, Dana told us that Barry had a girlfriend. In October, she asked us if we could get a ticket for the girl for Praise Gathering. We agreed, and Dana made arrangements for us to meet up with her at our hotel. Just before we left for Indianapolis, Dana phoned.

"Call me as soon as you meet her, and tell me what she's like. Barry Shafer deserves the best. In fact, he deserves *perfect*. This girl needs to be perfect."

Somehow our plans for the meeting went awry, and we never laid eyes on the girl. We ended up leaving her ticket at the desk. When we arrived home, Dana was on our doorstep.

"So what's she like? Is she witty and clever? And fun? Barry's the funnest person in the world. He needs somebody fun. Does she love the Lord? Nobody loves the Lord more than Barry Shafer. Is she cute? Is she pretty? Is she right for Barry?"

Wayne and I were ready! "Oh, I don't know," I said, taking my time. "I guess you could say she's"—I'm milking it for all its worth—"she's cuddly." Wayne shook his head in agreement.

"Cuddly? CUDDLY?" Dana screeched, eyes flashing. "She's *cuddly?* What kind of a person is that?"

The next event in the saga of Dana and Barry was a ski trip by the same faithful foursome, followed the very next weekend by a visit by Barry to Nashville. It surprised me, since they'd just been together, but, as usual, we planned a big family dinner.

After the meal, as we sat around the living room, I noticed that Dana was sitting on the floor by Barry's chair. Was I mistaken, or was she leaning against his leg? Was I mistaken, or was she looking at him like he was Tom Cruise? Was I mistaken, or every time he opened his mouth was she confusing him with Billy Graham?

Then the clincher! He reached out and stroked her hair! This in itself could be the eighth wonder of the world, because Dana cannot stand to have her hair touched. From the time she was a small child, her hair was off-limits. I always blamed it on the fact that she had such heavy hair that it actually gave her pain to have it messed with. Whatever the reason, you just didn't go there. But Barry was going there! And she was behaving like a dopey little kitten. She was loving it! She was all but purring!

Later, we pieced together the story. She had turned around on the ski slopes to see him skiing toward her, and her heart leaped out of her body. She threw him down right there in the snow, did heaven knows what (a mother *doesn't* want to know!), and the rest is history.

Like I always say, when it comes to your children, you should just bite your tongue and pray (knowing in your heart you have the answers). I just don't always take my own advice.

Diamonds and Dump Trucks

Judy Carden

Bob and I had just settled in for a short winter's nap when our three little cherubs exploded into our bedroom, bouncing up and down on our bed.

"Santa came! And he finished all of his cookies and milk," Aubrey squealed. "It's Christmas morning!" yelled Danny. "Hurry, hurry," five-year-old Ryan pleaded, bouncing high and landing smack in the middle of his father and me.

Fifteen minutes later, we were positioned around the Christmas tree, waiting to hear the magic words from Dad, *The first gift of Christmas goes to* . . . At long last, the festivities were under way.

Soft sounds of Christmas carols and squeals of delight filled the air, as, one by one, the children tore open their gifts.

Then came the moment when all eyes were on me, as Bob handed me a perfectly wrapped petite box.

"Open it," urged the children.

"Oooohh," I gasped, as I lifted a brilliant pair of diamond earrings from the box and put them in my ears. As I glanced around the room, though, I couldn't help but notice that the boys had exchanged worried glances. Danny smacked himself in the forehead and said, "Diamonds. Oh, no."

We continued our celebration until just one gift remained underneath the tree. It was clumsily wrapped, with much too much Scotch tape, and it had a tag that read "To Mom—from your boys."

For the second time that morning all eyes were on me as I ripped away at the layers of paper and tape and ceremoniously lifted their gift for all to see: a set of colorful plastic trucks! Three, to be exact.

"They're for me and you and Danny," Ryan informed me. "But they're not diamonds. Wanna play anyway?"

"They're better than diamonds," I said in between sobs.

And then I removed my earrings, grabbed a yellow dump truck, and said, "Last one to the sandbox is a rotten egg." Because, you know, diamonds are forever—but little boys are not.

What Did *You* Do Today?

Phil Callaway

I have been a husband for nearly ten years now, so needless to say I know virtually everything there is to know about my wife's needs. For instance, I know that she can get by without sleep for three days and three nights—but definitely not without chocolate. I also know that she needs flowers, nurturing, romance, protection, a listening ear, clean laundry, and clothes that fit. Whereas my basic needs are . . . well, pizza.

It is a quarter to five right now, and I'm sitting at my desk thinking about my need for pizza. It's been one of those days at the office. A computer blip swallowed half the morning's work, and nothing went right after that. I had no time for lunch. Deadlines loom. Reports beckon. And my stomach growls. It is saying, "Hey, give us pizza. We need pizza."

As the clock struggles toward 5:00 P.M., however, the growling is muffled in visions of home. Dinner will be store-bought Coke and homemade pizza. Toppings will include large hunks of pepperoni, layers of ham, and enough cheese to blanket Switzerland. The crust will be light, yet crunchy, flavored with a generous pinch of oregano. When I arrive, Ramona will be waiting at the door, her hair permed, her lips pursed. The children will be setting the table, newly washed smiles gracing each face. "Hi, Daddy!" they will say in unison. "We sure missed you."

Following dinner, the children will beg to be put to bed early. "We want you and Mom to have some time alone," they will say. "You've probably had a tough day."

As I park the car, however, I realize that something has gone terribly wrong. For one thing, half the neighborhood is in our yard. As I enter the house, I find the other half. They are riffling through our refrigerator. In the kitchen Ramona is bent over the dishwasher, cleaning out the last of the silverware. The table is piled high with laundry, and the stove holds not even a hint of supper.

Several times in my life I have said things people did not appreciate. This is one of those times.

"So what's for supper?" I ask. "Roast beef?"

There is silence.

I sit down beside the laundry and make an even bigger mistake. "So," I say, "what did *you* do today?"

Sometimes my wife moves very quickly. This is one of those times. Ramona stands up straight, brandishing a sharp fork.

"What did *I* do today?"

She walks swiftly across the room—still holding the fork.

"WHAT DID I DO TODAY?"

She hands me a piece of paper. A piece of paper women everywhere should own. Then she stands over me as I read it.

WHAT I DID TODAY

3:21 A.M.–Woke up. Took Jeffrey to bathroom.

3:31 A.M.–Woke up. Took Jeffrey back to bed.

3:46 A.M.–Got you to quit snoring.

3:49 A.M.–Went to sleep.

5:11 A.M.–Woke up. Took Jeffrey to bathroom.

6:50 A.M.–Alarm went off. Mentally reviewed all I had to do today.

7:00 A.M.–Alarm went off.

7:10 A.M.–Alarm went off. Contemplated doing something violent to alarm clock.

7:19 A.M.–Got up. Got dressed. Made bed. Warned Stephen.

7:20 A.M.–Warned Stephen.

7:21 A.M.–Spanked Stephen. Held Stephen. Prayed with Stephen.

7:29 A.M.–Fed boys a breakfast consisting of Cheerios, orange juice, and something that resembled toast. Scolded Jeffrey for mixing them.

7:35 A.M.–Woke Rachael.

7:38 A.M.–Had devotions.

7:49 A.M.–Made Stephen's lunch. Tried to answer Jeffrey's question, "Why does God need people?" Warned Stephen.

8:01 A.M.–Woke Rachael.

8:02 A.M.–Started laundry.

8:03 A.M.–Took rocks out of washing machine.

8:04 A.M.–Started laundry.

8:13 A.M.–Planned grocery list. Tried to answer Jeffrey's question "Why do we need God?"

8:29 A.M.–Woke Rachael (third time).

8:30 A.M.–Helped Stephen with homework.

8:31 A.M.–Sent Stephen to school. Told him to remember his lunch.

8:32 A.M.–Had breakfast with Rachael. Porridge.

Rest of morning–Took Stephen's lunch to him. Returned library books. Explained why a cover was missing. Mailed letters. Bought groceries. Shut TV off. Planned birthday party. Cleaned house. Wiped noses. Wiped windows. Wiped bottoms. Shut TV off. Cleaned spaghetti out of carpet. Cut bite marks off the cheese. Made owl-shaped sandwiches.

12:35 P.M.–Put wet clothes in dryer.

12:35 P.M.–Sat down to rest.

12:39 P.M.–Scolded Jeffrey. Helped him put clothes back in dryer.

12:45 P.M.–Agreed to baby-sit for a friend. Cut tree sap out of Rachael's hair. Regretted baby-sitting decision. Killed assorted insects. Read to the kids. Clipped ten fingernails. Sent kids outside. Unpacked groceries. Watered plants. Swept floor. Picked watermelon seeds off linoleum. Read to the kids.

3:43 P.M.–Stephen came home. Warned Stephen.

3:46 P.M.–Put Band-Aids on knees. Organized task force to clean kitchen. Cleaned parts of house. Accepted appointment to local committee (secretary said, "You probably have extra time since you don't work"). Tried to answer Rachael's question, "Why are boys and girls different?" Listened to a zillion more questions. Answered a few. Cleaned out dishwasher. Briefly considered running away from home.

5:21 P.M.–Husband arrived, looking for peace, perfection, and pizza.

I am finished reading now, but Ramona is not through. "Of course, not all my days go this smoothly," she says, still clutching the fork.

"Any questions?"

Often when Ramona and I are at public gatherings, she is asked The Question: "Do you work?" I'm glad she is not holding a fork at this point. Sometimes I wish she'd say, "Actually, I work days, nights, and weekends. How about you?" But she doesn't. She's a kind woman. She practices what I preach. Once, however, she confided that she wishes she had the eloquence to respond as one women did: "I am socializing three Homo sapiens in the dominant values of the Judeo-Christian tradition in order that they might be instruments for the transformation of the social order into the teleologically prescribed utopia inherent in the eschaton."

Then she would ask, "And what is it you do?"

Questions, Questions

Chris Ewing

It is my own fault, I suppose. Trying to instill a quest for learning in my children has led to my current sorry position of being in a growing state of educational inequality. In other words, I have reached the point where there are more questions I can't answer than there are ones that I can.

Remember the nursery rhyme "Twinkle, Twinkle, Little Star"? I changed it for my children in order to help foster the pursuit of science.

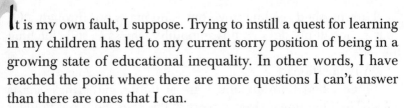

Twinkle, twinkle, little star,
How I wonder what you are.
Hydrogen gases swirling above,
Fusion fires that consume all love.
Twinkle, twinkle, little star,
Now we know just what you are.

My daughter asked, "Dad, if superconducting electromagnets generate magnetic fields millions of times stronger than the earth's, how come that doesn't mess up everyone's compasses?"

Hmm. Good question! Now, being a male and not wanting to display my ignorance in front of the children, I struggled for a plausible answer.

"Uh, well, by international law, I believe it is United Nations Mandate 4061, section 4, paragraph 13—and I quote: 'All large magnets, be they electrical in nature or not, must be installed so their magnetic poles align with those of the earth.' That keeps everything in sync, so there is no conflict in magnetic fields and all compasses remain pointing to their true polar direction." Whew! "Oh wow, Dad, you sure are smart."

The really tough questions, however, come from the youngest minds. "Daddy, what makes clouds?" *No problem,* I think.

"Well, when water evaporates, it rises into–"

"Daddy, what's 'vaporates mean?"

"E-vap-or-rates. That is when water turns into a vapor, which is kind of like a gas, and it goes into the air."

"Gas like you put in the car? From the gas 'tation?"

"Well, not really. The gas you put in the car is a liquid, like water." (I involuntarily wince at the memory of catching some youngster trying to fill the car's gas tank with the garden hose.) "But we will not EVER try to put water in the car again, will we?" I reinforced.

"Okay," he said. Sure. Right.

"Anyway, there are also gases that are like air. You just can't see them because the molecules are so far apart that they are invisible and you can see right through them."

"What are mol-kules?"

"Those are the little tiny pieces that make up everything in the world."

"Even me?"

"Even you."

"But will *I* become in-divisible?" This conversation had, as usual, rapidly gotten out of control.

"What?" I asked.

"Indivisible. So you can't see me anymore. Like the air."

"Oh. No, you don't get to be invisible until you are five years old." A shocked expression flashed across his face. "Kidding, just kidding," I quickly reassured. "You won't become invisible."

"But I want to be invisible!" he whined.

"Sorry! Sorry I tried to be nice and explain something to you! Now, do you want to know about clouds or not?"

"Yes," he sighed, "that is what I have been wanting and wanting!"

"All right. Clouds are just water that floats up in the air. When they get too much water in them, it rains or snows."

"Oh."

"And when clouds come down to the ground, that is fog." That perked him up.

"Then we get to drive in a cloud?"

"That's right."

"Cool!"

Sheesh. What it takes to get through to some people.

I recently attempted to assemble a toy my son had received for his birthday. In the instructions were words that made my blood run cold: "Some patience may be required." *Oh, great,* I thought. When something starts off like that, you instinctively know you are in trouble. And, as usual, the manufacturers understated the obvious. A *lot* of patience was required, and even then, the finished product didn't quite turn out as expected. Seems I had left out a tiny plastic piece—the one that had rolled off the table and was immediately gobbled up by the dog.

So it is with a family. "Some patience may be required" is an understatement. An unbelievable amount of commitment, hard work, and love is required—and things still never quite turn out as expected. We can just pray that the finished product is functional and durable and is something we can be proud of—even if a few little pieces have turned up missing.

Payback

Veda Boyd Jones

It didn't start out as revenge. Looking at the destruction around me, I said what mothers have said for centuries: "Wait until you have children of your own." My three sons swore they would never have offspring. In retaliation, I started a list of their misdeeds and told them that someday they will know what it was like to be on the receiving end. They protested that all their wrongdoings were accidents. But the list has been started.

As soon as the boys set up housekeeping, my husband, Jim, and I will knock calmly on the door. A 7.8 earthquake or a tornado will seem mild after Jim and I descend upon them with the list in hand.

We'll start screaming and arguing as soon as we enter the house, and it goes without saying that we'll be wearing gummy, black baseball cleats. Not only will we make marks on the kitchen floor, but we'll walk on the couch, too.

After we flip on every light in the house, we'll start at the top of the list. Clogging the toilet will be simple. There are several methods on the list to choose from. We can see if the Superman doll can overcome being flushed, or we can choose the more conventional manner and clog it with paper bathroom cups (so they won't know how many we've been using) or with a diaper or just three-fourths of a roll of toilet paper.

Armed with crayons, we'll draw pictures on the walls. I'm leaning toward a Picasso look-alike. Jim prefers pointillism. We'll use red Magic Marker in the middle of the tan carpet—where the couch can't be moved to hide it.

Spills are a cinch. I'll drop a jar of sweet pickles, one of honey, and another of apple juice on the kitchen floor. I'll leave the top off the popcorn popper so kernels and oil splatter everywhere. In the living room, Jim will knock over three full cups of hot chocolate with half-melted miniature marshmallows.

Jim and I have argued over the windows and have compromised, because we don't want to send the boys to bankruptcy court. We'll break only one window, but we'll make sure it's on the second floor.

We've also compromised about jumping on the beds. I don't mind the jumping, but I'm not going to hit my head on the window ledge and require stitches. We'll put ketchup instead of blood on the bedspread.

I'm not going to chop the bark off a redbud tree with a golf club, either. It doesn't seem right to hurt a living thing for the sake of a list and a promise, and I'm going to explain that to the boys. Our redbud is still living, but it's crippled and stands very lopsided. I couldn't do that to a tree.

But I will knock over a few plants. They always seem to survive a spilling, because they get new dirt in the clean-up process.

I hope the boys have screened-in porches. Jim gets the honor of knocking the screen door off the hinges (by accident, of course), since he always has to fix it. I'll just poke holes in the screens with Popsicle sticks so that insects—especially wasps—can get in.

Breaking a recliner will be a breeze. Jim and I will do that together so that one of us doesn't get hurt. We'll sit on the arms and talk, and we'll put our weight on the headrest until the chair turns over. I imagine it will take several falls, but we'll have plenty of time.

Speaking of time, we'll sneak into their bedrooms and set their alarms for 1:13 A.M. I never learned why they set our alarm for that special moment. That first night I thought I'd dreamed it. The second night I stayed up the next three hours wondering if it would go off again.

I wonder how the boys will feel about being pushed into the swimming pool—fully clothed, shoes on, and billfolds in back pockets?

There's something about boys. Parents who have a couple girls, even three, will have a different sort of life. For every girl, the mischief goes up linearly. With boys, the mischief is exponentially compounded.

My list will grow as the years go by, but I really hate to use it against the boys. I'd rather my sons just had children of their own.

And If I Die Before I Wake

Ken Davis

Parenting isn't for weaklings. Moms and dads must be stout of heart; they find that out quickly.

But there's one task that strikes fear and desperation into the toughest of them. You know the one: trying to enforce bedtime. Children have a deep, instinctive aversion to sleep. They'll climb any mountain, cross any river, swim any ocean, to avoid closing their eyes.

Our youngest daughter, Taryn, devised the strategy of calling out religious questions from the bedroom. It's the old Pharisee maneuver. One night, the fleeting tranquility of bedtime was broken by her inquiring mind's need to know. "Daddy, does God talk to us?" she shouted with Socratic intensity.

"Yes, God talks to us," I responded sagely. "Go to sleep. We'll discuss it in the morning." Being a fool. I imagined that would satisfy her.

"No, we must discuss it now!" Before I could frame an appropriate theological response, she added, "He said I could get up!"

How do you deal with that? Here's a child who doesn't know the meaning of the word *psychology,* and she's already deftly placed me in the palm of her hand, psyched out.

One night the bedtime battle reached epic proportions. It was a battle waged with weapons of quick wit and childish charm. In other words, I didn't stand a chance. I'd been struggling for thirty minutes, trying to get my other daughter, Traci, to settle down. Finally I put my foot down.

"Go to bed!" I commanded.

"I need a drink of water," Traci shot back without hesitation.

The verbal sparring match intensified. "You can't have water."

"Why?"

"You'll wet the bed."

"I've quit."

(How do they respond so quickly? Do they have a game plan? Do they pull random thoughts out of thin air? Is this the root of original sin? But I wasn't whipped yet.)

"You didn't quit wetting the bed," I countered. "You wet the bed just last night."

She was quick. "The cat did that!" She said it without hesitation, without blinking. Maybe she was going to be a lawyer.

I ignored the opportunity to laugh and embrace the teachable moment. Instead, I made my move to protect my authority. "Don't tell me the cat did it!" I bellowed. "The spot on your bed was the size of a large pizza! We only have a tiny little kitty."

"It wasn't our cat," she replied without missing a beat. She was a true professional; she was the best. Yes, she was going to be a lawyer.

And she was shocked—*shocked*—that I wouldn't believe her. I held her by the shoulders. "Look me in the eye," I insisted, "and tell me the truth."

Her bottom lip began to quiver, a huge martyr's tear welled up in her eye. "I'm sorry, Daddy," she sobbed. "But a big, giant cat took the screen off my window and jumped on my bed. He wet on my bed, and then he jumped back out the window." Sensing my skepticism, she continued. "He put the screen back on after he left; that's why it's still on now." I was speechless.

"He was a big cat!" she appended during my gaping silence.

I was coming to a slow boil. "I can't believe you'd lie to me like this." I scolded. "I want you to go straight to bed, and I don't want to hear a peep out of you." (I learned that one from my father. Evidently such sayings lose their power between generations; I could hear her in her bedroom making tiny little peeping sounds.)

Then, after a few moments of precious, lovely silence, a defiant little voice screeched from the bedroom. "Daddy, I want water, and I want it now!"

The gauntlet had been thrown down! My parental authority was up for grabs. I had only one option—I called on the sacred and hallowed words of parents across the reaches of time. "If I hear one more word from you," I roared, "I'll come in there and give you a spanking!"

"When you come," she sang out sweetly, "bring a glass of water."

I let out a great sigh, knowing when I was beaten. If *I* could think that quickly, I'd be a millionaire. "Go get your water," I laughed, "and then you get to bed or I'll come in there!"

But she wasn't done with me yet—not this night, not Traci. About twenty minutes later I realized I hadn't heard the pitter-patter of her little feet returning to bed. "Traci, what *are* you doing?" I called.

"Drinking water," she replied.

"No one can drink water for twenty minutes," I grumbled, as I stomped to the bathroom. I was wrong; children trying to avoid bedtime can do anything. These are the signs and wonders the Bible talks about in the Last Times. I opened the door and gazed upon a child who'd been quietly sipping water for twenty minutes. Her little belly looked like a basketball.

"You get to bed right this moment!" I barked.

This, of course, signaled a new phase in the negotiations. I closed my eyes and waited for the words I knew would come. They came. "I have to go to the bathroom."

Of course I had to let her go, or the giant cat would be back.

She still wasn't done with me. The next time I looked up, she was standing in the hallway, stark naked. She had her hands on her hips and that "whatcha gonna do about *this?*" look in her eye. Before I could respond, she took off. "Catch me!" she giggled as she zipped past me. I bolted out of my chair and bounded in clumsy pursuit, forgetting that God has equipped his naked children with the ability to turn on a dime.

She sprinted into the kitchen and hung a sharp right. I was wearing wool socks. On a linoleum floor with wool socks there is no such thing as a "sharp right." I lost control, spun out, and totaled my wife's new blender.

I walked away from the crash a bit shaken up, removing shards of glass from my body. Then, to my horror, I saw my naked daughter dash out the front door. What had started out as a power struggle between a parent and a child had now escalated into a neighborhood incident. This is how world wars begin. My daughter was running naked down the street, shattering the quiet of twilight as she sang, "Catch me! Catch me!"

I caught her about a block away from home. Then I remembered I was wearing only the moth-eaten woolen socks and a pair of old underwear.

I scooped up my giggling Godiva and ran the fastest hundred-yard dash of my life. Once back in the safety of our house, I laughed until it hurt.

I dared to inquire one day, "Whence cometh this dread of bed?"

"Monsters and prayers," said my daughter without looking up from her toys.

Monsters I understood. On more than one occasion I'd conspicuously sprayed "monster repellent" (water in an old Windex bottle) into the closet and under the bed to assure a safe night. But prayers? What could they possibly have to do with fear of the night?

The explanation forced me quickly out of the room. I needed to laugh without hurting her feelings. The child's prayer that begins "Now I lay me down to sleep" had been less than helpful during her formative years. One phrase in the prayer had embedded itself in her mind: "If I should die before I wake . . . " All the antics were to avoid that twilight zone where monsters live and people die.

CHAPTER EIGHT

Four-Legged Fun

They say a reasonable number of fleas is good fer a dog—
keeps him from broodin' over bein' a dog.
—Edward Noyes Westcott

One day two cats were watching a game of tennis.
"Hey," said the first cat, "I didn't know you liked tennis."

"Actually, I don't," responded the second cat. "The only reason
I'm remotely interested is because my father's in the racket."
—Anonymous

Dogs laugh, but they laugh with their tails.
What puts man in a higher state
of evolution is that he has got his laugh
on the right end.
—Max Eastman

What's That Smell?

Chonda Pierce

I wanted to kill that dog the first week we had him (which must be the terrible twos in dog years), but I didn't—but only for the children's sake.

My daughter, Chera, was eight years old when Disney did a remake of the movie *101 Dalmatians*. That Christmas she wanted a Dalmatian more than anything else in the world. Neither David nor I was too thrilled about something that eats and you-know-whats, but we figured a puppy would be easier to find than a Cabbage Patch doll.

Of course, I should have known when we picked out the puppy that he was going to be trouble, because the owner kept telling us how this was the last one of ten brothers and sisters. Why had everyone else skipped over him?

Since this was a Christmas present from Santa, David and I brought the pup home under cover of darkness.

"Maybe you can sing to him or something," said the woman who sold him to us. "To calm him down—since he's never ridden in a car."

I held the little freckled thing in my lap, wrapped in a blanket, and could feel him trembling through the covers. So as David drove, I began to sing, "You are my sunshine, my only sunshine." (It had worked for my son, Zachary, when *he* was two.)

The road back to our house was curvy, and one minute we were all leaning to the right, then we would straighten up, and then we would lean to the left. I was just singing about "how I had held you in my arms" when the little fellow bolted from my arms and landed on the dark floorboard where I couldn't see a thing but could feel him squirming around.

"Oops, he got away," I said.

"What do you mean *he got away?*" David asked. "He's in the car, isn't he?"

"Yes, but I mean I don't have him." I was groping in the blackness. "Turn on the light. He's somewhere down–"

"What's that smell?" asked David.

Then there came the loudest retching noise I'd ever heard from man or beast (and I have an older brother).

"Yuck! What's that smell?" David pulled onto the shoulder of the road and turned on the inside lights.

We found the tiny puppy standing there at my feet, trembling, surrounded by . . . well, let's just say everything was green and brown. David used an old piece of cardboard to clean up, although a shovel would have been better.

Not only did the new puppy get carsick, but he also was a whiner. We closed him off in the laundry room with a nice soft bed and plenty of water and food. But every time we walked away, he would whine.

"Shush," David begged, "Santa's coming tonight. Don't you want to be a good boy? Maybe Santa will bring you something." Not even the promise of goodies from the North Pole would shut up the dog. But when David went into the room to be with him, the puppy would lick his hand and stop whining.

"Oh," I said, "looks like he just wants to be with you."

"I could bring him to bed," David suggested.

"Or you could stay here with him," I voted.

So David slept on the floor of the laundry room on Christmas Eve–probably with visions of sugarplums dancing in his head. I tiptoed off to bed, and I heard him exclaim as I walked out of sight, "What's that awful smell?"

On Christmas morning David got up all red-eyed, his hair sticking out crazylike, but he had the video camera on his shoulder and was ready to go. When the children came racing down the steps, the little Dalmatian raced in a blur up the steps and right past them.

"What was that?" Chera wanted to know.

"It was a puppy!" Zach, who was four, cried out. "It was a puppy!"

They got to the bottom of the stairs and called the puppy. David kept the video rolling.

"What's he doing up there?" David asked.

Zach stood where he could peek up the stairs and answered, "Pee-peeing."

David grumbled.

"Come here!" Chera sang. "Come here, uh, boy? Girl?"

"Boy," David answered through his teeth.

"Come here, boy," Chera called out in her high-pitched voice, clapping her hands. The puppy raced out and tumbled down the steps and landed right on Chera's chest, knocking her back. He began to lick her face.

Zach petted him and said, "What's that smell?"

Right away Chera began to talk puppy talk, and the puppy seemed to understand. "Oh, you a good boyee. Yes, you are. Look at the little puppy. Oooooo! You such a happy puppy. Yes, you are. You like to lick my nose, don't you?"

"Ooo. He licked her nose!" cried Zach.

For the rest of the morning the puppy bounced around the house, up the stairs, down the stairs, under the tree, and over and through the mounds of wrapping paper. David followed him around with a wet cloth and some spray cleaner.

That night we watched *101 Dalmatians* (another of Chera's Christmas presents), and those puppies in the movie seemed so cute. They sat when they were supposed to, they ran where they were supposed to, and no one ever talked about how funny they smelled.

"So what are you going to name him?" I asked Chera after the movie was over. "How about Freckles? Or Pepper–like in the movie?" But Chera didn't seem to like either of those.

"Well, we have to call him something besides 'Hey-Boy,'" I pointed out.

"Naming a dog takes time," said David, holding a wet cloth. "The name has to fit, has to be just right–just right for Chera and . . . Hey-Boy. Me? I'd call him Leaky. But that's me. She'll come up with something that fits."

The dog almost didn't live long enough to be named. In the movie, the Dalmatians chewed up only the bad people's stuff, and everyone would clap and laugh at how clever they were. Our dog (Chewy would have been a good name) ate everything. When we went out, we left him closed up in the laundry room with plenty of food and water and a cozy bed, but that wasn't good enough for him. He chewed through the louvered door and went after the couch (Couch-Eater would have been another good name). He chewed off the sofa's front legs so that, when we arrived home, the couch had tilted forward and was lying facedown on the floor–dead. Couch-Eater had a cushion between his paws. That would have gone next, I'm sure, had we not interrupted.

During the next couple of weeks, the dog tore up a chunk of carpet (Carpet-Chomper, maybe), scratched the linoleum in the bathroom (Linoleum-Gouger), and ate the baseboard in the upstairs hallway (Baseboard-Muncher). I still don't know how he did that last one.

Then the day came when we were ready to move–to a house with a yard where we could drive a stake deep into the ground and tie a chain to it. "Bet he can't eat through that!" David said as he marched off to the hardware store to get what he needed to prepare our present home for sale. He came home with wood patch, carpet patch, a louver replacement kit, and a big throw rug to cover the hole in the living room. We stacked bricks under the front of the sofa–and then decided to abandon it. "Or we could take it along and let Hey-Boy use it as a chew toy," David suggested.

"I've got it!" Chera told us one day.

"Got what?" I asked.

"Got a name for him," she said, pointing to the spotted dog stretched out on his sofa, which barely was balanced on a couple of bricks.

"How about Smelly?" asked Zach, holding his nose.

"How about SPOT?" Chera said.

"Spot?" David asked.

"I get it!" said Zach. "Because he has spots!"

"No," said Chera. "Not Spot. S-P-O-T. SPOT. You told me, Dad, that his father's name was Sir Pepper. So we'll call him Sir Pepper Otis Theodore–SPOT!" She walked over and scratched the dog's belly, and he rolled over so she wouldn't miss a single spot. "Hey, SPOT," she said, "do you like that name?"

From then on his name was SPOT.

SPOT liked his new yard. David bought a doghouse and let the kids paint SPOT above the door. He put up a fence, and SPOT ran in circles in the yard until he beat a path around the edges. Sometimes David would plant bushes, and SPOT would dig them up. David would chase him around and around on the path the dog already had made. Sometimes SPOT would dig a hole under the fence and run off, and a neighbor would call to tell us that SPOT had just pottied on her bushes. Sometimes David called him names besides SPOT. I was sure that only confused the poor dog.

David and I could think of a dozen reasons we wanted to kill that dog. But then we had a couple of great reasons not to–Chera and Zachary. They loved that dog more than Nintendo and more than CDs. It didn't matter to them if SPOT chewed purses, dug holes, or tracked up the living room carpet. He could bark all night at a squirrel in a tree so that no one got any sleep, but they still loved that dog. We could go away for a week and come back in the middle of the night, and SPOT would jump up on the kids, lick their faces, and wag his tail. Zach would scratch him behind his ears, and Chera would talk her dog talk and SPOT would talk back to her.

One day I realized that what was playing out before me was unconditional love: I love you, no strings attached, no matter what. Since then, whenever I need to be reminded about unconditional love, I just watch those three together.

I've learned in my own life that it doesn't matter what I may have messed up–even if I tracked through the living room with big muddy footprints–God still loves me.

Unconditional Love–that would have been a good name for that crazy dog, too. But I don't think the doghouse was big enough to paint the name on it.

Help, Lord, There's a Cat on My Face!

Sheila Walsh

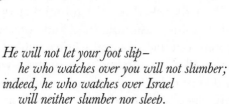

He will not let your foot slip–
  he who watches over you will not slumber;
indeed, he who watches over Israel
  will neither slumber nor sleep.

Psalm 121:3–4

With all my years of traveling, I've slept in some strange places. My great comfort when I'm far away from home is that the Lord never sleeps but always watches over me–whether I'm in Bangkok, Britain, or Boise, Idaho.

Some of the most powerful memories are from my days as a youth evangelist in Europe. In Britain, an evangelist or singer would never stay in a hotel after an evening meeting. Hospitality– and I use that word advisedly–would be extended from a member of the local church. That hospitality is what drove me to lift my eyes to my sleepless God to extend his help.

I remember staying with an old lady in Bristol, England, who had forty-three cats. I like cats, but forty-three are about forty-two cats too many for me. I drank my cup of cocoa with cat fur in it and then thanked my hostess and headed to bed.

"My little darlings will follow you!" she sang out after me.

I turned to see a plague of fur flow after me. "That's all right," I said. "I can find my room."

"It's where my darlings sleep, too!" She smiled as she delivered this good news.

Fluffy, Muffy, and the gang made themselves comfortable on the bed, in my suitcase, and in my toilet bag. We were a family.

As I went to sleep I prayed, "Lord, please keep these beasts off me while I'm sleeping."

I woke up to find that I was suffocating. I must be in a cave or a tunnel, I was drowning—no, it was worse than that. "Help, Lord, there's a cat on my face!"

Another town, another trauma. The couple that took me home after church seemed very nice—and almost normal. As we pulled into the driveway of their home, I listened, but not a bark or purr could be heard. Peace!

After supper the lady asked me if I minded sleeping in the garage. I said that was fine, assuming they had converted it into some sort of bedroom. But the man of the house pulled his car out of the garage and unfolded a camp bed in its place. It was November in England and very cold. I put on more clothes to go to bed than I had on during the day. (Where are forty-three cats when you need them?) Every thirty minutes the freezer would start up and *chug chug* till I longed for a cat to put in each ear.

In the morning, as I lay there stiff from cold and discomfort, the husband started his car to go to work and all the exhaust came flooding in. I thought, *I bet they're closet atheists, and they're trying to kill me!*

I stayed with a family in Holland for a week. They spoke no English, and I spoke no Dutch. The family shouted at me the whole time, apparently thinking it would make it easier for me to understand them.

I have lots of fun stories to tell and to laugh about in the comfort of my own home. But every story is held together by the common thread of God's faithfulness through it all. He was my constant companion.

Psalm 121 makes it clear that God never closes his eyes. He is always watching over you—and me—even if we sometimes get a little fur in our faces.

Hey, Dude!

John Ortberg

Sometime ago we went on vacation to a dude ranch in Arizona. My wife, Nancy, who grew up vacationing there, insisted that my experience would not be complete until I knew the exhilaration of a truly challenging horse ride. We went on a trail ride, but it was far too tame to count, as there was no possibility of falling and receiving a serious injury. The truth is that I have spent very little time around horses and have never actually met one I trusted, but of course I wasn't about to admit that.

So the next morning I rode out with five ranch hands to take the herd of horses to pasture about three miles away. I was very interested to meet my horse du jour. Often horses receive their name from some notable aspect of their temperament; when you get a horse named Pokey or Valium, you pretty much know what to expect. My horse was named Reverse, based on his particular eccentricity of going backward anytime someone was foolish enough to pull on his reins. I made a mental note not to do that.

The trip out to the pasture was uneventful. We dropped off the herd and were on our way back when one of the ranch hands decided to make a race of the return trip. His horse took off at full gallop, and the other four immediately started racing to catch up with him. Reverse started to make his move. Instinctively, I pulled on the reins as hard as I could. Reverse rose up on his hind legs and took a few steps backward—just as Silver used to do under the Lone Ranger—and then took off like a bat out of . . . a cannon.

For the better part of a mile, Reverse ran a dead heat. (The word *dead* sticks in my mind.) We were not sauntering or trotting—this was all-out sprinting as in a scene from a movie. The five ranch hands were college-age guys who lived on horseback all summer long, racing their horses as fast as they could. Reverse and I passed four of them. I say "Reverse and I," but the truth is, he was doing most of the work. I was just waiting to die. I was looking in the adjacent creek bed for the rock my head would split against once I was thrown off. Exodus 15:1 came to mind: "I will sing to the LORD, for he is highly exalted. The horse and its rider he has hurled into the sea."

While I was wondering how Nancy would spend the life insurance policy, the strangest thing happened. I realized there was a good chance I would survive this, and then it became one of the most exhilarating moments I had all week. I had a few moments of what Mihaly Csikszentmihalyi calls "flow"—my own private optimal experience. For a few moments I was completely captivated by a single activity. All I could hear was the pounding of Reverse's hooves; all I could feel was the rush of the wind in my face and the swaying rhythm of the gallop. Out of the corner of my eye, I could see the startled looks of the four horsemen of the apocalypse whom we passed up (a moment I enjoyed immensely). I felt *alive*—from my now-hatless head to the toes of my stirrup-straining feet. I started laughing from sheer adrenaline. By the time we pulled up to the fence, I knew this had been the ride of my life. I would not have missed this experience for anything.

Of course, when we pulled to a stop at the ranch (which, to my great relief, Reverse decided to do gradually), male pride would not allow me to indicate that this dash had been at all unplanned. "Yes, a decent mount," I said. "His wind isn't quite what it could be, perhaps, but never mind."

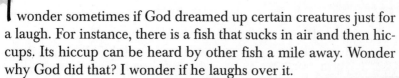

Anything for a Laugh

Marilyn Meberg

I wonder sometimes if God dreamed up certain creatures just for a laugh. For instance, there is a fish that sucks in air and then hiccups. Its hiccup can be heard by other fish a mile away. Wonder why God did that? I wonder if he laughs over it.

Then, of course, I wonder about the duck-billed platypus. When the first specimen was brought to England from Tasmania in 1880, the zoologists were mystified by the creature. Its two-foot-long body was covered with thick gray-brown hair (mammal?), but it had a flat tail (beaver?), webbed feet, and a wide rubbery bill (duck?)—and two spurs behind its rear ankles that secreted poison (snake?). The fact that this bizarre creature laid eggs caused the scientists to finally conclude that it must be a hoax. That theory was discarded, however, when a team of scientists discovered a whole pondful of platypuses in New South Wales. Those creatures could growl like dogs and lived most of their lives in the water, but they were also capable of climbing trees. Wonder what God was thinking? I wonder if platypuses make him laugh.

A little-known fact is that bedbugs bark when they smell human flesh. U.S. Army scientists came up with a scheme to use the bugs in Vietnam. The plan was to pack bedbugs in capsules rigged with miniature radio transmitters. The capsules were to be dropped on suspected Vietcong hideouts. If a radioman overheard their hungry barks, jets and artillery would be called in. The war ended, however, before the bugs saw active duty.

God is a wonder. I think he's also funny.

Cat Lovers Beware!

Patricia Wilson

I always dread the first ten seconds after my entrance into any gathering. That's how long it takes me to determine whether or not I know anyone in the room and whether or not we'll have anything to say to each other. At one end of the anxiety scale is not knowing a single soul in the room; at the other end is knowing only a single soul—and that soul not very well. Each situation calls for small talk. Long, in-depth discussions I can handle with aplomb, but I'd sooner hide in a corner all night than make small talk.

When I saw Phil waving at me from across the room, I heaved an inward sigh of relief. Although I didn't know Phil very well, I knew that he liked cats. His office was full of them, figuratively speaking. Posters of cats adorned the walls, stuffed cats sat on his chairs, and "catty" paraphernalia littered every available surface. Even his coffee mug was shaped like a cat! Being a cat lover of the first order myself, I knew we would have at least one subject in common.

No sooner had I joined him than Phil headed for the buffet and left me to chat with his wife, Tina. We talked generally about things like home renovating, living in the country, and raising kids and cats in the city.

"How many do you have?" Tina asked me.

"Well, I had three when Gerald and I were married and he had five, so we ended up with eight between us."

"Eight! How old were they?"

"My oldest fellow was ten, and Gerald's youngest was just two years old, and the rest fell in between."

She looked suitably impressed. "That must have been quite an adjustment."

"It was. At first, we had a lot of trouble with squabbling and spats, but eventually they got the pecking order sorted out, and they live together quite amiably now. Of course, there's still a flare-up now and then, but that's to be expected."

She smiled at me warmly. Encouraged, I continued on in my discourse. "It's not so bad now that we're down to four of them."

"Down to four!" She looked horrified. "What happened?"

"One of Gerald's boys was really homesick for his family in Montreal, so we agreed he could live with them. That left us seven at home."

She looked sympathetically at me. "You must have really missed him."

"Not really. I was just as glad to get the numbers down." A look of shock flashed across Tina's face. I ignored it and continued. "Anyway, within a short time, nature and attrition took care of the rest."

Tina's voice was warm with sympathy. She shook her head. "You're so brave about it. What happened to the others?"

I began to realize that she was a cat lover of the highest order. "Then we lost Vinnie—he was one of mine. Gerald found him in the barn, dead as a doornail. It looked as though he had fallen from one of the rafters. We were kind of surprised because they usually survive that kind of fall, but not poor Vinnie."

Her hand reached over and patted mine. Her brown eyes filled with tears. "It must have been a dreadful experience."

"Actually, I hadn't had Vinnie all that long, so it wasn't too bad. And we still had six left to keep us busy."

Tina's eyes narrowed, and she looked at me in puzzlement. I realized that I should be less flippant in my discussion on the demise of the cats. Trying to settle my face into a suitably somber expression, I continued on. "Then one of Gerald's older boys developed a terrible skin disease. We tried everything to cure it—it cost us a fortune in medical bills—but in the end, nothing could be done. We finally had to put him down."

"Put down!" Her voice mirrored the look of horror on her face.

I began to suspect that Phil's lady was rowing with one oar in the cat-lover's department. I answered her a little sharply. "Well, we didn't have much choice. There's only so much you can do, and then you have to be sensible about these things."

"Sensible!" She started to get up. "I think what you did is awful!"

"Well, so do I, but there comes a time when everyone has to make a decision like this. I had to do the same thing with an old dog of mine, and I cried for days afterward."

At this point, Phil returned from the buffet. "So, are you cat lovers comparing notes?" he asked cheerfully, obviously missing the look on Tina's face.

"We haven't gotten around to cats," Tina said tensely, "and I don't think I want to." She glared at me. "If this is how you treat your children, I'd hate to think about what you would do with your cats!"

CHAPTER NINE

A Little Bit Weird, a Whole Lot of Fun

The true object of all human life is play.
Earth is a task garden; heaven is a playground.
—G. K. Chesterton

That's the truest sign of insanity—
insane people are always sure they're just fine.
It's only the sane people
who are willing to admit
they're crazy.
—Nora Ephron

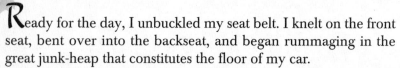

Air Bags, Seat Belts, and Change

Ken Davis

Ready for the day, I unbuckled my seat belt. I knelt on the front seat, bent over into the backseat, and began rummaging in the great junk-heap that constitutes the floor of my car.

I was desperately seeking my daily planner, which I often toss into the backseat rather than lugging it into the house. Without that book, sheer chaos was certain. I hadn't a clue where I was supposed to be or whom to call to find out where I was supposed to be. I didn't know what to do—my To-Do list was in the book. Everything was in the book. Without the book, my very existence could be called into question.

I was totally absorbed in rummaging through the artifacts on the floor. Half-eaten pizza, Happy Meal boxes, and sticky Dairy Queen cups flew in every direction. Did you know that if your face is on the carpet, your car could be accelerating down the street without your knowledge or permission? I didn't know that, either.

I'd accidentally left the vehicle in gear. My head was buried in the backseat, and my own backseat was elevated to headrest position. That sector of my anatomy, it should be noted, is sight-impaired.

I found the planner! Still facing backwards, I popped up with a victorious smirk. Then I noticed from the corner of my eye that various objects seemed to be moving slowly past the side window. Suddenly it hit me: My car was rolling! I spun quickly to stop the car, but a lamppost beat me to it.

Have you ever had your air bag go off?

I have, and I'm here to tell you it's nothing like TV commercials would have you believe. Those commercials present the air bag as something you'd activate purely for the entertainment value, like playing with a giant undulating marshmallow. Hollywood's special-effects wizards create this illusion by showing the deployment of the air bag in super–slow motion. Your kids beg you for a try. It looks like a great new ride for the amusement park.

My air bag wasn't even remotely like that. The slow motion must have been out of order. I didn't hear it coming, I didn't see it coming. It was just suddenly there. *Whap!* I had no idea what happened. All I knew was that my nose hurt worse than it had ever hurt in my life.

If I were designing cars, I'd install some kind of warning system. Perhaps one of those synthetic voices. "Your air bag is set to deploy in ten seconds," it would intone calmly. "We suggest you get out of the car."

After the air bag hit me, I kept my eyes closed for ten minutes. I had no choice in the matter–my glasses were embedded in my head. And I still had no clue what had happened. The car was full of powder, and the air bag had deflated. Through my tears, I only wondered why a huge hanky was now hanging from my steering wheel.

A bad word formed in the back of my head, stood up, and began making its way through the aisles and hallways of my brain, all the way to the front office where the lips are. Yes, it seemed almost certain I'd be starting my day with a curse. Now, I know what some of you are thinking: *No way! How could an inspirational author have a swearword in his head?*

Because I'm human, that's how. I still haven't reached that point in my pilgrimage where Scriptures come to my lips whenever my nose is broken. And my best guess is that you haven't, either. If I were to suddenly reach out of this book and punch you in the nose, I doubt that your reflex response would be, "Praise the Lord! I just want to thank God for your dynamic fist!"

If it's any comfort to you, the word in question never crossed the threshold of my lips. Before it came out, I started to laugh. I laughed until I cried. Why not? The tears were already there. For some reason, the term *air bag* took hold of me. What a ridiculous term! Twenty years ago no such phrase existed. Had I driven a car home and told my mother I had an air bag in my car, she would have responded in horror: "That's not a kind thing to say!"

How things change. What didn't exist yesterday is a household word today. As I laughed, my mind began to run free. (Don't worry; it has no air bags.) I began to laugh at my seat belt. When I was a child, there was no such term as *seat belt,* either. My mother was the safety device in our car. If I wanted to stand on the front seat, perch on the headrest, or drool out the window like our dog—no problem. In the event of an accident, my mother would save me with her arm.

Actually, it didn't even require an accident. Whenever she hit the brake, her arm would simultaneously arc toward me like a loose boom on a sailing ship. *Whap!* Talk about your tough love. "Why'd ya do that?" I'd snort through my bleeding nose.

"I kept you from going through the windshield," she'd reply with a look of heroic satisfaction.

"Can I go through the windshield next time?" I'd beg, still nursing my bleeding nose and sporting a shiner I'd never be able to explain to my friends. Very few kids, I believed, had ever died going through a windshield, but I suspected that thousands were victims of the long arm of the mom.

That's exactly why I loved riding with my grandma. She had that *thing* under her arm—that fleshy, soft forerunner to the air bag thing. When Grandma stepped on the brakes, her arm would come flying back, and I'd be smothered in gelatinous flesh. Everything would go black, and air would temporarily be cut off. But I didn't get hurt. Oh, I'd smell like Noxzema for a few days, but I could live with that.

My point is that nothing stays the same; everything changes. Grandma is no longer with us. If I understand heaven correctly, she no longer has the natural air bag. Automobiles have air bags, side-impact air bags, and switches for disengaging air bags. Parents are required to use infant seats to restrain children in cars. In my day, an infant seat was something you put a diaper on.

Change is everywhere. Even things that are dear to us change. Grandmas and grandpas die. Friends move away. The stock market falls. Only an unchanging God remains; he will never fail.

Coloring the Night Away

Marilyn Meberg

My friend Pat and I had agreed to spend the evening together, engaged in some wild and woolly activity yet to be determined. As we discussed various options, I became increasingly aware of my fatigue from a very demanding week. From that fatigue came a most soothing, novel, and appealing idea.

I announced to Pat, "I want to buy crayons and a coloring book and spend the evening coloring." She stared at me for a minute, trying to hide the look of incredulity on her face. Then, assuming her best therapist voice, she asked what kind of coloring book would please me and how many crayons I wanted. Pretending not to notice her clinical tone, I said I wanted at least twenty-four different colored crayons, and I would know the coloring book when I saw it.

With a kindly affirmation from Pat that spending the evening coloring might indeed be pleasant, she agreed to the plan. She did ask, however, if I thought smoking cigars while we colored would add a dimension of the adult to our activity. Since neither of us have the faintest notion of even how to smoke—much less how to smoke a cigar—we quickly gave up that idea as not only impractical but unappealing as well.

True to expectation I found the perfect coloring book for me. It was called *The Huckleberry Finn Coloring Book. Huckleberry Finn* has always been one of my favorite novels, and I was instantly gratified by my purchase. Pat chose a coloring book of Disney characters that I thought was a bit beneath her level of sophistication, but I didn't think it would be kind to say so.

Armed with my new coloring book and a box of twenty-four crayons (Pat had to buy her own; I told her I absolutely would *not* share mine), I settled down to one of the most soothing and delightful evenings I've had in ages. While I determined the perfect color combination for the Widow Douglas's dress, as well as for the apron of her sister, Miss Watson, we listened to Christmas music. Even though it wasn't yet Thanksgiving, and in spite of feeling slightly confused, I enjoyed it enormously.

I think it only fair to report that I was ready to quit coloring long before Pat was. In fact, I suspect she took up her crayons again after I left for home that evening.

I love the fact that God is a God who encourages *relationship*, not just with himself, but with one another. Jesus modeled that for us in the richness of his relationships with the twelve disciples. We are indeed rich when we have many friends, and I'm thoroughly convinced that God loves us, encourages us, nurtures us, and supports us through other human beings. They can almost become to us Jesus with skin.

May we not become so busy, harried, and overcommitted that we neglect that part of our soul that is fed and sustained by friendship.

Pacified

Patsy Clairmont

When I was a child, I talked like a child, I thought like a child, I reasoned like a child.

1 Corinthians 13:11

Recently I had the most mirthful thought; it came to me during church. A man stood up during the service and walked down the aisle toward the back carrying his young child. The toddler obviously was not impressed with the sermon. To keep everyone from knowing the extent of the child's displeasure, the father had corked him. A pacifier protruded from the little one's mouth, keeping his fussiness firmly bottled. His face appeared a tad red from holding in his opinions, but the pacifier did seem to accomplish its purpose.

Now here's my thought: *I'd like to manufacture adult pacifiers.* What do you think? It makes me want to honk and to giggle. Too outrageous, you say? Well, not so quick.

Don't you know some pretty fussy people that you'd like to ... cork? C'mon now, be honest. Why, those rubber stoppers might prevent unnecessary dissension, promote goodwill among humankind, and even breed greater contentment. Are you catching the vision?

I can recall a number of times I should have taken a couple of good swigs on a pacifier instead of a couple of verbal swings at an antagonizer. We would all have been better off if I had. My joy certainly would have increased, for I have found that my first words are not always my finest choices. Instead, my reactive whirl of words has the capacity to be outlandish. More often than I'd like to admit, my verbal response is based in an unsteady emotion such as hurt. (And hurt can be as fickle as love.) In my attempt to hide my hurt

177

and protect my vulnerable (and prideful) heart, I have used lashing language that puts others *en garde*. My reaction conveys an inaccurate message. It shouts "I'm angry" rather than confessing "I'm hurt."

Also, the sharp edge of lashing language can wound the recipient. In the heat of the moment, that can be somewhat satisfying. *Touché!* Yet, when our feelings cool off and our brains settle down, we almost always regret our knee-jerk (emphasis on *jerk*) reaction.

That's where the pacifiers fit in. Imagine how differently events would have unfolded if pacifiers had been applied appropriately. For example, picture Peter in the Garden of Gethsemane. Instead of whipping out his sword to whack off the soldier's ear, Peter would have raised his hand indicating a five-minute time-out. Then he'd reach for a small leather sack tied to his waist and pull out a well-worn pacifier. After several reflective pulls on his binkie, he would realize how inappropriate lashing out would be and instead turn to the Lord for direction.

See, this idea has merit. In fact, I can envision these teensy comforters being installed as standard equipment on automobiles. Honk, honk. Then, when the guy on the highway gets in our way, we push a button (instead of laying on the horn), which, in turn, releases our binkie from above our heads. We grab on to our pacifier, and after several deep slurps, we feel prepared to continue on our journey more ... well, pacified.

And what about school? Don't you think every high school should attach binkies to the desks? Then, when belligerence is the 'tude of the moment, teachers and students alike could unwind during a binkie break. Or maybe they could have a binkie room or a pacifier parlor instead of a detention hall. That way, the rebellious could ruminate rather than rumble.

I'd manufacture different colored pacifiers to go with our outfits, moods, and decor. I'd give the mouthpieces as gifts—tons of them. I'd offer them personalized, iridescent, flavored, and gold-trimmed. I'd organize pacifier conventions and even have marathons to reward the person who stays plugged the longest.

Only one thing niggles at me about this idea—the last words of 1 Corinthians 13:11: "I put childish ways behind me." Oh, phooey, that kinda spoils my frivolity.

How about you? Playing any childish games? Need to grow up?

Peculiarity Breeds Content

Becky Freeman

Do you really—I mean *really*—think so?" I asked my husband sincerely.

"Oh, Becky, *everybody* thinks so," Scott stated unequivocally.

So what was the subject of our discussion? It was my husband's opinion—and, according to him, the rest of the world's opinion—that I am a *peculiar* person.

It's not all that bad to be labeled "peculiar," really. Webster defines *peculiarity* as "something that belongs to only one person, thing, class, people; a distinguishing feature." I rather like that definition. *Unique* has a nicer ring to it, but *peculiar* will do just fine.

One of my most distinguishing features of late is my fingernails. You see—oh, how can I explain this?—I have none. There. I've admitted it. And I don't mean that they are short or bitten down to the nub. I mean, for the most part, they are nonexistent.

It all started when we went to the Christian Booksellers Convention in Denver, Colorado. Our publicist told my mother and me to be prepared to sign nearly two hundred copies of our book *Worms in My Tea.* "Wow!" I shouted into the phone. "Do you really think that many people will want to get copies of our book?"

"Oh, sure," she answered. "We're giving them away."

Well, even if it was a freebie-giveaway deal, the event still fell under the category of a "book signing." And if my hands would be on display for two hundred bookstore managers, I intended to make memorable encounters. I would begin by having my own nubby nails professionally covered up with the most beautiful fakes

I could afford. Thus innocently began a vicious cycle I am still coping with six months later.

From the day I walked into the beauty salon, I should have seen the handwriting on the wall. When the manicurist kept insisting that I relax, stating that I was one of the most tense manicures she'd ever sanded, I should have politely taken my leave. Instead, I courageously squeezed back tears and nodded toward the patch of blood oozing from my index finger directly beneath where Attila the Beautician's file was flying back and forth at warp speed. But I have to admit that, as soon as the swelling and bruises subsided (on my fingers, not the manicurist), my new set of acrylic nails indeed looked gorgeous.

By the time I arrived in Denver, I found myself using copious gestures when given the opportunity (yes, even making opportunities) for the sheer pleasure of waving my new nails around. Pointing was a great deal of fun. So was scratching Scott's neck. It wasn't until I was asked to sign an actual book that I realized there was going to be more to owning fingernails of length than I had bargained for. I came at the page, pen in hand, from a variety of angles. However, with my newly extended appendages, I may as well have been writing with a large pogo stick. My signature would not have passed preschool penmanship.

After signing the one hundredth book, I began to experience some success by squeezing the pen tightly between my knuckles. But my fingers eventually grew numb in that position, and I'm afraid it finally began to affect my thinking processes. Originally, my desire had been to come up with catchy individual greetings above my signature, like "Wormly Yours," "Love, Laughter, and Joy," and "May you find laughter in all your worms." I preferred that no two messages be exactly alike. After the one hundred fiftieth book, my mind began to wander, and I found myself writing odd salutations from bits of hymns I'd sung in childhood. I vaguely remember signing one book "All Glory, Laud, and Honor, Becky Freeman." I know the recipient of that copy is still shaking her head, wondering exactly what message I was trying to convey. I have no idea, but it was certainly heartfelt.

Scott took this new change in my hands' personality in stride—

until one night when he was trying to get to sleep and heard me crunching away on what he assumed was a bag of tortilla chips.

"Becky," he moaned, "cut it out. What are you eating at this time of night anyway?"

"My fake nails," I answered matter-of-factly. "Want a bite?"

I have never had a problem with nail-biting in my entire life. At least not until I acquired the artificial variety. Suddenly nail-biting took on an almost gourmet flavor. I've chewed off acrylic nails, gel nails, and plastic nails. All delicious. The problem is that, with each set of nails I bite off, my natural nails also peel off one layer at a time. My real nails now look as though my hands have been through a meat grinder, so I'm forced to cover them up when I go out in public. Now do you understand the vicious cycle I've begun?

You can see why my husband—and a few other people, too—have come to believe I am peculiar. I have to admit, since becoming a "real author," my life seems to be combing new depths of peculiarity. One moment I feel saucy and intelligent, ready to conquer the world—like Diane Sawyer. The next minute I am unpinning a dry-cleaning label from my dress while approaching the podium to speak—suddenly Minnie Pearl again.

I have been privileged to meet incredible people, and, at moments, I've even been treated as a near-celebrity. But 98 percent of the time I'm a housewife who lives in a cabin in the boonies with a husband, four kids, two dogs, a bathroom that needs scrubbing, and a frozen chicken that needs thawing.

Even though sophisticated people and agencies occasionally telephone our home/office/school/zoo now, I haven't even bothered to change the message on our answering machine to try to make us appear more businesslike. I mean, who do I think I could fool anyway? Executives and neighbors are all greeted by the identical message, delivered with as much Southern hospitality as I can dish out: "Hello, you've reached the home of the Freeman family and other wildlife." I side with Popeye the Sailorman on this point—"I am what I am."

And what does Scott think of all this? He shakes his head in wonder at what has transpired and pretends he has serious doubts about me and my grandiose adventures—at least in public. But my husband is always the first one I want to see after an exciting bit of news or an interesting encounter or an unusual experience or a new idea. Why? Because, in truth, no one—not one soul on the face of this earth—has shown as much pride and joy at the fact that I am a peculiar woman as has my own husband. He's consistently my best friend and cheerleader, even when my ideas seem harebrained to everyone else.

Just the other day, Scott and I took a walk together down our country road, holding hands. "Becky," he continued on a subject we discuss often, "you are *so* weird. I never met a person in my whole life as strange as you are. But you do intrigue me. When I come home, I don't know whether you're going to tell me you've got another book contract, or that you've run over the neighbor's mailbox, or that you tried to sterilize all our toothbrushes and ended up boiling them into one big plastic glob. I've got to stay around just to see what happens next."

Yes, we've finally accepted the fact that our love is a many-peculiared thing, but it took us a while to embrace it.

Traffic Ballet

Marilyn Meberg

This morning I was in my kitchen doing the mildly mindless things I do each day between 7:00 and 8:00 A.M. I flipped on *Good Morning America* to see if they knew anything I should and settled into my final cup of tea.

Am I ever glad I did! There was a segment that caused me to whoop with laughter and delight. I couldn't wait to tell you about it. In fact, I didn't even finish that cup of tea! I've dashed to my desk instead. Here's what set me off . . .

They interviewed a guy named Tony from Providence, Rhode Island, who is a traffic cop. He described how neither he nor any of the other guys on the traffic detail could bear one duty each of them had for at least an hour a day. They had to stand in the middle of a busy intersection directing traffic, and he said it was so boring and uneventful he could hardly endure it. He decided to try to spice up this dull task with something that would at least entertain himself and make the hour go faster.

He began experimenting with exaggerated hand and arm movements, which led to rhythmically syncopated body swings to go with the movements of his limbs. Finally, after only a few days, he began twirling from left to right, startling drivers with his flourishes of "hurry up," "slow down," or "stop!" It ultimately led to occasionally doing full body spins, which culminated in the splits.

Motorists grew to appreciate his antics so much that they honked and clapped until he had so many enthusiastic fans it created traffic jams, which only increased his need to twirl, flourish, and point to get cars moving. To avoid the hazards his accumulation of fans presented, Tony was assigned to different intersections each day so no one would know for sure where he'd be performing.

As this interview was going on, we, the viewing audience, were treated to a video of Tony's "intersection ballet." Buses and cars were whizzing past in such proximity to him I wondered if he had ever been hit by any of the vehicles. The question was posed to Tony, and he said that he bounced off the side of a moving bus once because he lost his balance during one of his twirls. He said he suffered no bodily harm from the experience, but that it did inspire him to do a bit of practicing of his twirls in the basement of his home that night.

What a perfect example Tony is of how to practice a laugh lifestyle. A laugh lifestyle is predicated on our attitude toward the daily stuff of life. When those tasks seem too dull to endure, figure out a way to make them fun; get creative and entertain yourself. If the stuff of life for you right now is not dull and boring but instead painful and overwhelming, find something in the midst of the pain that makes you smile or helps you giggle anyway. There's always something somewhere—even if you just have to *pretend* to laugh until you really do!

You need that joy break, so take at least one every day. Hey, how about twirling and flourishing in your kitchen, grocery store, or office? It works for Tony.

Drunk without Drinking

Barbara Johnson

When I was preparing to undergo some minor surgery recently, the doctor warned me that the anesthesia might make me a little goofy, even hours after the surgery was completed. For a moment I wondered whether anyone who knew me and thought I was already pretty goofy would even notice. Then I remembered that it's my husband, Bill, who's the peculiar one, being an only child and all.

The doctor said that, when I left the hospital, I was not to drive a car, sign any contracts, or make any irrevocable decisions—because I would be considered legally drunk for twenty-four hours after the surgery. Never having had a drink of alcohol in my life, I had no idea what to expect. *Just think,* I told myself, *you're gonna be drunk without even taking a drink!*

The idea was so amazing to me that I started imagining I was drunk even before the surgery started. When I arrived at the out-patient desk, the receptionist shoved a stack of papers toward me and told me to "fill them out and check the things that apply, and then sign here, here, and here. Be sure to press hard because it's a triplicate form."

In my imaginary state of drunkenness, I had a little trouble following her rapid-fire instructions, but I finally completed them all. In just a moment the door opened, and a nurse called me in. As soon as she had me settled in a bed, three other nurses slipped through the curtain.

"Oh, Mrs. Johnson," one of them said in a low, excited voice, "we're so thrilled to have you here. When we saw your name on the admittance forms and realized it was you, we called you back early. All of us have read your books. I even have one of them here, and I was hoping you would sign it for me."

I wanted to beg off, pleading imaginary drunkenness, but she was a nurse—and she would know I hadn't had any anesthesia yet. So I signed her book and then looked expectantly at the four of them, wondering what would happen next.

They stood around my bed, their faces glowing with friendly smiles. Suddenly my little cubicle had taken on a party atmosphere. I wondered if it was because I was drunk—and then I remembered that I wasn't, at least not yet.

"Barb, could we pray with you before your surgery?" one of the nurses asked.

Enthusiastically, the four of them joined hands, and the two nearest to me clasped my hands in their own, and they prayed the sweetest prayer I'd ever heard. (Of course, I thought I was inebriated, so just about everything was sounding pretty good to me at that point!)

Outside the curtain, I heard a man clear his throat. "Oh, Dr. Brown!" one of the nurses said, peeking out of the curtain. "We're just saying a little prayer for Barb. Would you mind waiting a minute?"

Evidently he agreed, because she returned and the prayer continued.

In just a moment the nurses' prayers ended, and the anesthesiologist stepped up to my bed and gave me a reassuring pat on the arm. He, too, said a little prayer, asking God to be with all of us in that operating room. Under ordinary circumstances I might have become a little apprehensive, knowing that the moment had come for the surgery to commence. But he held my hand, and in my imaginary drunkenness—and having just heard the nurses pray for me so thoughtfully and sincerely—I managed to flash him a smile before the lights went out.

To be honest, I don't think I was ever "drunk" during those twenty-four hours after my surgery, but I certainly was on a high. I kept remembering those thoughtful nurses and how they had surrounded me with their love and held my hands in theirs—and then sent me off to lala land with their prayers echoing through my mind and filling my heart with peace. The joy that this memory brought me erased any discomfort the minor surgery might have caused.

By that evening, I was feeling fine—and even a little mischievous. Knowing that Bill had been warned by the doctor to beware of my expected intoxication, I could tell he was constantly watching me out of the corner of his eye. For just a moment, I was tempted to put a lampshade on my head and dance a jig on the sidewalk, and then call up a real-estate agent and sell the house. But just imagining how startled Bill would be was enough fun. And besides, being peculiar is *his* job.

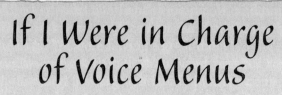

If I Were in Charge of Voice Menus

Chonda Pierce

I had a great idea the other day. It came to me about ten minutes into a fifteen-minute wait on the telephone. I had just called the telephone company to add the call-waiting feature to my service. But when my ear began to ache (and my finger, too, from pushing all those buttons), I believed I had had enough call-waiting to last me for a long time and hung up.

That's when it hit me: Just think how much time I could save if I had some sort of calling menu on *my* phone. Why, I'd have time to do great things—sleep, for instance. Or I could take up fun and creative hobbies, like sleeping. (It's not that I'm lazy, but if I had enough sleep, then I could do really, really great things like clean my house.)

It took a long time to set up my menu selections, since I had a lot of prerecorded messages to record. (Of course, they weren't prerecorded until *after* I had recorded them. But wouldn't that make them *post*recorded?) Anyway, once I had the system set up, I was so excited to see how it would work that for the whole first day I just sat and listened to the calls come in.

Ring-Ring-Ring!

"Hello. This is Chonda. Welcome to my new voice menu system. I'm soooo excited about this and about the new freedoms and possibilities this brings to me as a working mother and wife and to you as someone who has lots of busy things to take care of and a desire to get on and off the phone as quickly as possible. To facilitate both our goals, please listen carefully to the following menu options and press firmly the button that most applies to the purpose of your call. I thank you from the bottom of my heart for being a big part of this new direction as I move into the new millennium. Just follow my directions. This will be easy, painless, and much faster than trying to call the water company just to ask how many days are in the current billing period."

I was trying to be light and humorous while at the same time taking a jab at what really gets my goat.

"If you would like to leave a simple message of 25 words or less for me, press one now. If you have an even shorter message for David or the children, press two now.

"If you are calling to make a delivery, press three now. If you are calling to make a delivery but you are lost, press four now.

"If you are my dentist calling to remind me of a cleaning I scheduled months ago and have simply forgotten all about, press 21 now, or if you've determined that a root canal is our only option, press 22 now.

"If you are calling to discuss the general happiness of my children, about their day in school, whether they've received all their shots and vaccinations, or about Zach's last report card, press 34 now.

"If you're calling because you don't think I'm raising my children correctly, you can hang up now.

"If you're calling because you'd like to go shopping, press 45 now.

"If you're calling because we went to high school together and you haven't seen me in years, but you happened to see me on TV this week and thought I could get you free tickets to the Grand Ole Opry this Saturday night, press 59 now.

"If you've dialed the wrong number, press 16 now.

"If you're calling to see if I'd be interested in buying either bottled water or a security system for my home, press 44 and then quickly step away from your telephone.

"If this is someone from my small group at church reminding me of our next meeting, press 38 now. Or press 39 if you know for sure we are having snacks.

"If this is Zachary's principal, sorry about that overhead projector. Press 84 now to listen to a more formal apology.

"If this is someone from the Gallup Poll, press 53 if you favor a voice menu like this, 54 if you disapprove, 55 if you strongly disapprove, and 56 if you did not get this far into the message.

"If you've never liked the Beatles, press 41.

"If you'd like to start a recycling program in your neighborhood, press 81.

"If you are currently involved in, or have a desire to learn more about, a carpooling program for any grade school children in the Barfield area, press 62.

"If we have ever been involved in the same carpooling program before, press 84 now to listen to a more formal apology.

"If you know of a good, quality facial soap that you would be willing to recommend, press 27.

"If you owe me any money at all, press 77 now. I'll get right back with you.

"If you love chain letters, press 51, then press any three numbers at random, and within a week you should receive at least a million phone calls from complete strangers.

"If you have any hot tips for *America's Most Wanted,* you'll have to press *66 and take an oath before continuing this call.

"If you have a hangnail that's been bugging you for some time, press 47. If it's a brand-new hangnail, press 46.

"If you have a family member who has a problem with rhinotillexomania, press 12. For a definition of rhinotillexomania, press 92. If you laugh, press 93.

"Mom, if that's you, press 67, then enter the number of times you have already called me this week and the percentage of those calls that have occurred before 7:00 A.M.

"If this is an emergency, press 69 and please hold for further instructions.

"If this message has made you late for any sort of meeting, press 84 to listen to a more formal apology.

"Thank you for your time and attention to these options. I wish only to make things convenient for you and myself—*especially* myself. As we continue to grow here, we will continue to update this menu, bringing you more and more options so that every need is met. If you would like to add other options, press 89 and leave some of your favorite numbers. If you'd like to talk with someone in person, that just won't be possible, so you'd better find a button to push. If you'd like to repeat this menu, press 99 now."

BEEP! Someone chose a button.

"Hello. This is Chonda. Welcome to my new voice menu system. I'm soo ... "

I snatched up the telephone, "Mom, is that you?"

"Hi, honey," Mom answered.

"Why are you listening to this again?"

"I didn't catch it all the first time," she said. "What was that you said about Zachary's principal?"

After a little bit, I found out that my mother had a doctor's appointment scheduled for the next day (I made a note to enter that as button 33 later), and she was a bit worried about going by herself and talking with doctors who looked more at her chart, which was as fat as a phone book, than at her.

"I just like hearing your voice," she said. Taped or not, it didn't seem to matter to Mom. So I turned off the machine, and we talked for another hour. I guess I can put my housecleaning on hold.

Peanut Butter Yogurt and Raspberry Sauce

Marilyn Meberg

Go and enjoy choice food and sweet drinks, and send
some to those who have nothing prepared.
Nehemiah 8:10

One of the most delightfully peculiar experiences that will be forever squirreled away in my store of memories occurred some years ago when we were living in Fullerton, California.

I was indulging in one of my favorite taste treats—peanut butter frozen yogurt slathered with raspberry topping. As I was just dipping my spoon into this incomparable concoction, the door of the shop opened suddenly, and a tiny elderly lady burst through it. She scanned the shop for a second and then darted over to my table, pulled out the chair across from me, and sat down.

Before I had quite grasped what was happening, she leaned across the table and whispered, "Is anyone following me?" I looked suspiciously behind her and out into the parking lot from which she had emerged. Then I whispered back, "No, there's no one in sight."

"Good," she said, and with that she slipped out her teeth, snapped open her purse, and dropped the teeth into its depths.

Throughout this unexpected scene my spoon had remained frozen between my dish and my mouth. Galvanized into action by the melting of my yogurt, I put the spoon into my mouth. The little lady fixed her eyes on my spoon and then on my dish. I asked if she had ever eaten peanut butter yogurt with raspberry sauce. Without even looking at me, she said that she had wanted to try it all her life but never had. I calculated that "all her life" was probably some eighty years. I asked her if she'd like me to get her some.

Without a moment's hesitation, she said, "Yes," never taking her eyes off my yogurt. By the time I returned to our table with her order, she was nearly halfway through my original dish. I found this amusing, especially since she offered no explanation. I started eating what would have been hers, and we slurped along in companionable silence.

Across the street from where we were eating was an establishment for senior citizens that cared for those in fairly good health but in need of watching, as well as for those in poor health who needed constant attention. I classified my little yogurt companion as an inhabitant of this home. The minute she finished her yogurt, she began rapid preparations to leave. She whisked her teeth out from the environs of her purse, popped them in place, and headed for the door.

Concerned about her crossing the busy intersection alone, I asked if she'd let me accompany her. She was out the door and into the parking lot so fast I almost had to run to keep up with her. As I had surmised, she made her way into the senior citizens' building and scurried down the hall. The only thing she said to me was that she had to hurry or she'd miss lunch.

I stopped at the nurses' station and asked the girl behind the counter if she had noticed the little lady I had come with. She said, "Oh, yes. That's Felisha; she a real live wire." Then she asked if I happened to be a relative. I told her that Felisha and I had just met at the yogurt shop less than an hour ago. The girl's eyes twinkled as she asked, "Did you by any chance buy her a dish of yogurt?" I was a bit startled as I admitted that I had. The girl laughed and told me that Felisha knew every trick in the book.

I have revisited this memory many times throughout the years, not only for the deliciously quirky experience it provided, but for the example Felisha provided. Here's a little woman who knew how to get the most out of life—even to the point of my paying for it! I'll confess to you right now that Felisha is my model for "at the home" kind of living. When that day comes for me, I intend to join as many strangers as I can who will buy me peanut butter yogurt and raspberry sauce, or whatever else they may be eating. According to Nehemiah, that's a scriptural concept!

Live!

Luci Swindoll

I found a clever poem. I don't know who wrote it but there's a lot of the truth in it:

> *There was a very cautious man*
> *Who never laughed or played;*
> *He never risked, he never tried,*
> *He never sang or prayed.*
> *And when he one day passed away,*
> *His insurance was denied;*
> *For since he never really lived,*
> *They claim he never died.*

For those of us who "really live," it is hard to imagine why some people don't. I'm amazed at those who tell me they can't remember the last time they laughed. They confess, "We were never allowed to laugh in our home while I was growing up, so I just don't know how."

Playfulness is one of my favorite attributes in people. One morning a simple phone call cheered me up in the middle of paying bills. It was from some little kid who had the wrong number.

"Hello," I said.

"Hi."

"Well, hi, who is this?"

"Me."

"Oh—okay. Who would you like to speak with?"

"You."

194

"All right! How ya doin'?"

"Good. How *you* doin'?"

"I'm doing great. How old are you?"

"Four. How old are you?"

"I'm sixty. Would you like to marry me?"

"No. I gotta go now. You're too old. Bye."

"Bye."

You *may* feel too old to get married, but you should *never* feel too old to have fun. Laugh. Play. Risk. Try. Get out there, and really live!

Notes

The compilers acknowledge with gratitude the publishers and individuals who granted permission to reprint the stories found within the pages of this book. In a few cases, it was not possible to trace the original authors. The compilers will be happy to rectify this if and when the authors contact them by writing to Zondervan, 5300 Patterson Ave. S.E., Grand Rapids, MI 49530. Each piece is noted in the order it appears in the book.

"One Man's Treasure" is taken from *Wrestling for Remote Control*. Copyright © 1996 by G. Ron Darbee. Used by permission of Broadman & Holman Publishers.

"Light His Fire" is taken from *Marriage 911* by Becky Freeman. Copyright © 1996 by Becky Freeman. Used by permission.

"Pearly Gates" taken from *If You Want to Walk on Water, You've Got to Get Out of the Boat* by John Ortberg. Copyright © 2001 by John Ortberg. Used by permission of Zondervan.

"Pause for Concern" is taken from *Out on a Whim* by Dave Meurer. Copyright © 2001 by Dave Meurer. Used by permission, Bethany House Publishers.

"Showdown at the Hoedown" is taken from *Marriage 911* by Becky Freeman. Copyright © 1996 by Becky Freeman. Used by permission.

"A Day at the Beach" taken from *I Can See Myself in His Eyeballs* by Chonda Pierce. Copyright © 2001 by Chonda Pierce. Used by permission of Zondervan.

"Slapstick" is taken from *Marriage 911* by Becky Freeman. Copyright © 1996 by Becky Freeman. Used by permission.

"Kids: The Original Workout" taken from *Chonda Pierce on Her Soapbox* by Chonda Pierce. Copyright © 1999 by Chonda Pierce. Used by permission of Zondervan.

"Bet I Can!" taken from *The Best Devotions of Marilyn Meberg* by Marilyn Meberg. Copyright © 2001 by Marilyn Meberg. Used by permission of Zondervan.

"Yes, Ma'am!" by Sheila Walsh taken from *The Women of Faith Daily Devotional* by Patsy Clairmont, Barbara Johnson, Marilyn Meberg, Luci

Swindoll, Sheila Walsh, and Thelma Wells. Copyright © 2002 by Women of Faith, Inc. Used by permission of Zondervan.

"Birthday Countdown" taken from *The Best Devotions of Barbara Johnson* by Barbara Johnson. Copyright © 2001 by Barbara Johnson. Used by permission of Zondervan.

"You'll Never Have to Dust Again" taken from *I Can See Myself in His Eyeballs* by Chonda Pierce. Copyright © 2001 by Chonda Pierce. Used by permission of Zondervan.

"What Part of 'Ten Items or Less' Don't You Understand?" taken from *Chonda Pierce on Her Soapbox* by Chonda Pierce. Copyright © 1999 by Chonda Pierce. Used by permission of Zondervan.

"Gourmet Napping" is taken from *Lemonade, Laughter, and Laid-Back Joy.* Copyright © 2001 by Becky Freeman. Published by Harvest House Publishers, Eugene, OR 97402. Used by permission.

"Chatting with Martha Stewart about *My* To-Do List" taken from *Chonda Pierce on Her Soapbox* by Chonda Pierce. Copyright © 1999 by Chonda Pierce. Used by permission of Zondervan.

"The Bra of My Dreams" is taken from *Silver in the Slop* by Cathy Lee Phillips, copyright © 1999 by Patchwork Press, P.O. Box 4684, Canton, GA 30115. Used by permission.

"Step Right Up" is taken from *Normal Is Just a Setting on Your Dryer* by Patsy Clairmont, a Focus on the Family book published by Tyndale House Publishers. Copyright © 1993 by Patsy Clairmont. All rights reserved. International copyright secured. Used by permission.

"Face-lift" by Barbara Johnson taken from *The Women of Faith Daily Devotional* by Patsy Clairmont, Barbara Johnson, Marilyn Meberg, Luci Swindoll, Sheila Walsh, and Thelma Wells. Copyright © 2002 by Women of Faith, Inc. Used by permission of Zondervan.

"To Bean or Not to Bean" taken from *The Best Devotions of Marilyn Meberg* by Marilyn Meberg. Copyright © 2001 by Marilyn Meberg. Used by permission of Zondervan.

"Snaggletooth" taken from *The Best Devotions of Luci Swindoll* by Luci Swindoll. Copyright © 2001 by Luci Swindoll. Used by permission of Zondervan.

"Look Good, Smell Good!" taken from *Chonda Pierce on Her Soapbox* by Chonda Pierce. Copyright © 1999 by Chonda Pierce. Used by permission of Zondervan.

"Big Hair Day" is taken from *Silver in the Slop* by Cathy Lee Phillips, copyright © 1999 by Patchwork Press, P.O. Box 4684, Canton, GA 30115. Used by permission.

"Slippery Slope" is taken from *Women in Tune* by Betty Malz, copyright © 1987 by Betty Malz. Used by permission of Baker Book House Company.

"A River Runs Down It" is taken from *Mama Said There'd Be Days Like This* by Charlene Ann Baumbich. Copyright © 1995 by Charlene Ann Baumbich. Used by permission.

"Gourmet Goodies" is taken from *Sportin' a 'Tude* by Patsy Clairmont, a Focus on the Family book published by Tyndale House Publishers. Copyright © 1996 by Patsy Clairmont. All rights reserved. International copyright secured. Used by permission.

"Putting on the Ritz" is taken from *Silver in the Slop* by Cathy Lee Phillips, copyright © 1999 by Patchwork Press, P.O. Box 4684, Canton, GA 30115. Used by permission.

"The Trouble with Peanuts" by Barbara Johnson taken from *The Women of Faith Daily Devotional* by Patsy Clairmont, Barbara Johnson, Marilyn Meberg, Luci Swindoll, Sheila Walsh, and Thelma Wells. Copyright © 2002 by Women of Faith, Inc. Used by permission of Zondervan.

"Bare Witness" is taken from *I Used to Have Answers, Now I Have Kids.* Copyright © 2000 by Phil Callaway. Published by Harvest House Publishers, Eugene, OR 97402. Used by permission.

"Good Grief!" is taken from *Welcome to the Funny Farm* by Karen Scalf Linamen, Fleming H. Revell, a division of Baker Book House Company, copyright © 2001. Used by permission.

"Bite My Tongue!" taken from *Confessions of Four Friends Through Thick and Thin* by Gloria Gaither, Peggy Benson, Sue Buchanan, and Joy MacKenzie. Copyright © 2001 by Gloria Gaither, Peggy Benson, Sue Buchanan, and Joy MacKenzie. Used by permission of Zondervan.

"Diamonds and Dump Trucks," *God Things Come in Small Packages for Moms,* by Judy Carden, et al., 2000, Starburst Publishers, Lancaster, PA 17601 [www.starburstpublishers.com]. Used by permission.

"What Did *You* Do Today?" is taken from *I Used to Have Answers, Now I Have Kids.* Copyright © 2000 by Phil Callaway. Published by Harvest House Publishers, Eugene, OR 97402. Used by permission.

"Questions, Questions" by Chris Ewing is taken from *An Owner's Guide to Fatherhood,* published by Promise Press, an imprint of Barbour Publishing, Inc., Uhrichsville, Ohio. Used by permission.

"Payback" by Veda Boyd Jones. Copyright © 2002. Used by permission.

"And If I Die Before I Wake" taken from *Lighten Up!* by Ken Davis. Copyright © 2000 by Ken Davis. Used by permission of Zondervan.

"What's That Smell?" taken from *I Can See Myself in His Eyeballs* by Chonda Pierce. Copyright © 2001 by Chonda Pierce. Used by permission of Zondervan.

"Help, Lord, There's a Cat on My Face!" taken from *The Best Devotions of Sheila Walsh* by Sheila Walsh. Copyright © 2001 by Sheila Walsh. Used by permission of Zondervan.

"Hey, Dude!" taken from *If You Want to Walk on Water, You've Got to Get Out of the Boat* by John Ortberg. Copyright © 2001 by John Ortberg. Used by permission of Zondervan.

"Anything for a Laugh" by Marilyn Meberg taken from *The Women of Faith Daily Devotional* by Patsy Clairmont, Barbara Johnson, Marilyn Meberg, Luci Swindoll, Sheila Walsh, and Thelma Wells. Copyright © 2002 by Women of Faith, Inc. Used by permission of Zondervan.

"Cat Lovers Beware!" is taken from *How Can I Be Over the Hill When I Haven't Seen the Top Yet?* Copyright © 1989 by Patricia Wilson. Used by permission of Upper Room Books.

"Air Bags, Seat Belts, and Change" taken from *Lighten Up!* by Ken Davis. Copyright © 2000 by Ken Davis. Used by permission of Zondervan.

"Coloring the Night Away" taken from *The Best Devotions of Marilyn Meberg* by Marilyn Meberg. Copyright © 2001 by Marilyn Meberg. Used by permission of Zondervan.

"Pacified" taken from *The Best Devotions of Patsy Clairmont* by Patsy Clairmont. Copyright © 2001 by Patsy Clairmont. Used by permission of Zondervan.

"Peculiarity Breeds Content" is taken from *Marriage 911* by Becky Freeman. Copyright © 1996 by Becky Freeman. Used by permission.

"Traffic Ballet" taken from *The Best Devotions of Marilyn Meberg* by Marilyn Meberg. Copyright © 2001 by Marilyn Meberg. Used by permission of Zondervan.

"Drunk without Drinking" taken from *The Best Devotions of Barbara Johnson* by Barbara Johnson. Copyright © 2001 by Barbara Johnson. Used by permission of Zondervan.

"If I Were in Charge of Voice Menus" taken from *Chonda Pierce on Her Soapbox* by Chonda Pierce. Copyright © 1999 by Chonda Pierce. Used by permission of Zondervan.

"Peanut Butter Yogurt and Raspberry Sauce" taken from *The Best Devotions of Marilyn Meberg* by Marilyn Meberg. Copyright © 2001 by Marilyn Meberg. Used by permission of Zondervan.

"Live!" by Luci Swindoll taken from *The Women of Faith Daily Devotional* by Patsy Clairmont, Barbara Johnson, Marilyn Meberg, Luci Swindoll, Sheila Walsh, and Thelma Wells. Copyright © 2002 by Women of Faith, Inc. Used by permission of Zondervan.

The Funniest Stories from Today's Funniest Women

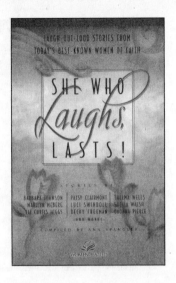

She Who Laughs, Lasts!
Laugh-Out-Loud Stories from Today's
Best-Known Women of Faith
Compiled by Ann Spangler

If you believe that "a cheerful heart is good medicine," then get ready for a potent prescription! *She Who Laughs, Lasts!* collects the funniest stories from today's funniest women of faith, who candidly recount their own foibles and follies as a way of reminding you that laughter can be faith's best friend.

Softcover 0-310-22898-0

Pick up a copy at your favorite bookstore today!

ZONDERVAN™

GRAND RAPIDS, MICHIGAN 49530 USA

WWW.ZONDERVAN.COM

Soul-Stirring Stories to Lighten the Load and Strengthen the Heart

Don't Stop Laughing Now!

Stories to Tickle Your Funny Bone and Strengthen Your Faith

Compiled by Ann Spangler and Shari MacDonald

"The cheerful heart has a continual feast," says the author of Proverbs. *Don't Stop Laughing Now!* is the sequel to the best-selling *She Who Laughs, Lasts!* It offers the same winning recipe, blending laughter and inspiration into a delicious meal of fun and faith for readers hungry for more joy in their lives. Contributors include a variety of authors such as the hilarious Barbara Johnson, Patsy Clairmont, Chonda Pierce, and Becky Freeman. These true-to-life stories will take readers from giggles and laughter to heart-soothing tears and back again, infusing them with encouragement to help them make it through even the toughest day.

Softcover 0-310-23996-6

Pick up a copy at your favorite bookstore today!

GRAND RAPIDS, MICHIGAN 49530 USA

WWW.ZONDERVAN.COM

A Glimpse into the Lives of Old and New Testament Women

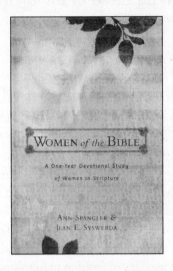

Women of the Bible

A One-Year Devotional Study of Women in Scripture

Ann Spangler and Jean E. Syswerda

Women of the Bible focuses on fifty-two remarkable women in Scripture—women whose struggles to live with faith and courage are not unlike our own. Far from being cardboard characters, these women encourage us through their failures as well as through their successes. You'll see how God acted in surprising and wonderful ways to draw them—and you—to himself.

This yearlong devotional offers a unique method to help you slow down and savor the story of God's unrelenting love for his people, offering a fresh perspective that will nourish and strengthen your personal communion with him.

Hardcover: 0-310-22352-0

Pick up a copy at your favorite bookstore today!

GRAND RAPIDS, MICHIGAN 49530 USA

WWW.ZONDERVAN.COM

Women of Today Can Find Inspiration and Encouragement in the Lives of the Women Who Lived in Bible Times

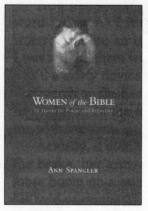

Women of the Bible:
52 Stories for Prayer and Reflection
Ann Spangler

These are the inspiring stories of 52 female characters in the Bible taken from the popular book *Women of the Bible*.

Women of the Bible: 52 Stories for Prayer and Reflection uses a weekly devotional format to offer contemporary Christian women an opportunity to study the legacies of women in Scripture. Some—such as Eve and Mary—are prominent and well-known biblical figures. But even the lives of the lesser-known women—such as Tamar, the daughter-in-law of Judah, who disguised herself as a prostitute—offer provocative and fascinating stories. What shines through in this inspirational book is the author's respect for these gritty, intelligent, and occasionally flawed women.

Each woman's life story is briefly recounted in an enchanting storytelling voice, helping readers see how these ancient stories still have meaning centuries later. Included is an introductory section listing each woman's name, her character, her sorrow, and her joy, as well as key Scriptures pertaining to her life. Then her story is told, followed by a section outlining her legacy of prayer.

Hardcover: 0-310-24493-5

Pick up a copy at your favorite bookstore today!

ZONDERVAN™

GRAND RAPIDS, MICHIGAN 49530 USA

WWW.ZONDERVAN.COM

Study the Scriptures from a Different Perspective

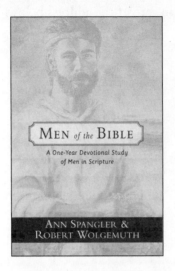

Men of the Bible
A One-Year Devotional Study of Men in Scripture
Ann Spangler and Robert Wolgemuth

Men of the Bible takes a close-up look at fifty-two men in Scripture–complex flesh-and-blood characters whose strengths and weaknesses often seem strangely similar to our own. Heroes and villains, sinners and prophets, commoners and kings ... their dramatic life stories provide us with fresh perspective on the unfolding story of redemption and offer glimpses into the way God works in our lives.

Hardcover: 0-310-23944-3

Pick up a copy at your favorite bookstore today!

GRAND RAPIDS, MICHIGAN 49530 USA

WWW.ZONDERVAN.COM

We want to hear from you. Please send your comments about this book to us in care of the address below. Thank you.

GRAND RAPIDS, MICHIGAN 49530 USA

WWW.ZONDERVAN.COM